Thunder of Freedom

THUNDER
OF
FREEDOM

*Black Leadership
and the
Transformation of
1960s Mississippi*

Sue [Lorenzi] Sojourner with Cheryl Reitan

Photographs by Sue [Lorenzi] Sojourner

Foreword by John Dittmer

UNIVERSITY PRESS OF KENTUCKY

The University Press of Kentucky

Scholarly publisher for the Commonwealth,
serving Bellarmine University, Berea College, Centre College of Kentucky, Eastern
Kentucky University, The Filson Historical Society, Georgetown College, Kentucky
Historical Society, Kentucky State University, Morehead State University, Murray
State University, Northern Kentucky University, Transylvania University,
University of Kentucky, University of Louisville, and Western Kentucky University.
All rights reserved.

Editorial and Sales Offices: The University Press of Kentucky
663 South Limestone Street, Lexington, Kentucky 40508-4008
www.kentuckypress.com

17 16 15 14 13   5 4 3 2 1

Cataloging-in-Publication data is available from the Library of Congress.

ISBN 978-0-8131-4093-3 (hardcover : alk. paper)
ISBN 978-0-8131-4094-0 (epub)
ISBN 978-0-8131-4095-7 (pdf)

This book is printed on acid-free paper meeting the requirements of the American
National Standard for Permanence in Paper for Printed Library Materials.

Manufactured in the United States of America.

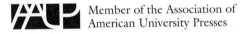 Member of the Association of
American University Presses

The images of Ozell Mitchell on the cover and on page 25, Ralthus Hayes on page
37, older Mileston women on page 68, and the Freedom Democratic Party Office
on page 158 were published in *Minds Stayed on Freedom: The Civil Rights Struggle
in the Rural South—An Oral History by Youth of the Rural, Organizing, and
Cultural Center* (Boulder, CO: Westview Press, 1991).

To the Holmes movement community
and its leaders,
to Henry, to Demitri Shimkin,
and to my family.

Contents

List of Photographs   ix
Foreword by John Dittmer   xi
Reflections on the Local Movement by Lawrence Guyot   xv
Preface   xvii
List of Abbreviations   xix

Part 1. Becoming Part of Holmes County
  1. From California to Mississippi, August–September 1964   3
     Their Stories: Sam and Laura Redmond
  2. What We Walked Into: Early Voter Registration Efforts, Winter
     1962–September 1964   23
     Their Stories: Ralthus Hayes; John Daniel Wesley
  3. Mileston, September–October 1964   45
     Their Stories: Shadrach "Crook" Davis; Norman and Rosebud Clark
  4. The Holmes County Community Center, November 1964–January
     1965   67
     Their Stories: Reverend Jesse James Russell

Part 2. Working with the People
  5. The Congressional Challenge and Marching for Freedom, January–
     July 1965   81
     Their Stories: Alma Mitchell Carnegie
  6. School Desegregation, Head Start, and the Medical Committee,
     Spring 1965 to Early 1966   103
     Their Stories: Kids Racing the Bug Sprayer
  7. Voter Registration, December 1964–December 1965   127
     Their Stories: McGee's Café

8. The Greenville Air Base Demonstration and the Community Action Program, January–December 1966   141
   Their Stories: Rosie Head's Birthday Party; Reverend Joseph McChriston

Part 3. Building Political Strategies
9. Political Organizing, January–June 1966   157
   Their Stories: Mr. and Mrs. Burrell Tate
10. The Meredith March, June–July 1966   173
   Their Stories: Eugene Montgomery; A Group Gathers for a Countywide Meeting
11. The November 1966 Elections and Coalition Building, Fall 1966– January 1967   195
   Their Stories: Five People Comment about Henry Lorenzi
12. Reading "The Some People" Story and a Trip North, February– April 1967   211
   Their Stories: Movement Visitors to the Balance Due House

Part 4. Developing the Slate of Candidates
13. Selecting the FDP Candidates from Holmes, January–June 1967   225
   Their Stories: Robert G. Clark: The Day Is Coming
14. Black and White Issues with SNCC Workers, Summer 1967   239
   Their Stories: Edgar Love and the Tchula Shootout; Alec Shimkin's Reflection
15. The Success of the 1967 Holmes County Elections, September– November 1967   259
   Their Stories: Mary Lee Hightower; Robert G. Clark, at a Farmers Co-op Meeting; A Late-Night Meeting with Robert G. Clark
16. Changed Lives: Celebrating the Movement and Its People   273

Afterword   275

Acknowledgments   277
Chronology of Movement Events in Holmes County and the United States   281
Index   295

Photographs

Sue Lorenzi   7
Nathaniel Beddingfield and Micheal Head   15
Hartman Turnbow   17
Ozell Mitchell   25
Annie Bell Mitchell   26
The *Holmes County Herald*   30
Ralthus Hayes   37
John Daniel Wesley   41
Pecolia and Robert Head with their granddaughter Patricia   47
Hartman Turnbow   49
Daisey Montgomery Lewis   57
Rosebud and Norman Clark   64
Older Mileston women   68
Thelma "Nutchie" Head   71
Calvin "Butchie" Head   73
Fannie Lou Hamer   82
Fannie Lou Hamer with movement leaders   83
Children sitting on a tire   89
Children with a bike   90
Alma Mitchell Carnegie in her kitchen   99
The kindergarten   116
C. Bell Turnbow   119
Children outside the office   122
Otha Lee and other children   123
Dino West and Steve Ellis   125
Bernice Patton Montgomery   128
Edith Quinn   132
Boys hanging out in McGee's Café   136
Penny McGee   138
Alma Mitchell Carnegie   142

Curtis "Ollie" Hoover   146
Young women   151
Reverend Joseph McChriston   153
The Freedom Democratic Party Office   158
Pecan Grove neighbors   161
Burrell Tate   168
The Holmes County Courthouse   176
Eugene Montgomery   183
Reverend Willie B. Davis with his granddaughter   189
Walter Bruce   197
Reverend L. E. Robinson   201
Henry Lorenzi   206
Singing at a Countywide Meeting   212
Norman Clark and Robert Cooper Howard   227
Lawrence Guyot   233
Robert G. Clark   236
Edgar Love   240
The Lexington Protest   249
Alec Shimkin   255
Howard Taft Bailey and T. C. Johnson   260
Reverend Willie B. Davis   262
Etha Ree Rule   264
Robert G. Clark in the campaign office   268
Men laughing at a Countywide Meeting   274

Foreword

Sue and Henry Lorenzi first set foot in Mississippi in September of 1964. Earlier that summer nearly a thousand volunteers, most of them white college students, came down to work with local people and full-time civil rights activists in projects throughout the state. They staffed the community centers, taught in the new "freedom schools," and helped organize the Freedom Democratic Party, which challenged the state's white-supremacist delegation at the Democrats' national convention in Atlantic City. The attention of the world had focused on Mississippi that summer after the disappearance of the three civil rights workers in Neshoba County. When, nearly three months later, the bodies of James Chaney, Michael Schwerner, and Andrew Goodman were found buried under a dam, the state's reputation as the most violent and repressive in the nation was confirmed.

Nonetheless, Freedom Summer (as it came to be known) changed Mississippi. The summer project and the attendant national publicity, grudging compliance with the new Civil Rights Act, and the peaceful desegregation of a handful of public schools in the fall of 1964 marked the beginning of the end of the politics of "massive resistance" in the Magnolia State. Racism remained entrenched in the white community, and for a time a revived Ku Klux Klan ran wild in parts of the state. But by holding firm and refusing to back down in the face of intimidation and terror, movement activists had won the right to organize their communities, a major achievement in its own right.

It was by chance—and good fortune—that the Lorenzis ended up in Holmes County. Located about seventy miles north of the state capital in Jackson, Holmes is mostly rolling hill country. Its western sector, however, is rich Delta farmland, and there in the early 1940s a group of black sharecroppers purchased farms as part of the New Deal's Farm Security

Administration program. Assisted by field secretaries from the Student Nonviolent Coordinating Committee (SNCC), these independent farmers founded their own movement in the early 1960s. When the Lorenzis first arrived in Holmes, they met Hartman Turnbow and Ralthus Hayes, leaders of a group of fourteen Holmes County blacks who had defied custom and risked arrest by attempting to register to vote in the spring of 1963. As Lawrence Guyot has observed, no local movement in the state was "as broad based, indigenous, or contagious as in Holmes." The Mississippi Freedom Democratic Party achieved its greatest successes there, winning its first major victory in 1967 when a Holmes County schoolteacher named Robert Clark became the first African American elected to the Mississippi legislature in the twentieth century.

I first met Susan Sojourner in the late 1980s at her home in Washington, D.C. I was then doing research for my book on the Mississippi movement and had learned from several people that Sojourner had collected some primary source material relating to the movement in Holmes County. After we exchanged pleasantries, Sue escorted me to her basement, which was filled with file cabinets stuffed with documents and reel-to-reel tapes of interviews she had conducted in the late 1960s with local people active in the struggle. In short, it was a gold mine. I realized then that if I had been starting over, I could settle in with this wealth of material and write a book about what was politically the most interesting county in black Mississippi. But I was not starting over, and besides, the logical person to chronicle the Holmes County story was sitting next to me. I told Sue Sojourner that this was the book she was meant to write.

She had also taken hundreds of striking photographs, and after she moved to Duluth she mounted a photographic exhibit, "The Some People of That Place: Holmes County, Mississippi," which appeared in selected cities to great popular and critical acclaim. (Photographs from that exhibit are included in this book. Judge for yourself!) Sue took her exhibit to Holmes County so that the people who made that movement could see themselves in action. They responded enthusiastically and, as they had in the 1960s, encouraged their friend to write more about that time as well. Sue insisted that the story should focus almost entirely on the local people, not on outside agitators like her and Henry. Finally, at

the urging of several of us, including Constance Curry, another movement activist who has written widely and well about the freedom struggle, Sue agreed to tell her story as well. In the latter stages of her work,
Cheryl Reitan contributed her considerable talents as a writer and editor.
The result is this book.

Although it is one of several outstanding local community studies
(books by Emilye Crosby, Todd Moye, and Hasan Kwame Jeffries spring
quickly to mind), *Thunder of Freedom* is unique in that Susan Sojourner was a participant in the events she describes. Yet unlike the authors
of other memoirs, constructed mostly from memory years or decades
after the fact, Sojourner was compiling the primary source material for
this book—documents, oral histories, and photographic images—as the
events themselves were unfolding. Insofar as I know, no other civil rights
memoir combines the reporting of a journalist with the experience of the
organizer and the perspective of a historian.

Here we find unforgettable personal portraits of local people like
Alma Mitchell Carnegie, whose political involvement began as a sharecropper in the 1920s and who by the early 1960s was "the oldest person
to join every perilous Movement action." But we also see the human side
of Mrs. Carnegie, watching the *Tonight Show* with Sue, admitting that she
"loved" host Johnny Carson! The people of Holmes County come alive
in this book, the best we have on the daily lives of community organizers
who joined together across lines of social class to crack open Mississippi's
"closed society."

Susan Sojourner has written a remarkable book. Civil rights scholars
will be combing through it for new primary materials. (The oral history
sections are in themselves worth the price of admission.) Social historians
will take note of the experimental health clinic in Mileston. It became the
prototype for the community health centers of today, which provide primary care for more than 30 million needy Americans. Most of all, *Thunder of Freedom* will have enormous appeal to general readers interested in
learning more about this fascinating time and place, in which ordinary
people accomplished extraordinary things.

John Dittmer,
author of *Local People: The Struggle for Civil Rights in Mississippi*
and recipient of the 1995 Bancroft Prize in American History

Reflections on the Local Movement

Sue and Henry's credibility in Holmes County was impeccable. They were in the movement from the fall of 1964 to the fall of 1969, and they are still identified with the community center at Mileston; they are identified with those first campaigns; and they were close to Hartman Turnbow and Ralthus Hayes.

They didn't get trapped up in the fact they were white. They knew what moved the different forces in the county and could stay out of the fights. They had the ability to listen and do it well. That's what made them the best organizing team in Mississippi.

They were always referred to as a twosome. People said Sue-and-Henry like it was one name. They had an exceptionally high reputation among organizers in Mississippi. All of the SNCC staff agreed with me on that point: John Green, Hollis Watkins, Willie Peacock, Bob Moses, and the rest.

There was nothing quite like Holmes County's political organization in all of Mississippi; in fact there was nothing like it in the South. When SNCC considered organizing a broad southern movement, the central question was, Should we create more Holmes counties or more SNCC membership groups? The movement in Holmes County controlled every scintilla of what was political and what was economic. There have been other movements, but nothing as broad-based, indigenous, or contagious as in Holmes.

Sue-and-Henry were about the job of energizing and transforming people so those people could energize and transform others. They helped Holmes County set up precinct captains and neighborhood block captains and in that manner transformed the political process. They believed that the greatest political capital we had was the people.

Sue-and-Henry were the catalyst that built the most powerful black political organization possible in Holmes County.

Lawrence Guyot,
former Student Nonviolent Coordinating Committee
field secretary, chairman of the Mississippi
Freedom Democratic Party, 1964 to 1968,
and member of the board of directors of
Veterans of the Civil Rights Movement of Mississippi

Preface

My experience in Holmes County gave me my identity as a white, middle-class outside agitator who was transformed by the black people I worked with. From the first day my husband Henry and I entered Holmes County, Mississippi, in 1964, I scribbled notes into my journal. I kept carbons of my letters sent north and copies of the newsletters I wrote for our supporters, to preserve a record of our sixteen-to-twenty-hour days working in the movement. When the intensity of the struggle lessened slightly in 1966, I allotted some of my civil rights work time to my own writing, capturing scenes, and listening to the people. Later, I was given a new, top-of-the-line, reel-to-reel recorder that I used mainly for documenting meetings, although I also taped thirty or so personal interviews.

After my conversations with local people, I wrote down their words whenever I could, sometimes within an hour after the session, reproducing the best I could their phrasing, style, and diction. These words are important. Pure and relatively raw, they speak volumes about authentic movement people. Excerpts from those detailed observations of individuals, as well as other "snapshots" of life in the movement—all written from 1967 to 1969—appear as sections titled "Their Stories" at the ends of chapters. I also shot hundreds of black-and-white film images of the local people I was interviewing.

The local leaders encouraged me. They asked me to read something of their history to an early Holmes County Freedom Democratic Party organizing meeting for the 1967 election campaign, the first in which blacks had a chance of winning. I read parts of it aloud for them. Entitled "The Some People of That Place," it was written using no names or places, yet all knew it was about the Holmes County movement people. This book is based on the story I read that night.

In 1969, Henry and I sorted and copied our work papers, documents, and files. We left the full set of originals with Holmes leaders and, planning to someday write about Holmes, we stored our copies and my negatives in Pittsburgh. We set off on thirteen months of foreign travel before settling in Washington, D.C., where our son Aaron was born. Henry suddenly died in 1982, never having had the opportunity to revisit our Holmes materials. Our Holmes book was left to me.

It is my hope that this book brings to the world an understanding of Holmes County's place in the history of the civil rights movement and the essential role of the local people.

Sue [Lorenzi] Sojourner

Abbreviations

ACLU	American Civil Liberties Union
AFSC	American Friends Service Committee
ASCS	Department of Agriculture Stabilization and Conservation Service
CAP	Community Action Program
CDGM	Child Development Group of Mississippi
CMI	Central Mississippi Incorporated
COFO	Council of Federated Organizations
CORE	Congress of Racial Equality
FDP	Freedom Democratic Party
HCCC	Holmes County Community Center at Mileston
LDF	NAACP Legal Defense and Education Fund, Inc.
MACE	Mississippi Action for Community Education
MCHR	Medical Committee for Human Rights
MFDP	Mississippi Freedom Democratic Party
NAACP	National Association for the Advancement of Colored People
NCC	National Council of Churches
OEO	Office of Economic Opportunity
SCLC	Southern Christian Leadership Conference
SNCC	Student Nonviolent Coordinating Committee, 1960–1967/Student National Coordinating Committee, 1967–197? ("Snick")

Part 1

Becoming Part of Holmes County

You need to tell how it was before the movement, what led up to it.
Write about back before the movement come and how life was for a Negro
    in Mississippi.
Take the man on the plantation, how he get up at five in the morning and
    get behind that mule
and work in the field until they ring that bell at twelve o'clock noon and he
    stop for dinner.
Then he go back to work at one o'clock when they ring the bell again,
but then they don't ring that bell no more after that
because he know to stay out working 'til the sun go down.
You gotta tell all that and how they was lynching and beating on Negroes
and just what life was like down here.
And then how it built up to the movement that come.

The reason that Negroes have stood up is they's not scared.
The lynchings and killings frightened the Negro
and kept them scared for a long time.
But the lynchings were different from now.
A lynching was just one Negro dead.
Each one that got lynched was just one Negro gone.
But this now, this is something that we is in together.
We was all together trying to do something.
So every time they come shooting or bombing
it just made us all mad and more determined to go on.

—Hartman Turnbow, as told to Sue Lorenzi,
September 1967

1

From California to Mississippi
August–September 1964

We whizzed along in our cozy little car. It was August 14, 1964. It was a fine night. Lightning displayed all the mountains hidden in the blackness beyond us. Puppydog smelled like dog. He jumped into the back and arranged himself comfortably on the many cushions. We had left Los Angeles the previous night, after ten o'clock. The day had been hot and hectic because my husband, Henry, was doing some final repairs on our 1959 Simca. He got it started and running semifine. Henry and I took turns driving and sleeping, and the next day we looked for a place to picnic and sleep in the shade.

It grew hotter. My brilliant idea was to drive forty-five miles out of the way to a national park, which evoked in my midwestern mind green grass, blue lakes, and shade trees. But in the middle of Nevada, in the middle of the desert, Valley of Fire State Park was just that—a hell of a valley of scrubby, sizzling fire.

The next days took us into the unceasing, sweltering heat of Lake Mead National Recreation Area and then on to an all-too-brief dip in the clear, clean water of Bear Lake in northern Utah. We traveled to Yellowstone to watch Old Faithful piss, and that's where we finally determined this was not our route.

Our path and our emotions swung us high and low. It might have seemed to some that we were on vacation. We were free of the usual obligations of school, job, and family. Two months earlier, I had graduated from the University of California–Berkeley, and we'd officially tied the knot.

We had started out on our new life together, packed up, closed our

3

apartment, and finalized plans for getting to Mississippi, where we hoped
to become civil rights workers. Several thousand miles of round-about
driving were ahead of us, because on our way we wanted to visit family
and friends in Duluth, Minnesota; Chicago; Pittsburgh; New York; D.C.;
Nashville; and Tuscaloosa, Alabama, before crossing Mississippi's border.
We needed to explain our plans for the next year or two or more and
what the civil rights movement meant to us, and maybe talk about what it
meant to them. We needed to see them—my dad and our moms, brothers, sisters, nieces, nephews, cousins, old friends, and teachers. We needed
to hug them, talk to them, and bid them farewell.

Just a bit more than a week before we left Los Angeles, the bodies of
the three civil rights workers were found after their six-week burial under
an earthen dam in Neshoba County, Mississippi. They had disappeared
on June 21, 1964, and were already at the time believed murdered. James
Chaney was a twenty-one-year-old local black activist from Meridian,
Lauderdale County, Mississippi. Andrew Goodman was a twenty-year-old
white anthropology student who had just arrived in the state on June 20.
Michael "Mickey" Schwerner was a twenty-four-year-old white organizer
and former social worker; he and Goodman were both Jewish New York-
ers. It was determined that the three had been taken to an isolated spot
where Chaney was beaten and all three were shot to death. Their car was
driven into a swamp and set on fire. Their bodies were buried in a dam
under construction.

It was hard to conceive of our trip as a vacation as we dealt with
our thoughts about Mississippi and the murders that had captured the
nation's attention. Still, in spite of the violence, Henry and I were clear
about what we needed to do. In the year before we set out, we had spent
many hours discussing all the possible work projects we could choose for
the time when I finally got my degree and he left his job. Since the September 1963 church bombing in Birmingham that killed four little girls,
the civil rights movement had loomed larger than the other "do-good"
work we had been researching, such as overseas aid through the American
Friends Service Committee. We had rejected the newly established U.S.
Peace Corps. To become representatives of the U.S. government in those
racist, Vietnam times seemed impossibly abhorrent.

We felt the overwhelming tide of the civil rights movement and knew we needed to be part of it somewhere for at least a year. We were on our way to find out if, and where, the Council of Federated Organizations (COFO) wanted to use us, since we had opted not to join them for their Summer Project but to arrive at the time most other outside workers were leaving. COFO was created in 1961 and reenergized in 1962 by several groups to create a united front of all the local, state, and national protest groups working in Mississippi. The groups that joined together were the Student Nonviolent Coordinating Committee (SNCC, "Snick"), the Congress of Racial Equality (CORE), and the state and local branches of the National Association for the Advancement of Colored People (NAACP). The Southern Christian Leadership Conference (SCLC) was also involved, playing mainly an educational role.

As we drove on, we were unable to ignore the increasing tension of the dangerous work ahead, although Puppy was a leavening agent. We had brought him because I could find no one in Berkeley who wanted to keep him. I hoped to find someone to take him among those we were going to visit. In the end, there were no takers. Puppy was destined to become a sweet but dumb, white middle-class mutt at the front lines of organizing in the Mississippi Freedom movement.

I wondered if Henry and I were ready.

I was born Susan Harris Sadoff. When I married Henry John Lorenzi, I accepted "Lorenzi" only with difficulty, tagging it on to the end of my other three names.

In 1964 I was twenty-three and Henry, twenty-nine. We had met in 1962 when we both worked in southern California's aircraft industry—he as a nuclear physicist and I as a temporary dropout from college, employed as a technical calculator and then junior mathematician.

Henry was raised in Pittsburgh and was proud of his peasant-class Italian Catholic immigrant family, whose women farmed and whose men worked in mines, mills, and construction. He had lived with his three siblings and five cousins in their urban farmhouse headed by two sisters (Henry's mother and his aunt) and their husbands. Henry's parents and upbringing were from a different world from mine. Henry was much more prepared for hardship and poverty than I was. His perspective on class had revolutionized my thinking. Actually, before I met Henry, I'm not sure I was even aware that I was middle-class.

At twelve years old, Henry was stocky and strong. He played football in high school for four years, achieving star status when he made the all–Western Pennsylvania team as a defensive linebacker. He carried hod for his Italian stonemason uncle in Pittsburgh. He studied math, engineering, and physics at the University of Pittsburgh, finishing with a master's degree in nuclear physics in 1959. He continued to pursue mathematics and philosophy after leaving the university. His insights informed everyone he met—on essentials of compassion and decency, human behavior and organizing. Everyone who experienced Henry knew that his medium was ideas, talk, talk and listen, listen, listen.

My family was Jewish. Unlike the Orthodox family that my father was raised in and had rebelled against, we were Reform Jews. We attended temple instead of synagogue, went to Sunday school, not Hebrew school, and were confirmed and not bar mitzvahed. Girls in those years were not offered bat mitzvah, although I attended Sunday school several years beyond confirmation, sixteen years in all. Along with the Jewish celebrations, family connections, and socializing came a clear sense of being Jewish. Although I developed no deep religious sensibility or historical grasp beyond the stories of the holidays, I knew justice and fairness were essential tenets. At that time, I didn't feel discriminated against. Actually I wasn't even aware of the Nazi horrors of the decade of my birth.

In our majority-Jewish neighborhood on the south side of Chicago, I wasn't particularly conscious of that Jewish identity. But when I was in sixth grade, our family moved to a less-Jewish Chicago suburb, and that move was followed by three more moves in four years. I learned about being Jewish in a Christian country and in Christian public schools. High school in Salt Lake City for a semester was followed by our move to a small, inland Maine town without a single Jew but with a hateful student who introduced me to startling anti-Semitic epithets. My final high school years were spent in the beautiful, historic Massachusetts coastal town of Marblehead, which had a long history of anti-Semitism. Our family became one of a small number of Jewish families there.

Another part of my identity came from being born in the South, in Tennessee, where my mother was born. Her Byelorussian parents had emigrated from Minsk and operated a general store in a small town in western Tennessee. I was born in Nashville, where my parents had met in

Henry and I moved to the shack in Balance Due in 1965. Here I am walking on the swaying footbridge, the most direct way to get there from town. This photograph was taken by Henry.

high school. My Tennessee tie to Mama made me feel special, even better than my older Chicago-born sister and brother.

Before I went to high school, I often visited Nashville to see my aunts, uncles, and grandmother in their big apartment building. For many years Alicene, a black woman, came in most every day to clean and cook for Aunt Freda and Uncle Julius. In Chicago, my mother had different cleaning women come in, maybe once a week. Most were black, some were white, and they always came to clean, not cook for us. Not until much later, in high school, did I begin to notice black conditions in the South or the North and make connections.

Still, I considered myself somewhat knowledgeable about the world, and I thought I'd become a teacher or a writer. As a third grader I started *The Family Reporter,* a newsletter I mailed to my out-of-town relatives. As a fifth grader, I got shoulder pads to keep playing football with the guys in the alley. My father made me quit. It was the beginning of my family's intolerance of me as tomboy, a trait that proved impossible to erase. I did find balance, though. In high school in Marblehead I was editor-in-chief of the newspaper, and later I worked on the college newspapers in Madison and at Stanford.

My father's staunch Republican ideas and politics determined a lot of my political beliefs. In the early fifties, he was a civil engineer at a sheet-metal company, where he also worked as the chief management negotiator with the union. His dinner-table expressions of frustration and outrage over negotiations were vivid to all of us. Having to deal with the union was an annual event that brought out a side of him I somehow managed to forget until it returned the next year. But I didn't fully forget the images of those bad union guys who made my Dad so upset. Imprinted on my brain, the images affected my attitudes for decades.

I arrived at the University of Wisconsin–Madison in 1959. It enlarged my worldview mainly by allowing me to make good and varied friendships, especially with several diverse students. I carried my father's conservative influence with me to a university noted at the time for its radical student activism. In the 1960 presidential campaign, while 99 percent of the girls in my dorm were for Kennedy, I was for Nixon. But even though I went to the airport to cheer at Nixon's arrival, I did little as an activist or organizer.

I heard the civil rights news of the Woolworth lunch counters and the mobbing of the Freedom Riders, but it wasn't much more than faint background for me. A new freshman, I navigated classes among the thirty thousand students, learned about beer suppers, and sailed a Lake Mendota dinghy. In my second year, I earned entry into the small classes of the newly formed Honors Program.

Still, I was overwhelmed by the large student body, or perhaps I longed for a new location, as was the pattern in my high school years. So in my junior year I moved to California to attend Stanford, naively believing that Stanford would be a small school because it was half Wisconsin's size, with sixteen thousand students.

My move to California introduced me to the idea of protest. In 1961 I met Al (Allard) Lowenstein, one of Stanford's deans. He had written a book called *The Brutal Mandate*, about southwest Africa, which opened my eyes to the oppression of blacks, and he was recruiting volunteers for the Mississippi civil rights movement. Al was a very dynamic guy, an impressive person, especially to a twenty-year-old. At Stanford I joined other students for my first political action, a protest against the House Un-American Activities Committee. My memory is of waving signs and shouting on the steps of a government building in San Francisco.

At the end of the spring 1962 quarter, I dropped out of school and moved in with my parents in the San Fernando Valley. I could not return to Stanford. It cost more money than I could find and, besides that, it intimidated me. The students were so blond; their lives and attitudes seemed formed by affluence far beyond my own experience. Also, the competition was brutal. For the first time in my student life I was outclassed scholastically; I dropped a whole grade point. But I got along well with my roommate, Mary Brumder, who impressed me with such resources as owning several horses at home and boarding one to ride at school. She was intelligent, down-to-earth, and had a fun sense of humor. We became close, often talking into the night about civil rights, life, and traveling. When she took the spring quarter off for a European trip, I missed her greatly. I was also upset because I couldn't figure out a way to travel with her.

That summer, I got a job at North American Aviation, where I met Henry, who was six years older than I. At first my parents liked him a lot.

Then, as we got more serious, Henry's not being Jewish became an issue for them. I didn't really want to get married, as I felt marriage was not the best institution for a woman. But either way, being married to a non-Jew or living in sin, I had to deal with my family's disapproval and my own justifications. Once again, I chose to change environments. I wanted to find a space in which to think. So while considering my long-term future, work, and Henry, I decided I might as well do the obvious and return to school to finish my degree.

By that time, I was an established California resident and as such I could pay a mere seventy-five dollars a semester studying at the University of California–Berkeley. With my accumulated credits from Madison and Stanford, I entered in February 1963 and hoped to graduate by December, although I later extended my studies to graduate in June 1964. In the process I pleased my parents by again enrolling in school and also putting four hundred miles between Henry and me. My studies at the three universities ranged from political science to Slavic language and literature, journalism, and English, which Berkeley mongrelized into a bachelor's degree called International Information and Political Theory.

I moved into an efficiency apartment in a backyard garage of a Berkeley home. I wasn't a college student in the same way as before. I had a thirty-hour-a-week job as a telephone operator and went to classes. Much of my time, besides working and studying, was communicating with Henry. He spent hundreds each month on our phone bill as we tried to work out what we would do after I received my diploma. He wanted to quit work as a physicist. He had a strong need, as I did, to do something that mattered.

Spending time with Henry caused a bit of turmoil. I had guilty feelings when I visited Henry in L.A. and didn't call my parents, even though I was so close to their home. When I told my parents Henry stayed at my place when he came to visit me in Berkeley, it made them uncomfortable. And then my landlord evicted me for having a man in my apartment. After all, it was 1963. I found another place in Oakland that wasn't in anyone's backyard.

In September 1963, four little girls were murdered in the Birmingham church bombing. In outrage and out of respect, Henry stayed away from work for several days. He needed space to think and focus on whether working on civil rights was indeed the project we'd been seeking. He did go back to work, but within a few months he quit his job and moved to Berkeley, where we took up our ongoing discussion of our future life and work together.

For appearances, Henry rented a room for himself. At the same time he moved into my Oakland apartment. He was too overqualified to get a position at the Berkeley radiation lab, even just counting collisions, so he worked one or two overnight clerking shifts at a nearby busy motel. We had time together and pursued whatever leads we could find on overseas and southern civil rights projects.

After my Stanford roommate Mary returned from Europe in 1963 and graduated, we were back in touch. By 1964, when I was focused on graduating, Henry and I introduced Mary to our friend Vince, and the four of us had some good times together. By late spring 1964, Mary had concrete plans to go to Mississippi for Freedom Summer. Indeed, her plans were much farther along than ours. She enrolled in the June 1964 COFO orientation at Oxford, Ohio, and was assigned to work in Holmes County. Her decisions inspired and helped us to finally decide that the civil rights movement was our choice for our focus after my graduation. The movement was all over the news, on everyone's mind—the most important volunteer effort going on in the country. We believed it was the project for us, the place we could make a significant impact.

By June, the issue of our getting married had to be faced when my parents said they were definitely coming up to Berkeley for my graduation. My misgivings about the institution of marriage weren't as strong as my objection to having my mother and father see Henry and me sharing an apartment. In the not-quite-final hour, Henry and I arranged to meet Mom and Dad in Carmel, halfway between L.A. and Berkeley, the day before graduation. The morning of the meeting, we drove down the California coast with me serenading Henry, Mary, and Vince with my bordering-on-manic rendition of "Love and marriage, love and marriage, go together like a horse and carriage." We arrived and found a judge to officiate in his courtroom. He shocked all of us when he pronounced us man and wife in the name of "Jesus Christ Our Lord and the State of California." After such a strange "state" ceremony, we celebrated with a dinner overlooking the gorgeous Pacific. The next day we all drove back to Berkeley for the graduation and Mom and Dad's introduction to our now "legal" apartment.

Our life together from the very beginning was an intense relationship of constant discussion, learning, courtship, and love. And on our path from Berkeley to Mississippi, it continued. We drove on.

Through the dark, the car slowed a bit as we chugged and gingerly crept south across the Tennessee border into Alabama. Governor George C. Wallace's WELCOME sign displayed both the American and the Confederate flags in equal status. It was September 22, 1964. The road was pitch-black. No houses could be seen for miles. It felt as if we were entering foreign territory.

Henry and I rehearsed. "What are you going to tell the cops if they stop us here or in Mississippi?" I asked.

"If we're headed south, we're going to visit Andy Silver," he answered, referring to my childhood friend, now a graduate student at the University of Alabama–Tuscaloosa, a son of my father's best friend. My dad and "Uncle Iz" had graduated in engineering together from Vanderbilt in the early 1920s.

"If we're headed west, we're going to see Mary," he said.

"Mary isn't a very good name to give," I replied. "She's affiliated with that treasonous SNCC."

Our true destination was indeed Holmes County. Although we had some names of COFO contacts in Jackson, we intended to stop first to see Mary in Holmes, about seventy miles north of Jackson, to get our first Mississippi bearings. We weren't in Mississippi yet, and I couldn't figure out why it seemed so different, why we both felt so jumpy. I wondered if I wasn't making up whatever was frightening me, but I couldn't stop holding my breath—on the dark road, in the dimly lit, lonely gas station. In daytime, it may have been a nice, calm, sunny, friendly-as-the-dickens small town.

My mind raced. "Are those cops in front of us?" The tension became a pang between boob and belly button. We should have prepared not just lines but an actual prearranged plan of action. In crossing that Deep South border, things had changed. Policemen were definitely not our friends. But Andy sure was. When we made it to his house in Tuscaloosa, we felt safe. Relieved, we slept well.

The next morning, sitting on the can searching for the paper, with my

sleepy eyes barely open, I perceived a new item. The shaving kit! Instanta-
neously, I realized Henry had done what all northern bearded "agitators"
had been advised to do. I cried.

Henry laughed at me from across the tub, "It took you long enough!"

"That's not fair. I hadn't opened my eyes yet."

"You've been up for fifteen minutes!"

We packed, the beardless stranger and I. He didn't look at all like
the man who had made love with me the previous night. Or the previous
year. In careful preparation for our journey "in," he had determinedly
and deliberately shaven off the two years' growth on his chin.

We prepared to leave. We left a final note for Andy, indicating our
time of departure and instructions in case we did not call at the appointed
time, in case we got "lost" in Mississippi. It seemed overdramatic, but I
described in detail the car with its license number, Henry—his clothes,
his height, his newly clean-shaven face—and myself in seersucker dress.
Puppy I mentioned, but Andy could describe Puppy by himself. With
precautions settled, we eased into silence, each contemplating this entrance into danger and the increasing tension in internal organs.

Twelve miles west of Ethelsville, Alabama, I was disappointed to find
the same hot, yellow sun still glaring, the same bright blue sky, the same
green scrubby brush, the same dusty clay shoulders on each side of the silvery roadway, and the same whisper of cooling breeze moving the heavy
heated air. We were in Mississippi, but I would not have known it without
my map. I rolled down the window and gulped air that tasted quite the
same as any fresh country air. Mississippi looked just like Alabama, where
it had felt semi-semi-safe and thus like America, maybe. With careful, anx-
ious fear, we drove in. We tried to detect any changes of air, atmosphere,
and scenery as we crossed over the state line. I strained to see something that coincided with my internal feelings. This was indeed a different
world, a completely unrelated section of the country that was not really a
part of my home USA. I wanted something compatible with my fantasies.
We saw a green pickup truck driven by a wholesome-looking, respectably
clean and alert-seeming white farmer. But two .22 caliber rifles were on
a rack above and behind his front seat. The state seemed to require only
one license plate on motor vehicles. In the back. Most Mississippians
filled the front bumper slot with a colorful Confederate banner plate.

It suddenly became urgent to find a gasoline station, and that's when I felt the new tensions rising within again. Where could we stop with our foreign California plates? Where would be safest—a place with a lot of people or a few? Finally we decided it was absurd. We'd been driving and stopping for more than a month without worrying about it. We spotted, in the dusty clearing by a field off on my side of the road, a grocery shack with two gas pumps in front, tended by two clean-looking country boys. Henry pulled in; Puppy and I rather immediately got out. The dog wagged his tail. We hoped his innocence would rub off on us. No one could accuse him of advocating for civil rights.

The slow-paced country sound of the young man's speech snapped me into the soon-to-become-automatic boldness (covering fear) and meekness (bordering on extremely polite obsequiousness) for dealings with white folks. To my smiling, nodding, polite drawling question, he pointed me toward the restrooms behind the store building. The signs startled me. I passed what looked like an old tool-tire-rag-and-junk room with a "Coloreds" sign over it. Amid its clutter were a filthy sink and commode. The "White Men's" door was open and, though none too clean itself, the room served its single function. Puppydog followed me into my properly designated room, "White Ladies." I smiled an encouraging, "Good dog," as he lifted his leg inside the sacred sanctuary.

A few hours of driving later, we saw a small green sign that said, "Leaving Leflore Co. Entering Holmes Co." We passed places with names like Egypt, Sidon, Cruger, and Horseshoe. We didn't know then that they were plantations.

Excited to be close to the end of our journey, we finally entered Tchula, the town of Mary's mailing address. We saw its wretched shacks beside the dusty, crumbling road and drove the last long eight miles to Mileston, which wasn't a town but first a tiny green metal sign on a steel post and then two gas pumps right up close to the porch of a weathered, low, barnlike house or store. Except for several skinny, long-haired hounds, it looked deserted in the late-afternoon, still-hot sun. The Jax beer sign, old empty pop bottles scattered around, and a battered Coca-Cola sign encouraged us.

We stopped. Inside I faced the wondering stares of a large, silent black woman and a small, wide-eyed girl. I use the word *black* and need

Nathaniel Beddingfield and Micheal Head watch TV in the house next to the Beddingfields' store. Nathaniel's parents, who managed the store, were often unable to get goods from white suppliers because they sold to SNCC organizers.

to note that in 1964 black people were also called Negro and colored, but they weren't called African Americans.

A huge old wooden fan, at least three feet high, had a belt and motor that made tremendous noise in the nearly deserted store. It managed to shift the heavy hot air only slightly. I hesitated, but Mary had said to ask at Beddingfield's store and the lady there would know her.

I was conscious of my white, white skin. I asked about Mary. I explained that Mary was a white civil rights worker, an old friend of mine, who had said to stop here and ask for directions to the new community center. Mrs. Beddingfield didn't warm perceptibly, but she showed recognition and pointed to the gravel road that went over railroad tracks. "Just right over there," she said. "You can't miss it."

We turned around and down a dusty road to a weathered wooden once-red railroad stop. A sign hanging by one nail was barely legible: "Mileston." Not five hundred yards farther, we saw a church and next to it a construction area with a building already well formed. Unloading lumber and materials from a truck bed were white people—and the girl with them was Mary. We had arrived.

Abe Osheroff, the California–New York–Spanish Civil War veteran carpenter we'd heard about from Mary, appeared in the door. He nearly knocked us over with his bounding enthusiasm, especially when he saw Henry's muscles, heard of his construction and hod-carrying experience, and realized our plans were undefined. He was friendly and affectionate.

"I swear he looks like a redneck with that head of black hair, red face, and short stocky body," he said of Henry. Abe's carpenter partner Jim Boebel had cut his hand on a saw and had not been able to work for a few weeks. Abe really needed us—Henry, most of all. At this point, the only other help around seemed to be one fragile-looking old local carpenter, Mr. Robert Head. All the rest of the help seemed to be Abe.

We learned to address local elders with respect. We used "Mr." or "Mrs." and their last name to address them instead of calling them, as the local whites did, by their first name only. Our peers, and those younger than us, we called by their first names. Almost immediately, I shortened my four names to Sue Lorenzi, and we became known in common usage as "Sue-and-Henry" or "Henry-and-Sue."

Abe and Jim had left their Venice, California, business for five months to build a brand new movement community center at Mileston. In his fifties, Abe was an old man in the eyes of the summer workers. A political radical since at least the 1930s, Abe knew the organizing importance of safe meeting places and transportation. He had raised twenty thousand dollars from friends to buy building materials and a new pickup truck. Then he asked COFO where in the state he could build a movement center. Holmes—with its many independent black landowners who had already been "Moving" for more than a year—won out.

After visiting a while, Mary directed us to Flora and Dave Howard's, near the new community center. Starting the next day, they would give us a place to stay in their home before we went to the COFO office in Jackson to be assigned. The Howards had the area's only home phone, and their house was the base of much movement activity. Their family

Hartman Turnbow, a Mileston farmer, inspired many with his fiery oration during the first stage of the movement. He was the first of the First Fourteen to speak up to the sheriff. When night riders came to burn down his house, he jumped from his bed, grabbed his rifle, and shot back.

included eight children, who, when we arrived, were running around the large, handsome Mrs. Howard. She had just come inside from her long, hot day of picking cotton and was wearing khaki long pants, a skirt, a T-shirt, and a cabana straw hat. She greeted us warmly.

Our next stop was Hartman and C. Bell Turnbow's house on Dawson, which had been home all summer for Mary, Abe, Jim, and sometimes other volunteers. The bold local leader and fiery orator Mr. Hartman Turnbow came in from the field soon after we arrived. Henry and I were invited to stay overnight. Solid and barrel-chested, Turnbow loomed larger than his five feet and ten inches. His huge energy dominated. He spoke in unusual turns of phrase that we soon came to call Turnbowisms.

About six months earlier, I had heard a tape of him on KPFA, the radical Pacifica public radio station in the San Francisco area. His words flowed rapidly with lilting energy. They tumbled from his mouth, often indecipherable to my inexperienced ears. That spring 1964 broadcast was taped for us by our friend Vince, who knew we were seriously considering Mississippi work, although none of us had any idea then that we would be working in the same local movement as this dynamo. We heard Turnbow testifying about being a Negro who had attempted to register to vote in 1963 Mississippi. He repeated the story as he traveled to build the movement.

In the radio tape, Turnbow described trying to "redish" (register) to vote at the courthouse in Lexington, the Holmes County seat. It had taken three or four days for the fourteen women and men, mainly independent farmers, just to get into the circuit clerk's office and be given the "test." Soon after, his house was firebombed at night by white men they called night riders. These raiders terrorized blacks in 1960s Mississippi just as others had terrorized southern blacks in the 1800s. A month after the courthouse attempts, the fourteen found out none had "passed." No one got registered. But neither had anyone been killed. Hartman Turnbow's name had not been in our heads during our month of driving, but arriving at his house to his presence was a great and special welcome to the county, the state, and the movement.

That evening, a situation upset us. Mrs. Turnbow was in great pain after picking cotton all day. She had gotten up at 5:15 a.m., made breakfast, and was out in the field picking from 6:00 a.m. to 6:00 p.m. Her back hurt so much that she was lying flat on the floor. Not only was the doctor thirty miles away in Greenwood, but it felt treacherous to Turnbow to take her there. "They're out to get Turnbow," the other workers told us. "He's got no lights on his truck. All they need is to catch him alone at night—then he's dead! He made a public statement that he'll never get arrested at night . . . or arrested, at all. He's a proud, stubborn man." Taking Mrs. T. to a doctor was a big decision because it was a threat to their lives.

The Turnbows made up their minds to set out for Greenwood. Turnbow unloaded the truck of several hundred pounds of newly picked cotton and loaded in Mrs. T. He put a revolver in his pocket and told Abe he could use the automatic. They chugged away.

Then we white outsiders—Mary, Henry, me, and Abe—sat in the living room of the deserted home with a rifle leaning against the one door and other weapons hidden for the moment. The dogs growled. We perked up our ears and covered the window over the sink with newspaper.

Headlights flashed in at the front porch. Dogs barked.

"Out with all lights," Mary directed us. "You can't see with lights like that on top of you. You've got to stay out of the lights to stay alive."

"Up with the gun. Goddamn whites," said Abe, referring to those whites who worked against the blacks and the movement whites.

Someone came toward the house. It was a Negro. I felt relief.

"Douse the goddamn lights!" someone shouted.

"Is this where Hartman Turnbow lives?" a dark-skinned, well-dressed girl asked. She introduced herself as Turnbow's daughter. She blinked in apparent disbelief at the unfamiliarity of the surroundings—of white folks in HER front room!

So ended our first day in Mississippi.

Their Stories: Sam and Laura Redmond

Fantastic in his opening up and giving with the stories, Sam Redmond's talk flows. In the right atmosphere, and with enough rein, he uses beautiful sound effects . . . durruph, durruph, durruph . . . wheez-um, wheez-um . . . horses, birds, guns, dogs all with a different, perfect sound.

In the family's living room is a painting of a setter dog that looks like their dog Kate. The date on the painting is 1916. There's a lighted framed picture of John F. Kennedy and Jackie, a graduation picture of the Redmonds' son Ben, photos of kids, school friends of kids, and grandkids.

While we talked, Mrs. R. was ironing in the living room. A neighbor, Doris Alexander and her children, Jereldine, Florence, and Angie, the baby, were in and out of the house. An old man was there. Sam was patching his own pants and kids were listening to the record player.

Mrs. R. told me how nice it once was in Mileston, how at the Mileston school they all used to have big exhibits and they canned all kinds of things. Annie Bell Mitchell, Leola McIntyre, and Mrs. Carnegie did the canning, along with Mrs. R.

Sam was born in 1903, the only child of a man and a woman who lived on a white man's place. "We moved up along on Durant Road and rented a place we was to buy, but the man wouldn't sell it," he said. "They do you like that when they see you can make a good crop and probably will be able to pay off the land and buy it. So momma got up and bought some land over by Ebenezer Road, 'tween Lexington and Jessie Williams' place, off across from that old store."

"South from Lexington but close in," said Laura. "You can see the Lexington clock from Sam's old house."

Sam said, "Ed Wilburn Hooker (one of the most powerful whites in the county) always told my poppa, 'John, you ruint that boy. He don't need nothing.' But my poppa always said, 'Well, I don't know that, and he's the onliest son I got and it ain't gonna be my cause if he be needing.' So poppa always helped me out.

"Momma always fussed, but she gave me too. But it was poppa that always gave without a word. I'd say, 'I need fifty dollars.' And poppa would go on up round by Mr. Hooker—momma cooked for the Hookers some—and he'd say, 'Let me have fifty dollars, Sam needs some money.' Then Mr. Hooker would say, 'Why, John, that boy don't need nothing! You leave that boy alone!'

"Poppa let me work whatever I wanted and whatever I made was mine, free and clear. If I made six bales, then that six bales was mine. Or if I made two, then that was what I had. Finally I got so I gave them a little help on their land note. But it wasn't them asking. 'Twas me feeling ashamed."

Sam told a story about whites who were going to shoot at houses owned by black families, just for sport. "Last Halloween, the whites was going to come in a trail, shooting up the place, starting at Turnbow's," he said. "But they checked to find out at the store if any of the niggers got ammunition. The man at the store say he sold all out of ammunition. That stopped them. They didn't come. It used to be that Negroes couldn't buy ammunition. Then they black market it. Go down to Jackson and buy lots of it and sell it up here to Negroes for a good price."

Sam told me he had eleven children—all boys, no girls. The two oldest, W.M. and Lonnie, were by his first wife, and the rest by Laura. Some of the others are Sam Jr., Willie (Whit), Lynn, Leonard, Bill, Pemcy, and Ben. Richard (Stout) is the youngest.

Sam's folks raised Lonnie. "Lonnie's a whole story in hisself," Sam said. "I tell you that boy is something else. That boy is lucky. Now he's always got five or six pair of dice that he carries with him in his pockets. And he's got a big, new, what is it now? . . . Oldsmobile car. And, too, all his three kids has good clothes, and his wife don't work nothin' but to see after them three little ones. He don't do no work but gamble.

"He caught himself getting some little old job so as to cover, because they is hard on you in Kansas City. If they see you are not working, they just always after you, harassing, picking at you, think you are gambling. But that Lonnie, he got himself a big old pair of hip boots and some little job washing cars in a place. And when he goes in the back to shoot, he carries his boots right back there with him . . . right beside him. They say Lonnie don't wash but maybe one car in a whole week's time. When they come in to check about him, he's always there with his boots, and they say, 'Fellah, you say you work here?' And he says, 'Yeah, sho' do.' And he goes on in front and starts splashing some water. So they leaves him alone. . . . Lonnie is doing well. Why that boy is big. What's he weigh now, Laura? Probably 350 pounds. And he's not but my size.

"After momma and poppa died and the place split up for building lots and one sell here and there, I kept it some but not so long ago, I sold off the rest—some fifty-five acres. It helped to pay some notes on this place here."

Sam hunts with white folks—Mr. Sheppard, Mr. Bubba Cunningham—who come down to hunt on his place. White folks hunt on horseback. He had long stories about his bird dog Kate. They had it fixed for her to stay in the house, on an old saddle blanket near the heater. "Dog is smart. She can do everything. She'll go with the wind. She's not a pointer; she's a setter. You'd think a covey was in the brake, and that dog was sitting in the cotton patch. Sure nuff, that's where the birds be. Birds even nest in the garden some. They natural smart. It gets too moist for them down by the lake, and they come up here to hatch. Then they go back down to the brake."

Everyone knew Kate was the best bird dog ever, and people were always trying to buy her. Someone offered $125 for her, but Sam wouldn't sell. His hunting stories went on and on . . . hunting rabbits, quail, squirrels, hunting with whites, selling rabbits to a white (a lady who only wants small ones and doesn't know that some of the big ones are just as tender as the small ones), and how to have good relations with whites.

"Westfield Plantation is posted for no hunting," he said. "But I go up and ask the man. I say, 'I'm not coming in stealing, not bother nothing. I just want to hunt rabbits.' He let me. That's the right way to do. To ask the man first. Rabbits in there. And mallard duck. They just too fat eating all them beans and everything. Just too fat to even be good. I also killed some deer in there.

"Laura's mama's German shepherd dog used to stay at the farm and bring in the cows. Kate used to tend to the baby while Laura was in the field. Dogs is smart, can teach them anything.

"I used to need seven dollars a month to pay for the bus for the kids to school. I'd go out and kill me some rabbits, quail, and paid for it right in that one day's hunting. I don't like possum or frog. Possum is nasty. It will eat anything. It even eats dead things. Now a coon is clean. It kills its own meat and loves the fish. But the possum is something else. Don't give me no frogs neither."

2

What We Walked Into

Early Voter Registration Efforts, Winter 1962– September 1964

When Henry and I arrived in Mississippi in 1964, the civil rights move-ment had the attention of the nation and the world. Nearly a thousand outsiders, mainly white, mainly college students, had come into Missis-sippi to join COFO's Summer Project and work on voter registration, freedom schools, and local organizing. Movement strategists hoped the outside workers would bring the movement to the attention of their fam-ilies, hometowns, and the press, so the world could see what workers in Mississippi had been facing every day.

In 1960 black college students in Greensboro, North Carolina, staged lunch counter sit-ins at Woolworth stores where black patrons weren't served. A year later the Freedom Riders, an interracial group of civil rights activists, launched a series of bus rides from Washington, D.C., into many southern states. Amid often violent white citizen and police reaction, the Freedom Riders were testing the new Interstate Commerce Commission regulations banning segregation in public transportation facilities.

These direct-action demands for service spread throughout the South and inspired blacks all over the nation. The students formed SNCC in spring 1960 to sustain the momentum and to publicly and dangerously confront white supremacy. President John F. Kennedy sent federal troops into Mississippi in 1962 when rioters at the University of Mississippi (Ole Miss) tried to prevent James Meredith, the university's first black, from gaining admission.

When we arrived in Mileston, we came into the heart of Holmes County's civil rights activity. Two years earlier, in 1962, a number of

Holmes County black farmers had begun taking steps of their own that joined them to the struggle already sweeping the South. The Holmes farmers' acts were local and definitely movement actions. Several of the farmers drove the thirty miles to Greenwood to see what was going on at the Freedom Meetings that SNCC organizers were holding. Earlier that year, SNCC had set up a headquarters in Greenwood for organizing in the Mississippi Delta, not just in Leflore County but also in other counties such as Sunflower and Coahoma. SNCC worked where local leaders had been identified and were active. The leaders and organizers taught and led, and they protected each other. They opened up new areas of their counties with meetings, voter registration training, and distribution of food to the hungry. They also helped confront the arrests and violence.

In winter 1962, a few Holmes farmers at a time made bold journeys on remote roads where being seen, stopped, and identified with the organizing effort could bring physical and economic harm. Ozell Mitchell, Alma Mitchell Carnegie, and Hartman Turnbow from Mileston ventured to those Greenwood meetings. Afterward Ralthus Hayes, Ben Square, and others joined them. They asked organizers to come to Mileston to help set up a meeting.

The danger increased when they invited the organizers to Holmes. Over the next several months, a growing group of Holmes farmers went back and forth to the Greenwood meetings to learn of the movement and to consult with SNCC organizers. Mileston folks had conversations with friends and neighbors to persuade them to hold their own regular Mileston meeting. Ozell Mitchell was a member of the deacon board of the Sanctified Church in Mileston. Persuading church deacons Northalee McIntyre, Sam Redmond, and P. K. Dulaney to open up the church for the Mileston meeting was not impossible, but much discussion was required in the face of increasing church burnings throughout the South.

Jack and Mattie Louie, a farming couple living on the former plantation Marcella, opened up their home to John Ball, a young SNCC organizer. By early March 1963, essentials such as a meeting place, local leaders, and at least one outside organizer were all falling into place for the first Mileston meeting. During March, varying numbers attended the weekly voter education meetings at the Mileston Sanctified Church. Then on Monday, April 8, perhaps as many as forty attended. It was decided to

Ozell Mitchell, a Mileston farmer, was one of the first Holmes County blacks
to attend the 1962 meetings in Greenwood. He helped the young SNCC organizers set up a voting rights meeting in Holmes.

Annie Bell Mitchell and her husband Ozell were among the First Fourteen in Holmes, who dared to try to register to vote in 1963.

make the first attempt to register to vote the next day at the courthouse in the Holmes County seat, Lexington. At least twenty-five volunteered to meet and drive together to Lexington—a historic first action for Holmes. The next morning, only fourteen of those who had promised showed up. But that was enough for a movement that always worked with what it had. They became known as the First Fourteen. They met at Ozell and Annie Bell Mitchell's farm a few miles north of Mileston.

In Holmes and most other Mississippi counties at that time, less than a handful of Negroes had been "passed" by the white voter registration clerks and listed in the county registration books. Those circuit clerks held the fort against what they must have felt was a black onslaught. Facing Holmes's 72 percent black population, Circuit Clerk Henry B. McClellan used an eighteen- or twenty-one-question registration form, complete with a question asking for an interpretation of a section of the Mississippi constitution. He was strict for blacks but offered help for the whites.

Even before getting the form, a Negro had to screw up the courage to approach the courthouse—to walk up to it alone or in a group, aided at some point by the young black organizers. Simply asking for the right to vote was an almost revolutionary step. If it was successful, the results would ultimately, though a long way down the road, bring voting power to the majority. But the system had been denying blacks their voting rights, oppressing them, and stifling them in most every arena for hundreds of years. Approaching the courthouse marked a person as a troublemaker who wanted change that would wreak havoc on the white system. One could get hurt—and many in Mississippi in the 1950s and 1960s had already been beaten and even murdered for trying to register to vote. Right up to 1963, whites tried to keep registering to vote a secret from the black community. Some didn't know about it. Those who did also knew it was risky. But even though the blacks at the first Mileston meetings knew that asking for the registration papers was dangerous, they were learning how to fill them out.

Holmes County had more independent black landowners than any other county in the state—more than eight hundred. Also unusual was that more than one hundred of those farms were on the rich delta land. The ownership of delta land by blacks originally came about through a Roosevelt-era program that broke up several plantations, including the nearby Marcella, Dawson, Choctaw, and Mileston plantations, into plots sold with house, barn, mule, and tools. The program gave long-term, low-interest loans to impoverished sharecroppers and black and white day laborers. The four former plantations near the community center were made up of all black landowners. Most of the First Fourteen had lived on the project farms of the Farmers Home Administration (FHA) since the late 1930s or early 1940s.

Mileston, because of its location on the highway and the railroad, and also because it had a small grocery store, was a recognized, named community. The other three former plantations were in rural areas.

So on April 9, a Tuesday morning, those fourteen farmers who were determined to try to "redish," and several more who went as drivers, pulled up onto the highway. The cars headed northeast to Lexington and the Holmes County Courthouse. All were local Holmes residents. Only one SNCC organizer, John Ball, joined the fourteen farmers that morning.

There were other Greenwood-based SNCC organizers working to open up Holmes—Bob Moses, Sam Block, Hollis Watkins, and Lawrence Guyot (or just "Guyot," pronounced "GHEE yacht").

Bob Moses was born in Harlem and studied philosophy at Harvard. He taught at the Horace Mann School in Manhattan before arriving in Mississippi in 1960 to become a civil rights activist. In 1961 Moses formed the Council of Federated Organizations. At the time that first Holmes group attempted to register to vote, Moses was the COFO director and a SNCC field secretary.

Sam Block was in college at Mississippi Vocational College in Itta Bena, near Greenwood, in the same county, Leflore. He started doing voter registration work in Greenwood in 1962 and became a SNCC field secretary. The Holmes leaders traveled individually and by twos and threes to Greenwood for meetings. They invited Block and Amzie Moore, a strong local leader from Cleveland in Bolivar County, to come to Holmes and help with the early voter registration efforts.

Hollis Watkins, the twelfth child of a sharecropping family, was from rural Lincoln County. At age nineteen, in 1961, he was recruited by Bob Moses as a SNCC voting rights organizer. He attended Tougaloo College, the historically black college near Jackson, which was active in the civil rights movement. He went to jail in 1961 for leading a sit-in at a Woolworth lunch counter in McComb.

Guyot was raised in the Gulf Coast town of Pass Christian, Harrison County, and was also attending Tougaloo College while working in the civil rights movement.

Of the SNCC workers helping to organize Holmes, only John Ball was actually living in the county at the time. He was from Itta Bena.

SNCC was proud that native Mississippians were doing fieldwork in the state. It's "one of the most encouraging aspects of our work thus far," stated the SNCC Field Work Report of spring 1963. "It shows that indigenous leadership can be developed in even the most difficult areas."

No explicit plans had been laid for getting into the courthouse. On arriving in Lexington that morning, Ball and the others parked away from the courthouse and walked quietly by twos and threes—not as an organized march, so as not to inflame the situation.

High Sheriff Andrew P. Smith was waiting on the courthouse steps with his auxiliaries. After hearing from the federal Justice Department that SNCC organizers had requested federal protection for a "courthouse attempt," Sheriff Smith had deputized thirty men earlier that morning. Smith confronted the group of blacks and asked what they thought they were doing. Turnbow was in no more of a leadership position than any of the others, but without a prior plan, he stepped forward and said, "We's come to redish."

Then Smith asked which one was going in first.

Turnbow later explained, "When the sheriff put his one hand on that blackjack and the other one on that gun and raised his voice, then that thirteen wanted to run. But running wasn't [for them]. They managed to stay. I got them out of struggling when I stepped out there and said, "I'll be first. Hartman Turnbow." That relieved them.

Turnbow was allowed to enter the circuit clerk's office, but he didn't receive registration forms before the office closed at noon for dinner. The group waited under the big tree on the courthouse lawn near the Confederate monument for that afternoon and over the next three (some say, four) days before they were let in. Each was called, one at a time, shown the "test" forms, and then berated by the circuit clerk.

Lexington's weekly newspaper, the *Holmes County Herald,* covered the county's first group registration attempt on the front page of the Thursday, April 11, 1963, edition. The paper ran a big headline, "Quiet Prevails Here after Tense Situation," published photos, and mentioned most of the First Fourteen blacks. More than half of the group—Alma Mitchell Carnegie, Sam Redmond, John Daniel Wesley, Reverend Jesse James Russell, Reverend Nelson Trent, Jack Louie, Rosebud Clark, and Hartman Turnbow—were pictured in four large photographs along the bottom of

The *Holmes County Herald,* Lexington's white weekly newspaper, covered the attempt of the first blacks to register to vote. Blacks weren't usually in the *Herald*'s pages unless they had violated some rule. Printing their names and photos was dangerous because local whites could target them for reprisals. Originally printed in the *Holmes County Herald.*

the front page. Others mentioned were Annie Bell Mitchell, Charlie Carnegie, Norman Clark, Chester Hayes, Ralthus Hayes, and Ozell Mitchell. John Ball, the SNCC organizer, was included. Some say Joe T. Mitchell was there. Between fifteen and twenty-five claimed to have been among Mileston's First Fourteen. Because the action took place over three or four days and an exact list was never made, there was room for confusion. I used the phrase "Fifteen of the First Fourteen" to reflect that inherent uncertainty; however, most in the movement referred to the group as "The First Fourteen." I worked with, interviewed, and spent time with those first movers, except for Reverend Trent, who left the county that first day.

Negroes weren't usually seen in the *Herald*'s pages unless they had violated some rule. Such coverage was not positive publicity or "good press." It was dangerous business for these beginners in movement action. Everyone's name was printed in the news story. From then on, every week, a circuit clerk's list of all who tried to register was printed in the *Herald,* thus announcing to the local whites, neighbors, creditors, suppliers, and employers just who the new troublemakers were—that is, who should be targeted for reprisals.

Turnbow, particularly, was targeted because he had spoken up to the sheriff. As he told it, "Right there, [my agreeing to go first] took the strain off them, but further down in the deal, I had to pay for taking the strain off them. That branded me. I didn't see the [sheriff's] point at first by asking who was first. But he was fishing for the leader. So when I stepped out and said I'd be first, then he just figured I was the leader. Then they just thought they'd give me a good hot time and burn me out . . . but it didn't work that-a-way."

Indeed, soon after those first movement actors finished their courthouse vigil and returned to their farms, night riders drove onto the Turnbow place on the main highway. Turnbow's land was not far from the Mitchells', slightly north of Mileston and easy for the night riders to find. They threw firebombs and fired rifle shots into the house, where Turnbow, his wife, and his teenage daughter were sleeping. In a bold and important action, Turnbow leapt up out of his bed, grabbed his rifle, and shot back. The whites scattered. Some say a few were hit and one was killed.

The Turnbow family was uninjured. They pumped and hauled water from outside to put out the fires caused by the firebombs. The worst damage was done to the outhouse. The sheriff returned (many believed he was one of the night riders) and arrested Turnbow for arson of his own home, along with Bob Moses, who was documenting the damage. Blacks and movement whites were often jailed on ridiculous charges in Mississippi in those times.

The U.S. Court of Appeals Fifth Circuit described the event: "About 3 a.m. on the morning of May 8, 1963, Hartman was awakened by the sound of an explosion. He grabbed his .22 caliber rifle and went into the hall and noticed the living room and back bedroom were full of flames and smoke. Going outside, Turnbow said he saw two men standing near the side of the house. One of the men had a pistol in his hand and immediately began firing at Turnbow who returned the fire until the intruder and his companion ran off.

"After several unsuccessful attempts to contact the Sheriff's office, Sheriff Smith was finally summoned to the scene and arrived at nine a.m. accompanied by a deputy and an F.B.I. agent. During the investigation by these officers, Robert Moses, a non-Mississippi voter registration worker, was taking pictures of the scene of the fire. One of the investigators told Moses to stop taking the pictures. While he was sitting on a chair inside a screened porch, Moses took Sheriff Smith's picture. Moses was immediately arrested and confined for interfering with the investigation. Later Turnbow was arrested on the charge of arson. . . . At the preliminary hearing Turnbow was bound over for the Grand Jury under a five hundred dollar bond."

John Doar, an attorney for the Justice Department's Civil Rights Division, was called into Leflore and Holmes counties. He was the division's attorney most sympathetic to the plight of civil rights advocates. "Because of Mr. Turnbow's involvement in voter registration," Guyot said. "John Doar vigorously defended Mr. Turnbow in every phase of the charges levied against him." By the time Turnbow was arrested and taken to the Tchula jail, Guyot had become involved.

Doar contacted Guyot about a formula to release Turnbow to Guyot through the use of a reciprocity bond. "This reciprocity bond was unusual," said Guyot. "It had never happened before." Guyot believed that when Turnbow was defending his wife and child, Turnbow killed one of the night riders. The state of Mississippi didn't pursue a murder charge against Turnbow; however, later, the death of a night rider was attributed to a heart attack.

In October 1963, when the arson charge against Turnbow was presented, the Holmes County Grand Jury voted not to indict him.

In spite of the night riders, the first organized action was a victory. None of the First Fourteen had been physically hurt or killed: that was the definition of victory in that time and place. Meet, plan, then take the action—that was their real success.

Henry and I often talked with the local leaders about their earliest movement experiences. While most gave similar accounts of the earliest years, there were differences in the stories of each of the leaders. Turnbow, who inspired people during the movement's first stage, gave rousing talks in Mileston. He also traveled to the newly established Third Sunday Countywide Meetings that rotated to newer communities, as well as the meetings that started in 1963 and 1964. Encouraging people who were already active, Turnbow also moved to action many who were deeply afraid of white segregationist violence. He described how he saw change happen: "That lynching I was telling you about—that one with the burning with the 'cetylene torch—that 'n was a turning point. It just . . . made a Negro mad, got to thinking he'd rather die any way but to be all burnt up with a torch while he's still living. But this now, this is something that we is in together. We was all together trying to do something." Back then, to whites, "organizing" was a dirty, bad word and "freedom" was even worse. And meeting was something that just wasn't to be done, shouldn't be done, "oughten not" to be done. Turnbow continued, "The Negro ain't gonna stand for all that beating and lynching and bombing and stuff. They found out when they tried to stop us from redishing that every time they bombed or shot or beat or cut credit, . . . it . . . just made him angry and more determined to keep on . . . and get redished."

Turnbow praised John Ball and all the SNCC organizers who supported the First Fourteen's actions. He was grateful to them. "I knew we had the right to go redish, but didn't nobody ever stir it up," he said. "Ever since I been a man, I been knowing I had a right to redish and vote. Different folks discussed it. That thing [was] discussed for fifty years, but nobody never made an attempt. So John Ball he come in here . . . that just kicked it off. I did [what I did] 'cause I wanted to vote. I was paying tax every year just like everybody else, and I couldn't vote over who was going to be over me."

Turnbow said he was aware of earlier actions like the Freedom Rides in 1961 and James Meredith's integration of Ole Miss in 1962:

> We knew about it. . . . There was lots of gossip when that was going on. . . . We figured that was right. Figured it need to been. We figured it outta done been. And just hoping it'd work out like it did. Lots of folks was hoping that. We just hoped it would spread. Just hoped more peoples would get into it. In other words, the Holmes County Negro is not crazy at all. Lots of them got more sense than the whites got. The Negro in Holmes County, he knowed he was being deprived of his rights all the time. . . . It just took a made-up mind.

While they stood on the courthouse lawn, with their "made-up minds," waiting near the Confederate monument and under the big tree, they caused all manner of people to wonder. People of their kind—some folks they knew—walked by them, keeping eyes down, not even tipping their hats or winking an eye. This was dangerous stuff, and everyone was afraid of what they were doing—afraid for them. Reverend Trent, a preacher of the county, came to stand under the tree with them on that first day. He didn't return. None of the others knew him or his people or how to find out whether he was safe. The *Herald* newspaper printed a short interview with him.

No one else in those four days came from the street to join the group. Sometimes other blacks looked at them from way across the square as if to say they were crazy fools and nothing could be gained by causing such trouble and meddling in business that was not meant for them. One of the hill farmers who came on the second day to Lexington to see the commotion was Eugene Montgomery. He was the husband of Bernice Patton Montgomery, and both were uniquely energetic and talented people. "I was standing on the other side of the square watching them crazy folks that day they went to the courthouse," Eugene Montgomery said. "I wasn't there the first day, but I was in town the second. . . . Word got out quick and everybody was talking about it. Yes, I thought they were fools," he went on. "I didn't think nothing was wrong. I was doing fine myself. I had money and could get what I wanted."

Yet, the First Fourteen stirred emotions in both the black and white communities. Some whites watched with anger. They said the only way to handle the mess was to teach folks their place, teach them a lesson with pain and hurt to keep them from stepping out of line. The night riders with their firebombs thought they were teaching Turnbow and all the local troublemakers that lesson.

Hazel Brannon Smith, the fair-minded white owner of the weekly *Lexington Advertiser*, the only newspaper in Holmes County in the 1950s, printed balanced reporting about civil rights issues. When the White Citizens Council had become active in the county, it set up the *Herald* to put Smith's paper and her unpopular views out of business. They wanted to stop her front-page reports and editorials on incidents such as the time a sheriff shot a black man in the back. In 1964 Smith won a Pulitzer Prize for courageous journalism.

After the courthouse attempts by the First Fourteen in April 1963, and the night riders' firebombings and Turnbow's jailing, fear increased on both sides. Whites were surprised and frightened by Turnbow's spirit. Blacks had been taught that in all situations the best way to get along was to be submissive and take whatever was dished out quietly, with grins and smiles and "thank you, sirs" thrown in. And people in the community of the First Fourteen who hadn't shared the struggle said, "You see. I told you so. It was nothing but a mess from the beginning. It serves you right. You shouldn't have gotten out of line. We can't go with you 'cause you ain't goin' nowhere 'cept straight to trouble."

The First Fourteen prayed and sang and stuck together and found their worries eased. Ralthus Hayes, a sharecropper who had become a successful manager of his own farm, described the attitude of the group. "The fact is all of us that did go up there wasn't without fear in no way. We had fear. We didn't know what they might do to us. But we just got up the courage enough to try and take the risk. We knew there was a danger, but we knew it was important to try to get registered to vote. That didn't mean we weren't afraid though."

They had known it wouldn't be easy—they had known that from the beginning. In fact, they had half expected the retaliations and arrests, so they were able to bear them and continue. For Turnbow, the arson attack on his house was terrifying, and yet the effect was the reverse of the night riders' intention. "This is the thing," Turnbow said. "They set my house on fire, but that just stirred it up. It just made it worse. Like putting more wood on the fire. It just made a bigger fire. Them people that done it, they thought, if they burn me out, it would just squash it. But it made it worser. . . . Everybody then was determined to go redish. They poured out. Didn't care what it cost. They go do it."

Despite the danger, fear, and harassment, the Mileston first movers felt victory in taking those steps together. They had planned and carried out an action—meeting in Mileston and driving to Lexington together to try to register. They knew the replication of such actions throughout Holmes County and the state and the South, piece by piece, would wear away at the system that barred them from voting and so much more.

Their Stories: Ralthus Hayes

One day Ralthus Hayes and I were talking about the First Fourteen and the events of April 1963. He remembered: "There were many Negroes who were around Lexington that day, watching to see what would happen, were afraid we were going to get beat up or like that. They had a lot of dealing with white people and were afraid of doing anything . . . just afraid of getting hurt.

"All of us that did go up there, we wasn't without fear in no way. We didn't know what they might do to us. But we just got up the courage enough to try. Courage," he explained, was "just something that some people had and others didn't have. The ones that went were scared all right, but they were willing to take the risk.

"All those that went knew how important voter registration was. Mrs. Carnegie—she went because she had faith in the movement. So, she might not have seen the full meaning of what it all was leading to, but she had faith.

"Those coming to class learned about how important it was to register to vote. They knew all about what was going on in Greenwood and other places. They read about it in the newspapers and saw it on the television—saw peoples up there marching and going to the courthouse. You

Ralthus Hayes, a low-key, steady leader, went to South Carolina for Southern Christian Leadership Conference training and came back to Mileston to teach citizenship, adult literacy, and voter education classes.

know how it goes—one goes up, sees some, and then he says, 'You hear what happen such-and-such?' And it gets passed on all around like that.

"It wasn't just new to all of us either. Fact is I had been going to meetings way back. And, you know, I had gone to try to register before. It was back in '54. There was a big meeting at Mound Bayou and Thurgood Marshall . . . was there at that meeting. That was in May. Let's see, just a few days before . . . well, the court gave that decision on May 17, and this was just a few days before that. He was there then talking to us, telling all the lawsuits and things the NAACP had been doing and did and what all was going to be did—how he was going to tell the president and Congress about us. He said he was going to take care of ole Miss, meaning Mississippi, the state. And he told us about registering to vote.

"When I went up to try to register, the circuit clerk gave me so much trouble with saying the books was closed and all that. But I didn't try to get others to go with me. See, it was different then.

"Mrs. Carnegie, she was going to a lot of those meetings in various places, and Ozell Mitchell too. They were going to the ones when they started them up in Greenwood. See, when they were up in Greenwood, the folks talked to them about how they wanted to come down and work in Holmes County too. Ozell Mitchell and Mrs. Carnegie carried back the word—talked with us that they knew. Then we worked and arranged for the meeting to be started at Mileston. The fact was that John—John Ball—he didn't think we should go yet. He didn't think the people were ready to go. But the people wanted to go up."

So, Hayes explained, they called Sam Block to come down. Sam was more experienced than John. They called Sam to come and the arrangements were made. The people who went were volunteers. There didn't seem to be any formal procedures for knowing who was going to go, except that John, who was leading the meetings, "asked for who all wanted to go. And then he taken their names."

Hayes explained how when they got up to Lexington, they all met at one corner on the square and lined up and walked across the street. Sheriff Smith came out of the door of the courthouse and met them on the walk at the south door. He asked them if they had a permit, and they told him that they didn't have a permit to march and that they weren't marching anyway. Then Smith told them to all go around and stand up under the tree. And they went around. Sam Block was the leader of the group and Sam was the spokesman.

Hayes was definite about no one getting into the circuit clerk's office in the morning, not even Turnbow, and that it was Sam Block who decided to go up to Greenwood when the office closed over the noon hour. The whites were all asking around, looking for Sam. Hayes guessed Sam had just decided he'd like to get back up to Greenwood. Not all the local people went up to Greenwood with Sam. Some stayed out under the tree.

When they got back after dinner, Sheriff Smith came out and asked who wanted to go in first. Hayes remembers Dan Wesley going in first and Turnbow second and that only those two went in on the first day. Hayes suggests that Turnbow's way of telling the story was just exaggerating a bit. Hayes didn't remember anything about Smith holding a blackjack or putting his hands on his hips. "Fact is we weren't thinking too much about who was first to go in or nothing. It didn't matter. No one was worried about being first. The first was just whoever Smith let in first."

The atmosphere on the square didn't seem strange to Hayes. Sam Block had called the Justice Department beforehand and they had notified Sheriff Smith that the people were coming up to register. Smith hadn't cleared the streets of whites, so they were on the street, along with many that Smith called in and deputized. Hayes said they looked upon the law enforcement as people there to protect them.

The people under the tree were free to come and go—to go get something to eat or drink or smoke—and then come back under the tree and wait. This was the way things went all the time they were waiting—all the four days. No new people joined on the second or later days.

Speaking of that first day, Hayes said, "I went off down to get some cigarettes or something and Mr. Weathersby's son, Chick Weathersby, he stopped me and said, 'You don't have to be afraid, Ralthus. Nothing's going to happen to you people. We're just here to protect you, to see that none of them hotheads start anything up.' He said that right out. I didn't stop and axe him nothing. He just mentioned it as I passed. He was one of the deputies. He wasn't wearing no gun or anything, but he was one of the ones that Sheriff Smith had deputized.

"Justice Department men were there too. One was sitting all day with his motor running, parked right over by us on the north side of the square. His car overheated, him having it running and just sitting there all day." The Justice Department men never came up and talked to any of the people under the tree, but when "McClellan went over to the car, [the men asked] why he was taking so long in processing the people. The men talked with McClellan a while. McClellan had been running out all day, going over to the café to get coffee every few minutes."

After we were there a little while, a Methodist preacher from Lexington came up and asked what we were doing. Then he stood with us under the tree talking with some of the others. He never did go in to get a form. Some whites, some of the ones that knew him from around Lexington, came up and talked to him. Then later they followed him home. He left out of the county that night. We didn't know where he had gone or what might have happened to him. It took us three days to find him. He was all right when we located him."

Their Stories: John Daniel Wesley

Mr. Wesley told me he didn't ever like to boast about himself or broadcast his business. "Sometimes I think I might not tell enough of some of the things I have done," he reflected. Even when enthused about a story, as when he told about army experiences in Germany and black-marketing whiskey, he used his usual matter-of-fact, bare-bones manner of speaking.

"Bob [Moses] and Amzie Moore and Hollis [Watkins], the one that sings, came in for that first [Mileston] meeting. There were quite a few people there. Then John Ball was coming in every two weeks or so. It wasn't the first time I'd heard of registering. We had talked on it in my Masonic lodge. Then we met that Sunday and planned to go up on the next Tuesday, I believe." The night before the First Fourteen tried to register, Wesley went up to Lexington to see someone in the hospital, and he saw the whites meeting at the city hall. "They had all been notified that we were coming. They had time to prepare. At the meeting," Wesley went on, "we planned how we would meet at Ozell Mitchell's, and they asked for volunteers. John Ball took the names. We were all volunteers. John and them notified the Justice Department and they called to Sheriff Smith and told him that some people—not specifying who—were com-

John Daniel Wesley was the youngest and most formally educated of the First Fourteen and the first to fill out and turn in the circuit clerk's form. The massive black
migration to the North in the 1960s left the courageous Wesley as one of the few black
young men available to join the movement struggle.

ing out to register on that day." The Justice Department had been called
to be there, "though, of course, they don't ever do anything but take
down notes."

Wesley drove to Ozell Mitchell's in his car and then got into Sam Redmond's car to go to Lexington. He knew Sam Redmond pretty well, even though Redmond was much older. He didn't really know much about Turnbow and couldn't remember his being at the meetings beforehand.

They planned to meet together at Lexington, but then "the cars had got split up some kind of way," Wesley said. "When we got there we parked over by the Holmes County Bank and some had parked over on the other side and some were down by that south street. We all gathered down around the corner at Beale and met there to start. A deputy stopped and then helped us to cross. When we got to the other side, Sheriff Smith came out of his door and came and met us. He told us to stop and asked us if we had a permit to march. We said 'no' and he said we'd have to disperse."

"Go around to the other side over by the tree and wait there," Smith said.

"John or one of them yelled out, 'Okay, in single file to the tree!' and Sheriff Smith said, 'No,' he wasn't going to have any marching there and we'd have to break up and disperse. 'Get over there not in a march.'

"We broke up and some went around one way and some went around the other, and we got over to the tree. When I got over there, Turnbow was already walking up toward the courthouse. So I don't know what happened there, what Sheriff Smith had said. I was too far in the back to hear what was going on. Few knew that actually I am the first one to have filled out the form."

Wesley wasn't too sure when they arrived, although he knew that Circuit Clerk McClellan's office closed at 11:30 for dinner; they hadn't really been there very long before it closed. Turnbow never got waited on, never got the form to fill out, and came back out when the office closed for dinner.

While they were there, reporters came and asked them about Samuel Block. They were questioning everybody about him, where he was. Wesley said, "They asked me if I knew Samuel Block, and I told them 'no, not personally.' They didn't ask me any more.

"The way it was, that I was first, was that when we got back to Lexington, there were just a few of us. Mr. Hayes, I believe, and maybe Mrs. Carnegie—just four or five of us. We walked up there and Sheriff Smith met us and said, 'Which one of you is going in first to register? That's what you came here for I guess.' And I said, 'Well, it doesn't make no difference.' And he said, 'Okay, you—go on in there first.' And so I was the first to go in there and actually fill out the form to register."

Wesley couldn't remember when the preacher from Lexington came over to join them—before or after some of the group headed to Greenwood for the dinner break. He knew that no one else except him had joined them, "though there were lots of Negroes up around there on the other side peeping around," Wesley said. "Some of our folks were afraid that they were going to come into our group and start batting at us and beating us up. When we were crossing the street, some Negroes came up and tried to stop us, tell us not to go across there.

"No, I wasn't afraid really, not of the guns. I didn't think we'd get shot in the street. Of course, it was tense and everything, you know. The Justice Department men were there. Two were standing by the one door and another at the other door. They were all around the place. You could kind of tell which ones they were. You could tell between them and the Holmes County men.

"No, there weren't many whites on the street. They had started gathering over there in front of that café that burned, but Sheriff Smith had gone over and told them to break up and not gather. Sheriff Smith really acted pretty good. He had been notified before we came that we were coming. But he didn't know who we were or what to expect. He made lots of whites deputies. They were all around. They had the guns."

Because he'd gotten in the first day and filled out his form, Wesley didn't have to go back and didn't go the next days after that. Wesley said, "Really very few were involved at the beginning and it was hard to get people out at that time. They were afraid their houses would get bombed and they'd get shot."

Wesley said the reason he'd gone up was that they all knew that something had to be done sooner or later, and it was just as well to do it then as later. But then right after they made their attempt, he thought, "We . . . moved too fast, without getting all the full details." He continued, "But then I see now I believe that we didn't start soon enough."

3

Mileston

September–October 1964

Eighteen months after Holmes County's first "movers" attempted to register to vote, Henry and I entered the county. There were many local people who were willing to struggle, who were gaining confidence, in addition to Hartman Turnbow. We joined Mary and the four COFO Summer Project volunteers who had stayed on, plus Abe Osheroff, who made no secret of his intent to entice us, especially Henry, into his exciting community center construction project.

Often in our first crack-of-dawn mornings, Henry did construction with Abe while I drove off with Mary, John Allen, Don Hamer, Larry Stevens, or Mike Kenney, the remaining outside whites who had been working in Holmes County for the COFO Summer Project. We visited local movement leaders in the delta and eastern hill communities: George and Willie Mae Wright in Sunnymount, Cora and Roby Vanderbilt in Old Pilgrims Rest, Austin Wiley in Mount Olive, and others. Many of the hill leaders had been drawn to Mileston in 1963 and early 1964 to learn about organizing their own communities.

In the rural, impoverished, black world at that time, organizing was mainly done without access to telephones. Communication took place at regular meetings or by going to see an individual at home or in the field. With the Summer Project came two-way radios for both cars and bases in movement offices or houses. Because Holmes COFO worker John Allen was doing especially dangerous work opening up the adjoining Carroll County, his car was equipped with a radio, more for the security of reporting problems to the base than for communicating ideas or arranging work or meetings with local leaders. We outsiders knew how much phones could help; we longed for them. Early on, I learned that there weren't phones in enough black homes to require a list, although I made lists of other longed-for "necessities," like the bathtubs I located in several Mileston movement homes. Navigating rural distances by car was a more difficult, risky way to communicate than using a phone. Early civil rights work meant driving—driving dirt roads, mud roads, no roads, and occasionally gravel roads. Pavement was found only in the white folks' parts of town, which we avoided whenever possible. Driving meant flat tires nearly every day, wishing for a two-way car radio, and getting stopped by the state patrol, who were always out to get movement workers.

The first people to organize in Holmes's hills, as in its delta, were the black landowning farmers. Hill holdings were often smaller than the forty acres that most often was the amount that had come from the Roosevelt federal program in Mileston; black holdings were usually smaller than those of whites. Most of the houses were run-down old shacks disconnected and isolated from each other and, seemingly, the world. The houses may have had a TV set, but no indoor toilet or running water. In some outhouses, the maggots sifted through shit within a foot of the seat.

Totally rural and almost exclusively black, these hill communities were often centered on a small, independent black church that provided life-sustaining strength to its members. Even though at least 125 such churches existed at that time in the county, it was risky to hold movement meetings in them. More than twenty black churches in Mississippi had been firebombed that summer, and it was the investigation of the burning of Mt. Zion Church in Neshoba County by Schwerner, Chaney, and Goodman that had led to their deaths in June.

At a citizenship meeting in the upstairs of an old store in Tchula, the delta town about six miles north of Mileston, workers attempted to organize a mass meeting and tried to encourage the development of local leaders. The upstairs room was the meeting place of the black Masons of Tchula. Joe Smith, their leader, was also the chair of the local NAACP. It was not an accident that the movement met there. The store was along Highway 49, south of the Tchula black neighborhood of Goose Hollow. We could hear the jukebox playing downstairs. The twelve of us at the citizenship class listened to John's talk about voting and organizing. He spoke in elementary terms, asking slow, measured questions, attempting

Robert Head with granddaughter Patricia and wife Pecolia. The Heads lived on the highway at Mileston with several children and grandchildren. Mr. Head, a carpenter, helped construct the Holmes County Community Center at Mileston along with Californians Abe Osheroff and Jim Boebel.

to get the tired and old to speak up. After their long day in the field, they sat silent, listening, some looking as if they might nod off.

"Where can we hold the meetings?" John asked.

"They's afraid," several lamented. "No one will come."

"They ain't no place but this one room heah that'd hab us."

"Maybe," John suggested, "we should wait 'til next meeting. You keep your eyes open, considering, and feel around for a bigger place . . ."

"Boy," one fellow bellowed, "We done felt."

We stood in a circle, crossed arms, held hands, and sang "We Shall Overcome." Feeling strangely as if we three whites had somehow cast ourselves as saviors, I felt sad. The gathering was so pitiful it hurt. In the North, I'd sung that song stridently, energetically, even offhandedly. In Holmes, where the song was so clearly needed, it felt bleakly futile.

By contrast, in Mileston, where the first movement meeting had been held at the Sanctified Church in March 1963, the energy was palpable. Abe had arrived in summer 1964 to build the community center, around the same time as the Freedom Summer workers came into the county and the state. Local farmer Dave Howard offered as a building site a piece of his soybean field closest to the church. Abe, Jim Boebel, carpenter Robert Head, and local farmers who could give time were shaping the center into a one-story, thirty-by-eighty-foot wood frame structure.

Abe and Jim were independent and unaffiliated with COFO. They planned to stay until the building was completed, but the project slowed when Jim injured his hand. Although he didn't have to leave the county or be hospitalized, Jim couldn't do his usual work. The time when the cotton ripened in August and September was called lay-by, and the farmers didn't have to work all day, so they had time to work on the community center. But the cotton was now becoming fully ripe and farmers had to begin their crucial picking. Abe needed an experienced construction laborer like Henry. So with charming persistence, he worked on getting our energy into center construction.

We hadn't been assigned to a location, but when we had stopped in New York en route to Mississippi to see COFO recruiter Al Lowenstein, he had alerted COFO we were coming. After we each had left Stanford, Al was my most direct contact with COFO. Once we got to Mississippi, Henry and I thought we would check out the scene at the Jackson office

Hartman Turnbow was a master orator. Here he speaks at a Third Sunday Countywide Meeting. Also pictured are James Moore (*center*), from Pickens, and Walter Bruce (*far right*), from Durant.

before settling in anywhere. So, as we awaited details of the next Jackson COFO orientation meeting, we happily worked with Abe and Jim on the building.

We were clearly needed in Mileston. The thirty-five COFO Summer Project workers in Holmes County had been based fairly evenly in the eastern hill communities and Mileston. By our September arrival, only five of the thirty-five workers had decided to stay on in Holmes for an undefined period. The others had already left the state, most returning to college.

One of the biggest Mississippi Freedom Democratic Party (MFDP) projects was continuing work on the Congressional Challenge. In fall

1963, SNCC had organized the Freedom Vote, which some called the Freedom Ballot. These mock elections throughout Mississippi were held to demonstrate to the state and the nation that blacks would vote if given the opportunity. SNCC centered their efforts on Mississippi, where racial discrimination was the highest and black registration the lowest. Students from Stanford and Yale volunteered to work on the Freedom Ballot to augment the forty SNCC members already working on it. Nearly eighty thousand blacks came out to vote.

That Freedom Vote gave the MFDP a message and some muscle. The Freedom Democratic Party sent its delegates to the 1964 Democratic National Convention to contest the right of the Mississippi Democratic Party to participate, claiming that their white senators and representatives had been illegally elected in a completely segregated process that violated both party regulations and federal law. The Democratic Party turned the challenge over to the Convention Credentials Committee, whose decision to televise the proceedings allowed the nation to see the testimony of the MFDP delegates.

The sixty-eight challenging MFDP delegates included Hartman Turnbow, who told his story about trying to register to vote. Fannie Lou Hamer, the powerful forty-seven-year-old sharecropper who turned herself into a SNCC and MFDP activist, delivered a stupendous oration. For eighteen years, she had worked as a timekeeper on a plantation in the same delta county, Sunflower, that was home to the infamous James O. Eastland, a powerful plantation owner, a U.S. senator, and the chair of the Senate Judiciary Committee. At the convention, she spoke eloquently of the shame to America of the life experienced by black Mississippians. She told of being arrested for attending a voter registration seminar and thrown in jail. Others were arrested as well: June Johnson, Euvester Simpson, Annelle Ponder, and Lawrence Guyot. Hamer told of horrific beatings she received in that jail. In the midst of her televised testimony, President Lyndon B. Johnson called an impromptu press conference to preempt the media's focus on her. Later that night, all the major networks broadcast her MFDP testimony in its entirety.

Most observers speculated that the MFDP would be seated. Then representatives from other southern states threatened to leave the convention and bolt the party if the challengers were seated. The MFDP ended up getting no seats at the convention. The MFDP representatives considered and flatly rejected the lopsided two-seat "compromise" offered them by the Democrats. The MFDP considered it a victory that the Democrats changed the national party rules so they would never again accept an all-white delegation.

September turned to October, and we learned more of Mississippi's political climate—how to sleep alert to every dog's bark, keep in constant touch with each other, and worry whenever we didn't hear from anyone who was away from us. Openly working on civil rights was dangerous. SNCC kept track of "incidents" around the state. Fifteen racist events in Mississippi were logged during the first two weeks of October 1964: almost daily arrests, bogus traffic tickets, and shots fired at buildings and homes. Serious incidents ranged from a black youth shot at by a police officer, a black man on his way to a movement meeting beaten with a blackjack and left in the road, a COFO worker Freedom House dynamited, a family evicted from a plantation, and a cross-burning in front of a home.

Abe and Henry focused on the building. Mr. Head, Mileston's lone carpenter who was not a farmer, had more powerful movement steadfastness than strength in his aging body. He contributed what he could to the construction. With most others out in the fields, Mr. Head was the only regular local construction volunteer.

Being able to settle into one county and meet its movement leaders and outside workers who shared their summer's experiences was a unique opportunity for us—a special Lorenzi–Holmes County orientation. As each day passed, it felt less necessary for us to explore movement action in other parts of the state. The trip to COFO in Jackson seemed less urgent.

During those first few days, simple events often hit me the hardest. When our car broke down, especially after dark, we undesirable whites lived with a constant patter of discomfort, as though something, we didn't know what, was missing—safety and security, perhaps. Our minds played out our choices: if we couldn't get the car to restart, walking down the highway was dangerous, but if it did start, the trip would be dangerous as well and often was postponed until light. These weren't reportable "incidents" but cumulative irritations that filled daily life with fear and frustration.

In some situations, whatever action I took was wrong, such as the time I sat in the darkening dusk on a highway at an old, dirty, tumble-down Negro repair shop where I knew white people shouldn't be seen. The black couple in the car with us that evening had sat in the back, separated from Henry and me in the front. Even we movement folks who were fighting for desegregation were afraid of what whites would do if a car carried both white and black people. That evening, I started talking to the fellows working on our car. One had a sister living in Los Angeles. Henry yelled at me to get back into our car. He said I was not only endangering myself by talking to them, but I was risking their safety if they were seen talking to me. I had put us all in danger by trying to be respectful and friendly. Rudeness, however wrong that felt, was the safer route. Constant awareness of the whites forced all our actions. We paid attention to whom we talked and with whom we drove when we ventured outside the safety of the black community.

Only a couple of weeks into our time in Holmes, an event occurred that drove home the isolation and danger we faced. One night after dinner, Mary and I stayed for a while at the old shack that COFO had set up as a makeshift community center in Mileston, a mile or two from the new center site. Henry had gone to the new site without us. I didn't know that the newly arrived SNCC project director Ed Brown was planning to use Henry's help. Ed wanted to deal with the persistent problem of the police harassment of the teenagers coming and going from their weekly Action Group meeting at Mileston.

That night, Henry joined Ed and Larry Stevens. They each drove a carload of youths the twenty-five miles to their homes in the hills. The three set out as drivers as well as adult protection and witnesses of what the patrolmen might do.

Mary and I arrived at the new center and learned of Ed's plan about twenty minutes after the young people, Henry, and the others had left. My fear rose. I was irritated that no one had told me about the plan. Mary and I went to the Howards' to wait. I sat alone in the darkness of the porch. The two-way radio crackled in the house, and we all raced to it. Larry's voice burst out from Turnbow's house. He, Ed, and the kids were safe, although evidently out of breath. Henry had been arrested. The words tore swiftly, coldly, through me, to my fingertips and toes. I felt scared self-pity, terror for Henry, and anger at them all. I sat in stunned silence, forcing back tears as I heard Abe arguing about their stupidity and Mary making calls to Jackson. The lit room whirled around me.

Abe snapped his fingers in front of my face and told me I should wake up, get moving, and start calling for bail money. The police had found a bread knife in the car and had arrested Henry on two charges, a "concealed weapon" and a "loud muffler"; the muffler offense was a felony in Mississippi. I envisioned months at the notorious Parchman Prison Farm for Henry, as he was obviously guilty. We had indeed traveled with Henry's mother's bread knife in our food supplies. Larry failed to tell us where they had found the knife. Mary said it was too late to radio back to find out. I worried they'd found it in the glove compartment or inside on the floor. Hopefully it was locked in the trunk. They figured the bail might be as high as three thousand dollars. I called Jules, Henry's lawyer-brother in Pittsburgh.

Abe ranted about the inefficiency and stupidity of Ed, the escapade leader. I wallowed in self-pity. That night, I slept at the old community center, cuddled Puppy, and barely spoke to anyone. I wished for Henry's body and lips. I decided to take cigarettes to him.

I awoke early and got to the Howards' ahead of everyone else. In the midst of my fright, I was most unnerved by my total dependence on everyone else. When we finally all came together, I wasn't very civil to Ed. "What in the hell did you think you'd accomplish?" I snarled. I wondered how Henry could have agreed to do something so stupid.

We argued and tried to find out about Henry's hearing. We called Judge Bridges in Thornton, Judge Kelly in Tchula, Patrolman Moody, Sheriff Smith, the jail, the Greenwood Highway Patrol office, then Judge Bridges a second time and all of them again. The runaround was complete and irritating. The telephone lines seemed against us as we couldn't get the Lexington operator to answer.

Finally Mary and I went to Lexington. I dressed as the worried wife, prettily and properly for the officials. I wanted visiting privileges. We had to be at his hearing because no lawyer would be allowed. We had to find him. We weren't sure where he was.

As we walked into the sheriff's office, a man slipped out. When I found out the man was the sheriff, I went after him and spoke politely, trying to find Henry. He was cold and angry. We found out later that when I was confronting the sheriff, Henry had already been acquitted. Incredibly, charges had been dropped, which was unheard of.

Henry had actually talked his way out of the situation. An impossibly good talker and compromiser, he had played up our having just arrived, our plans to go soon to Jackson, and the fact that we had no long-term plans in the county. He mentioned he might be getting a job teaching math or physics at Tougaloo, the black college near Jackson. When I finally spoke with Henry, he was so cocksure about how he had talked his way out of jail that he was irritated about my having worried Jules and his family.

That night in Lexington, we ate White Castle hamburgers and saw a bad movie. We argued some, talked of leaving Holmes and moving to Jackson. Later, alone, I seriously considered leaving Mississippi without Henry. The trauma had wiped me out. It truly was remarkable that he had gotten out alive. They could have had him if they had wanted. Later, we saw the event written up in the October Holmes SNCC incident report.

On a later night, as Henry slept I tried writing my thoughts. It was hard to see what we were accomplishing. Soon COFO would assign us somewhere, and I wasn't sure where I wanted to end up, or even if I wanted to continue. Full of conflicted emotions, I wished desperately to be alone, without Henry, although I knew I couldn't exist in Mississippi without him. Simultaneously, I wanted us to be together. Abe, with his decades of struggles in Spain, New York, and California, had once told us we should join the fight, no matter how futile, in order to live rightly on our feet, instead of nonhumanly on our knees. Remembering that, I felt guilty, wanting to be mature. But I also wanted to live the way I wished, which I knew was selfish.

Henry's arrest shook me, but work in Mileston continued. In mid-October, Henry and I finally attended the COFO orientation meeting in Jackson. We stayed with Edwin "Ed" King and his wife at their house. Ed, a white Mississippian, was the chaplain of black Tougaloo College. His face was severely scarred from a 1963 car accident, which had occurred under suspicious circumstances six days after the Mississippi civil rights activist Medgar Evers was assassinated. The accident shattered Ed's jaw and he was undergoing a series of operations.

The evening at their home was unnerving. Not only was Ed a white organizer; he was a white Mississippian, which made him even more of a renegade. Henry and I were considered white outside agitators. The house was small, and under ordinary circumstances, it would have been comfortable, but frankly I was scared. Our very existence was making white Mississippians angry, and the evidence of what could happen to civil rights workers was visible on Ed's face.

COFO's fall priorities were the central topic of the orientation meeting. At the top of the list were voter registration and the development of both county Freedom Democratic Party (FDP) offices and the state MFDP. Community centers were even farther down on their list than Freedom Schools—which were their schools for children run during the 1964 Freedom Summer. All of their projects were heavily invested in voting rights.

The year before, in September 1963, COFO-SNCC had held the statewide Freedom Elections, in which eighty thousand black Mississippians voted during the three-day period. Only a handful of Holmes County movement folks participated. The successful organizing effort brought unprecedented turnout for a mock balloting for governor and lieutenant governor. Aaron Henry, the black COFO chair, ran for governor on a ticket with Ed King, who ran as the lieutenant governor candidate. That mock election laid the foundation for a real statewide voter registration campaign. Following through, the 1964 Freedom Summer took on a massive voter registration and education project.

For me personally, the orientation was a tough event. I reacted with an irritated disdain that Henry and I were clumped together with a bunch of brand-new volunteers. COFO overlooked what we felt was our advanced, oh-so-hardened experience in Mileston. By the time of the orientation, we had built the beginnings of a relationship with the Mileston movement. More than that, we had lived with the fear of being shot, assaulted, or having our living space firebombed. We had faced police reprisals for being white workers in a black movement. Henry had been arrested on trumped-up police charges. Our time in Mileston seemed more like months than weeks, so we felt quite seasoned by our field experience.

Still, we had come to the orientation to meet COFO staff and other volunteers who had arrived after the summer project finished and to see where we'd be assigned.

Liz Fusco was the coordinator of Freedom Schools. The summer was over, and while some Freedom Schools were operating in other parts of the state, the ones in Holmes had closed. Working with a Freedom School meant leaving Holmes. After a day or two, my attitude bordered on snotty as I continued bristling at how our movement experience was disregarded. Liz was turned off by me; I was turned off by her. She rejected me as a teacher in her program.

Henry, on the other hand, was quite acceptable for a variety of assignments around the state, but we weren't looking for separate assignments. The orientation helped us determine that we did not want to work for COFO. Our taking on the Holmes County Community Center (HCCC) at Mileston was a mutual decision. It took pressure off the state COFO to staff it; in addition, we preferred to be under the direction of the Holmes local people than the state COFO from Jackson. We left with an understanding that we would work in Holmes for the time being—probably a year.

The grand opening of the HCCC was held October 18. Finally completed, after more than four months under construction, the center housed a library with nearly seven thousand northern-donated books in a small room immediately to the right of the front door, just off the front deck. In the back were a kitchen, a restroom, and a shower. Functioning indoor plumbing was a rarity in the community. Henry and I were given the sleeping-loft space above the kitchen. The remaining space in the building was open—the largest indoor area available in the county for blacks to use, and they did use it as they wished, for political change. We outside workers, local leaders, and state organizers were "ready" and were percolating plans for meetings and activities for adults and children.

On the Grand Opening morning, COFO staff from around the state began pouring in for what became an uncoordinated planning meeting. Amazingly—yet perhaps not so surprising for that group of leaders and organizers in that area—no one seemed to know who was running the show.

Abe and Mary, who were leaving that night for Jackson, decided to give a presentation designed as a farewell to the Summer Project and a welcome to the new SNCC-COFO staff. Local leaders Hartman Turnbow and Reverend Jesse James Russell were in charge of a Holmes countywide meeting and the kick-off of the MFDP fall campaign, respectively. Later,

Daisey Montgomery Lewis, a retired agricultural extension worker, became the chair of the trustee board and center director for the community center at Mileston. Howard Taft Bailey stands next to Lewis.

we "green" organizers regretted not having thought to even ask the guests for donations to support the new building.

Earlier in the day, a few Mileston teenagers had showed up to clear away the accumulated construction trash in front of the building. They carried benches into the center from the church next door, the Sanctified Church that had taken the brave step the year before to open its doors to the first movement meetings. Norman Clark arrived with a vase of flowers for the library. Nearly four hundred people began arriving from all over the county and the state. Matt Herron, an independent photojournalist who was documenting the movement, and other photographers came to cover the event for magazines and the general news.

Trouble soon showed up in the form of Moody, or "Mister Moody," the state patrol officer who always followed the movement, and a second patrol car with another officer. Around one o'clock, they drove from the highway past the church and the center on their left and on toward Dave and Flora Howard's house beyond. John Allen ran across the road with a camera to get a picture of them coming back. The two patrol cars sped back, screeched to a halt in front of John, and started questioning him. Seeing John's camera, Moody feigned ignorance and opened it, exposing the film.

Meanwhile, curious guests began to gather. Photographers raced out from inside the center, and the patrolmen seemed nervous. They ordered the crowd off the "highway," referring to the narrow dirt road. Then they warned John about being a wise guy. When they attempted to leave, Moody's patrol car peeled away first but was delayed by Turnbow's shiny black car blocking the road as it attempted to turn into the church driveway. The crowd roared with laughter. Moody didn't look too amused. He and the other patrolman posted themselves on the paved highway turnoff to the center and stopped every car as it entered, examined each license, and gave out tickets. Stokely Carmichael, SNCC field director in Holmes County, in his flamboyant way, walked over to the patrolmen to question them about their actions. They immediately arrested him for interfering with an officer. While they were at it, they arrested John and drove them both off to jail. The photographers hid behind bushes and in the soybeans to capture the scene with their telescopic lenses. Later, four or five patrolmen and Sheriff Smith and his dog stationed themselves on the paved highway, but by 3:30 p.m., all the patrol cars had left, perhaps chased away by our power of the press.

Inside there were speeches: "The work of the center is just begin-

ning," Abe said. "It can be the freedom center of Holmes County."
Turnbow said the building would be used in the struggle to secure justice
for the Negroes in Mississippi: "If we seek first the ballot boxes, then all
will be added to us. It is time for us to join together to help ourselves as
we joined together to build this community center." In his dedication,
Reverend Russell quoted the Bible: "I have surely built a house for you,
and a habitation for you to grow in forever."

Mrs. Victoria Gray of Hattiesburg, a strong state FDP leader, called
the community center at Mileston a "labor of love, not merely a building,
but a dream made reality, a reality above price." As one of the sixty-eight
MFDP challenging delegates at the August Atlantic City Convention and
one of the three MFDP candidates in the next month's Freedom Vote,
Mrs. Gray asked for the people's votes and campaign support for herself,
Mrs. Fannie Lou Hamer, and Mrs. Annie Devine. Just as the 1963 Freedom Vote had laid the groundwork for the 1964 Convention Challenge,
the 1964 Freedom Vote against the white Democratic representatives
would lay the groundwork for the 1965 Congressional Challenge.

After the speeches, the center's trustee board met and defined Henry's and my position, appointing us the community center managers under Center Director Daisey Lewis, who was to advise us and come to the
center as needed. She also was appointed to the board. Daisey was an
educated professional—a retired schoolteacher and county worker. She
and her husband Lee lived on his father's hill land, twenty-five miles east
of the delta in the Spring Hill community. The exact timing and duration
of our appointment to the center was not clarified by the board at the
opening.

That night Henry carried Puppydog up the ship's ladder that led to
our loft door in the community center. We crawled into our bed with new
responsibilities and daunting tasks ahead. Exhaustion brought immediate
sleep.

Thus began the sometimes harrowing, often delightful, days in
Mileston. Henry, Puppydog, and I had actually done it! We were fantasti-
cally active in the midst of Mississippi's furor. Our venture was exciting,
stimulating, challenging, and frequently frustrating.

Mileston movement leaders treated us well, caring for us as if we were
their grown children. Mrs. Caldonia brought us the first gifts, a roast,

some liver, and other goodies from her family's slaughtering. Mrs. Lewis brought us a sweet potato pie and turnips—yummies that neither of us had ever before even tasted.

At three o'clock one morning in the week following the grand opening, Turnbow's house was shot into again. I was up and out within hours of the shooting, calling for support in Washington and Jackson. I went to look at the scene in the afternoon and spent the rest of the day writing a report for the *Vicksburg Citizens Appeal.* For the next two nights, Henry and I were so jumpy we hardly slept.

As the days passed, the police harassed movement workers and local people with tickets and fear, but they were only partially successful. There weren't enough patrolmen to cover the increasingly widespread movement activity—the number of weekly meetings was by then in the double digits. The hub of the Holmes County movement, the community center, was deepening our understanding of the critical link between meeting places and community organizing.

Director Daisey Lewis and the COFO-SNCC workers—John, Don, Mike, and Ed Brown—agreed that Henry's and my major priority and responsibility would be the community center. We gained a satisfying sense of direction. Philosophically and politically, each of us was developing a consciousness and growing understanding of the distinct roles of outside workers and local people.

The Holmes County movement people had already organized themselves and knew their own needs, desires, and direction. They no longer needed to depend so heavily on outside organizers from SNCC, CORE, and COFO, as did counties with no local movement-leaning leaders. Individuals in those counties went looking for the movement when it came within range or when workers from outside organizations looked for potential leaders as they tried to open up a county. Basic growth was still needed in Holmes, especially in the many sections of the county as yet untouched by canvassing and voter registration efforts. But the year and a half during which Mileston leaders had been spreading the word to people in other Holmes communities had resulted in a strong core of around two hundred seasoned, active adults able to focus on new areas of Holmes.

When legal needs arose, we clearly relied on our affiliation with

COFO. When Henry was arrested, or the community center or the county FDP had legal problems, COFO lawyers were available and assisted us. The Jackson office maintained a wide-area telephone service line, which avoided long-distance charges for individual calls, and on that line COFO called each project in the state for updates several times a day. Our center was on its regular calling schedule. COFO also provided to us some center supplies such as minimal quantities of office items, books, food, clothing, and speakers. So although we had chosen a route based in Holmes and independent of COFO and others outside, our relationships with SNCC, CORE, and COFO were amicable and collaborative and could grow.

The drive and force of the local movement was the most exciting and tantalizing aspect of our independent stance in Holmes. The center was theirs, totally in their hands. They indeed had their own reality, identity, and energy. We worked directly and only for them. We had much to learn and to teach—as much as they had to give and get from us. It was a sizzling, productive experiment that engaged and enlarged our minds, hearts, souls, and bodies and those of the local people.

Their Stories: Shadrach "Crook" Davis

Crook Davis was a tall, powerful, dark-skinned, sharp, able man. He did not hold a great number of movement offices, but he was a steady backup whenever workers and leaders, such as Hayes, his neighbor on the Choctaw plantation, needed the protection of his strength and wits. He lived with his schoolteacher wife, Sarah, and their children in the house next door to his parents, Shadrach Sr. and Caldonia, who named their three sons Shadrach, Meshach, and Abednego. In her seventies, Mrs. Davis was still strong, active, and a widely respected church and movement leader.

Crook talked to me about those beginning days of the movement. He said he thought that the meeting at Sunnymount started up before the meeting at Mount Olive but that both communities had been involved early, as had Old Pilgrims Rest. Turnbow had gone out speaking to lots of communities, and so had Hayes and others. "It was something back in those years," Crook said. "Andrew Smith was fair and old McClellan, boy you should've seen his face and Pat Barrett and a bunch of those other men. You've seen some of these white folks haven't you? You know how they are. I bet they just can't figure you out, can they? Staying around with all the niggers. Having educations and degrees of coming down here.

"I don't think I'll ever forget their faces at that trial down in Jackson. That was some trial. And they had Bob Moses on the stand, questioning him. Barrett and a bunch of others. Judge Cox I believe it was, was questioning him. And when they went to asking about where he comes from and what he did before he come into Mississippi, you should've seen them. They just didn't know what to make about Moses. Well, they asked him the questions and it came down he had a college degree here and another degree there and he was teaching here and he had been teaching there. McClellan say he just didn't have no idea he was such a nigger like that and if they had known that . . . Well, anyway they ask him if he had been all that, why he do such a thing as come down to Mississippi doing all the troublemaking. He just sat there cool and quiet and he told them, 'Well, I was up there teaching and I started hearing how bad it was for the people down in the south and I read about the things going on down here and I just decided to come down and work to help my people.' You should've seen their faces.

"The trial was held in the Main Post Office building in Jackson. It was the trial for Bob and Hartman Turnbow and all of them, you know when they was arrested for having burned Turnbow's own house. This was after. They already had a trial before that little JP in Tchula. I was in there. It was me that put up a bond to get Bob out. See they grabbed and arrested Bob right away that next morning after the fire. Then they came and arrested Turnbow too. They really were rough on Bob when they took him, grabbed him up, swung him around, pushed and shoved him. They all stayed in [jail] for a while. We couldn't get them out. I don't know what, but then Guyot came up and got Turnbow's bond signed. Then they was holding Bob's trial at that little old place in Tchula. We were up there watching. There wasn't too many that would go in there. Just a few of us went. You know, all them niggers around there were saying, 'You better not go in there, better not fool with that mess,' acting scared and the fool.

"But shoot, I wasn't going to let them fools talk out me from going into that trial. All the others was sayin' you shouldn't put your name up on them papers. Then white people will stop your money at the bank. But shoot, I told them fools the bank wouldn't stop my money, and even if they did I got my brother up in Detroit and if anything happens to my money I can just call my brother. They got money and they'll send it to me to make a crop. Yes, I don't need to worry about them fool people down here.

"Bob Moses was cool. He was a fine boy. He just come to meetings and sits back quiet and wouldn't say much, just let the people talk. He would come in and talk softly, talk about how they had to go up and try to register and it was dangerous. He didn't talk big and loud, he just said his say and then he sat quietly. He went all over, to other parts of the county and to the meetings of the people."

Their Stories: Norman and Rosebud Clark

I paid a visit to Norman Clark, one of the First Fourteen, and his family, at their farm. I found Norman out back hauling some bushes. He was an average-sized man, in his midforties, not particularly tall, yet not short either. He wasn't either slight or stocky, but rather well proportioned, giving the basic impression of strength and wiriness. His smiling face was oval in shape, flat in features, and had a small mouth and chin, which almost came to a point. His rich reddish-brown color got brighter in the summer and deepened with his burn and tan, especially at the top—the back of his head where his hair was thinning.

He opened the barnyard gate wide so I wouldn't have to walk in the gray-black watery ooze of the hog pen. It extended, unfenced, back toward the barn. A large black-and-white sow lay midbelly-deep in the middle of the pool. We walked out back, behind the barn to the fence where his tractor with trailer bed attached was parked.

He got back on the bed and began pitching the cut shrubs, bushes, branches, grass, and wastes off the trailer and over the fence where, after they dried, he would burn them. He'd cut down most of the bushes and branches that had been in front of his house along the road near his driveway, where it'd gotten so overgrown it was hard to get into the drive through the tangle.

We went inside the house when he was done unloading his trailer, and

Rosebud and Norman Clark used their vehicles for farming, church, family, and movement activities. Both among the First Fourteen, they attended the earliest movement meetings, housed SNCC workers, and were bedrock movement leaders.

he immediately offered me something to eat or drink. There was food in the kitchen pans; one had two pieces of fried chicken, and a pan with six or seven pieces of boiled chicken sat on the stove burners. Biscuits were in the oven. Some cornbread was left in its pan sitting on an open shelf.

I asked for some water and we went outside to fill the pail. First he got me a glass and opened the chest freezer in the back room. It was jammed tight with food and seemed to need defrosting. Norman took a pick and broke off pieces of ice. He insisted that I use my own hands to pick up the ice for my glass.

Many times Norman is close, warm, friendly, and unguarded. He doesn't indicate at all a consciousness of my whiteness. But then at moments when I don't expect it, Norman and Rosebud will act in some little way that reveals how conscious they are that I am white. Norman's insistence that I pick up my own ice is an example. Frequently he calls me Mrs. Lorenzi. But that day he called me Sue.

Rosebud often treats me as one of the children, kidding me, disagreeing on personal matters, seeming to speak her mind. Once, we were at the center with Rosie and Elease and Rosebud scolded me for losing so much weight and told me how I used to have such pretty hips. She said, "If I were your mother, I'd take you over my knee and spank you." She was silent for a few moments after that and then said, "Listen to me, a Negro woman, talking about mothering and spanking a white lady."

Anyway, Norman and I walked outside, him with the pail, me with a glass of ice. He pumped water into my glass and then hooked the pail under the spigot and pumped it full. Back inside, the children came into the living room. Kayrecia was twelve years old, dark and lively. Quiet Marvis was thirteen and light bright. Inez, who was seventeen, mocked me. The two older boys, Richard and Lewis, were both tall, one slightly darker than Norman. They trooped through the front room and went off to the back room.

The atmosphere in the Clark household was not really chaotic or disturbingly noisy, but there was lots of activity. The portable radio played loudly. We talked in the living room. Mrs. Clark read the mail and teased Inez when she found two letters for her from two different boys in the service. Inez seemed to enjoy the banter. Norman asked me when Henry and I would start having kids. When I mentioned that it would mean we'd have to worry more about money and providing and planning, he disagreed. "You should have kids soon, before it's too late," he said. "You never can plan too much. You shouldn't look too far ahead. You know the Lord provides and you just don't know what might happen. You never know. President Kennedy he didn't know he was going to get shot when he did. You just can't plan."

Norman and Rosebud also talked about how when they came to the delta, that first year, they sold a cow for two hundred dollars and bought a tractor right away. Rosebud started talking about taking care of children, and Norman told her, "You'd better not be talking like that Rosebud or Sue won't never want to have children."

Norman told me about one night after Inez was born. "She was just a little baby," he said. "And was late at night, about midnight." Rosebud butted in, "What you mean midnight, it was two o'clock in the morning." Norman said, "Okay, about two o'clock in the morning she woke up and started hollering and screaming. We didn't have any milk in the house. We used to have Pet milk in the can. You know, Rosebud's milk wasn't much good. But that night, we didn't have no Pet milk in the house and that baby was just hollering. Well you know, I walked all the way over near to where Judge Brandon's house is, way out in the pasture, and found the cow and milked it for that baby. The baby was still screaming when I got back, and I gave her the milk." Rosebud said, "He just did that because Inez, that was his first girl."

4

The Holmes County Community Center

November 1964–January 1965

The regular Wednesday night Mileston community meeting was one of the first activities to move into the center building. It developed out of the 1963 citizenship classes on voter registration that local leaders Ralthus Hayes, Reverend Jesse Russell, and Willie James Burns taught. All were Mileston project farmers who had gone to South Carolina for teacher training by the SCLC.

The teacher training began with the Highlander Folk School, which established citizenship schools in 1954 in South Carolina to help adults learn to pass literacy tests on the way to voting. The schools spread across the South until the state of Tennessee moved to shut down Highlander in 1961, blaming it for much of the strife raging across the South. The SCLC carried on the citizenship schools, continuing to educate voters under the guise of adult literacy classes. SCLC staff including Andrew Young and Dorothy Cotton drove all over the South recruiting prospective students, who were then bused to South Carolina for a week-long training program. The citizenship schools clandestinely taught the fundamentals of practical politics, democracy, community leadership and organizing, civil rights, and the strategies and tactics of resistance and struggle. The program was designed to get participants to establish citizenship classes in their own communities.

Mileston's Wednesday night meetings, which began after Mileston leaders received SCLC training in 1963, were first held in the Mileston Sanctified Church. When the meetings moved into the center, right next door, it was a natural homecoming. No special celebration was held, but people felt that this meeting place was meant to be—this was what the

The older Mileston women sometimes gathered before the regular Wednesday night meeting at the Community Center at Mileston. *Left to right:* Alma Mitchell Carnegie, Annie Bell Mitchell, Caldonia Davis, Florence Blackmon, and Maude C. Vance.

movement community reaped from the lessons that activist Abe Osheroff brought to Holmes County.

Each community meeting began and ended with song. Song and music protected, cradled, and inspired those in the struggle. The movement standby "We Shall Overcome" closed every formal movement meeting. Everyone gathered in a circle, crossed arms, joined hands, and swayed out the many powerful verses: "We are not afraid. . . . Truth shall set us free. . . . God is on our side. . . . We shall overcome." A powerful effect was felt by all as we sang freedom songs like "Oh Freedom," "Go Tell It on the Mountain," "Ain't Gonna Let Nobody Turn Me 'Round," "If You Miss Me from the Back of the Bus," and "Like a Tree Planted by the Water, We Shall Not Be Moved." The music often brought individuals and the community through difficult times.

The spirit of the local people lightened those times. One day some lumber and blocks from an unfinished construction project were left on the floor of the main meeting room. Mrs. Carnegie, whose name was spelled like the steel mogul's but was pronounced "Car nuh GEE," came to the center that day for a meeting. Seeing a plank inclined on a block, the playful sixty-eight-year-old woman walked right up it. With arms gracefully swinging out, one hand daintily holding the skirt of her clean but well-worn housedress, she looked like a child curtseying. Her back straight as a rod and her feet in wide old-lady shoes, she firmly, gaily, quickly strutted—one foot in front of the other—up the low plank, then turned and nearly skipped back down. She took a joy in it like an eight-year-old child would—doing it just for fun.

Rosie Head and Elease Gallion were the first Mileston young adults to work at the center and were in their twenties when the movement sparked their hearts and minds. Rosie and her children Willie C., Dolly Mae, Shirley Mae, Luther Dale, Calvin "Butchie," Debora Denise, and Donald lived with her parents Robert and Pecolia in a house rented from the Mileston Farmers Co-op. It was on the highway, almost within sight of the center. Elease lived on her father's farm on the Mileston road, even closer to the center than the highway. Each had gone to the Greenwood freedom meetings in late 1962 and early 1963; the young SNCC organizers in Greenwood were definitely an attraction. Elease had also worked with the COFO volunteers in the summer of 1964.

At the center we worked together to set up social events and programs for children. Turnbow and the Russells were so concerned about education that we immediately established a daily kindergarten and a once-or-twice-a-week story time in the library. Like Puppydog, the kindergarten gave us great fun and a relief from harder struggles. Although training myself and the teachers was wearing and certainly not simple, it was wonderful to be reminded how much I loved and enjoyed little kids. I became absorbed with them, oblivious to all but the group I was working with. I forgot myself in my spontaneous interaction with them. Before opening the kindergarten, I rejuvenated a Ladies Auxiliary, which elected a kindergarten committee to help with handling the class and raising local funds. It often felt slower and more draining to report and explain to them the activities and needs of the kindergarten than just to solve the problems myself, as if I could. But, as with all grassroots organizing, the benefits of community ownership of the programs flowed from participation from "below up" rather than from "above down."

Soon after Rosie and Elease started, two young women from Tchula, Zelma and Clemma Williams, came every morning to volunteer. At first they were less comfortable with the venture than Elease and Rosie had been. Both Williamses were shy and quiet and definitely lacked hands-on experience with children, but they were willing and interested in learning. I happily let them take over whenever they would. Whenever activity lapsed, I had to struggle to not jump right in. At the beginning, fourteen four- and five-year-olds came; within a few weeks, attendance grew to thirty. One plantation owner told "his people" that he didn't want their kids coming to the center. But a few still sneaked their kids off to us. Henry built benches and low kiddy-tables out of tongue-in-groove boards. We had few materials, so I wrote letters to supporters in the North describing items we lacked: art supplies, toys, teaching manuals, records, and Encyclopedia Britannica filmstrips.

Then, in the very midst of kindergarten programming, every able-bodied person helped with the MFDP Freedom Election of October 30–November 2, setting up voter education for adults at the center. Fresh in our minds was the 1963 Freedom Ballot, when nearly eighty thousand Mississippi blacks had registered for the Freedom Vote and cast their ballots, and the Freedom Vote–elected delegates had attended the 1964 Democratic National Convention and demanded to be seated but lost. We were at it again. In this November 1964 Freedom Election, the Freedom Democratic Party ticket listed Lyndon B. Johnson and Hubert Humphrey for president and vice president, Aaron Henry for senator, and three candidates for Congress: Fannie Lou Hamer, Victoria Gray, and Annie Devine.

We organized center social events and coordinated health, clothing, and welfare programs. Unplanned emergencies, harassment, and legal issues constantly required our responses. At the same time, I started writing the first of several years of irregularly produced double-sided, legal-sized, blurred mimeographed newsletters to report on the activities of the Holmes movement, the community center, and Henry and me. An equally time-consuming task was sending the newsletters out to prospective and current northern supporters. Fund-raising, especially by letter, was a

Thelma "Nutchie" Head, a seamstress of note and a sister of Rosie Head, occasionally used her sewing machine in the center's library.

challenge. Once I got the letters mimeographed, they were often illegible because of either the ditto master or the machine. I ended up sending copies of the several pages to California, where my father could reproduce them for me at his job. Mr. Turnbow visited Abe Osheroff in Los Angeles for about a month and spoke at several events Abe had arranged to raise funds for the center. Dynamic and colorful, Turnbow told our story so well it was difficult for anyone to hear him without making a donation.

Early in our programming, the Free Southern Theatre, an integrated traveling troupe of sixteen professional actors, brought exciting entertainment to the community center. Performing what had never before been seen live in Mileston, they attracted more than one hundred people, who packed the center for each of the two shows. The audiences ate up the hilarious, familiar-to-home Purlie in *Purlie Victorious* by Ossie Davis, and they were attentive to Godot in Samuel Beckett's *Waiting for Godot*. They seemed to comprehend more intuitively than any intellectualizing college student might have.

Within a few months of our moving into Mississippi, my parents drove from Los Angeles to see family in Nashville. They stopped for a day in Mileston to get a feel for what their baby girl had chosen to do. Our time together was much too short, and Mileston may have been too scary for their comfort. However, seeing us in our building and meeting some local leaders must have eased some of their concerns, or at least gave them concrete images of Mississippi. My father was so appalled that we didn't have hot water that he went out to try—unsuccessfully—to find an electric water heater.

Not one of the local or nearby butane companies would agree to sell any gas for our heat or hot-water systems. They tried to freeze us out. On her way north, Mary Brumder checked to see whether any of the Memphis companies had licenses to install in Mississippi, but she had no more success than my dad. Henry and I wrote a report to the movement lawyers about the butane companies' service refusals. But when the winter nights turned bitter cold, the Mileston farmers finally rustled up a coal- and wood-burning stove. They set up the old cast-iron stove not quite in the middle of the main meeting room and cut a hole in the brand new twenty-foot-high ceiling. Norman Clark brought in the first load of coal. Others brought wood. Standing four and a half feet high with its impressive pipe, the stove's welcome heat attracted many to sit and stand close around it. They opened its clanking door and fed its fire. I began cooking fried-egg breakfasts on the weekends on its flat top surface. The kindergarteners started their session in the circle of the stove's warmth. More than chilly, many mornings were freezing cold. We'd planned to use the small, fifteen-by-twenty-foot, front room library for the children, but most of the time we worked and played huddling by the stove in the main meeting room. Henry got up early to fire the stove and get ready for the children.

Living as we did right inside the center, its work became truly an around-the-clock project. We tried to figure a way to fit in time for eating and resting. We tried locking the building and putting a "closed" sign on the door on Sunday mornings and two afternoons a week, but it worked only sporadically. I found myself using the closed time to write fund-raising letters. Many times during "closed" afternoons, Henry worked with dozens of people sorting and distributing the many tons of used

Calvin "Butchie" Head and other children often spent time playing in the community center library with its many donated books.

clothing sent by northerners wanting to help. Up to our ears in clothes, we and the leaders struggled to determine an order for distribution. The most needy among the plantation people, sharecroppers, and project farmers came in to make their selections first.

Around this time another donation arrived, this one from Duluth, Minnesota. It came from my sister and brother-in-law, the Duluth mayor, members of the Jewish community, and the NAACP chapter. Local drivers provided a shipping truck. Inside were canned goods, school supplies, encyclopedias, books for the library, furniture, more clothing, and dozens of other items to make the center a more welcoming place.

Henry's brother, Silvio Lorenzi, also helped us out. He often sent us a taste of home, fifteen-pound sticks of Genoa salami.

Just surviving took effort and energy. We drove the pickup Abe had bought for the center with construction money, but even though we rationed its center use, it drank many gallons of gas each day. And even though we were more tied to one spot than any of the other workers, a conservative estimate of our gas expenses alone, not including repairs and oil, was a hefty sixty dollars a month. Many blacks earned two dollars a day, and the price of gas was thirty cents a gallon. Food for the two of us and too many packs of cigarettes (though only twenty-five cents a pack) were our other major expenditures. We realized that to actually stay for a whole year, we would need funds well beyond the fifteen-hundred-dollar wedding-gift stash we'd come with. We weren't making a garden at the center and, although farmers were generous in sharing what they raised, grocery shopping was essential. Most times it was difficult—downright scary. Driving thirty miles to Greenwood's white supermarket felt a bit safer than Tchula's Piggly Wiggly, because Greenwood's larger size meant we were unknown. Beddingfield's in Mileston, like most Negro stores, was barely a market, with small quantities of limited stock on its shelves. Wong's grocery, the only middle ground, was only a slight step up.

Every day brought more work than we could do. We were doing education around the MFDP Congressional Challenge, scheduled for January. But more immediately there was another challenging electoral exercise—the federal Agricultural Stabilization and Conservation Service (ASCS)'s annual December elections for members of the ASCS committees.

ASCS committee members dealt with soil and water conservation programs as well as price supports and allotments for various commodities, such as cotton. These all-white committees assigned acreage allotments to each cotton farmer, which meant that allotments had always been disproportionately larger for whites. Not until the 1964 COFO workers researched the workings of this federal agency did the movement farmers find out that the committees were elected to their positions by the farmers. And the elections were open to all farmers who participated in ASCS programs—owners and tenants, black as well as white. To vote required no registration, no literacy test, and no poll tax payment!

In Holmes and eleven other heavily black, rural counties, the MFDP distributed information on the ASCS, encouraged local farmers to become candidates, and organized support for their campaigns. More than twelve hundred of the nearly two thousand eligible Holmes farmers voted. The results of the 1964 ASCS elections in terms of blacks winning committee seats were just so-so, but large numbers of blacks participated. That gave them great opportunities to learn and build individual and movement strength. Of the nine ASCS districts in Holmes, only one elected a Negro chairman. He immediately faced harassment: the bank repossessed his truck several weeks before its payments were due, and the man he rented his land from demanded immediate payment.

Along with all these program tasks, individual needs, and newly developed skills, we spent weeks preparing for the arrival of Josephine Disparti, a registered nurse from New York. The statewide Medical Committee for Human Rights (MCHR) was established in Jackson in 1964 as a base to serve the COFO summer volunteers. In the fall, it turned its focus to local efforts. In response to our center's request for medical help, the MCHR joined with the National Council of Churches Delta Ministry and opened an office in Greenville in the fall of 1964, bought a medical van, and hired nurses Kathy Dahl, Phyllis Cunningham, and Josephine Disparti. They assigned Josephine full-time to Holmes to develop the first movement clinic in the state.

When Josephine first arrived, she stayed at the home of Hartman and C. Bell Turnbow. Just days after her arrival, night riders drove by the house and shot into her bedroom window. An FBI agent and the sheriff came to the Turnbow home, but they didn't investigate the crime. They interrogated Josephine. They looked through her room, her closet, and her suitcases, obviously trying to find anything to charge her with. After a week or so, she moved in with a local black woman named Lila Forte.

Josephine helped organize and met weekly with the newly formed Holmes County Health Improvement Association. It started with only eight people but quickly grew to a fair-sized group of local people interested in health issues, classes, and improving their families' lives. Josephine worked to set up the clinic in our community center kitchen. The committee's first project was building a clinic room, separate from the kitchen and placed just behind the library in the front part of the main meeting room. With Josephine's help, the group investigated health and welfare problems and planned for solutions. Often new people, not yet drawn to the movement, became attracted to working on a new issue, in this case health, which expanded the reach and scope of our local efforts.

Luckily for us and the county, Josephine had been a school nurse and had done lots of home visits. The committee, Henry, and I helped get the word out that she would begin making house calls in January, but it wasn't a simple task. As a white outsider, already known to the sheriff and the FBI, she had to be careful. When a sick farm worker needed attention, someone would have to drive out to the plantation at night with Josephine hiding on the floor of the car. Holmes had an alarming number of high-risk pregnancies, because poor black women went without prenatal care. At that time most black children were still delivered by midwives who were supervised, and often humiliated, by white public health nurses. Health care was pay-as-you-go, and very few rural people could afford the charge, thirty to seventy dollars, for treatment at the emergency room.

Teens worked at the clinic, setting up the clinic equipment and helping people fill out their registration forms. Josephine was a role model for them and joined them in starting a health career club.

Set to begin offering services in January, Josephine was very much appreciated. She knew the job would be hard, because she was going it alone, the only nurse serving rural Holmes County blacks, and she was doing it without backup.

Firebombs and shots continued to be fired at movement homes and centers around Mississippi. In Holmes, movement farmers came from communities all around the county, two at a time each night, to guard our center building. The farmer-volunteers, with their rifles and shotguns, sat in the library, the only room in the building with a window facing the road in front of the center. Occasionally Tougaloo College students helped guard the center on weekends. They kept watch overnight while Henry and I slept in our loft at the back. The community center had become the known base for the movement and its meetings—those for the Mileston community and the countywide meetings, as well as smaller meetings among several leaders. It was also the hangout for the outside volunteers. Even with all the security measures, the center was a dangerous site. Yet there was a warm sense of community and a feeling of safety at the center. It was the place where movement ideas, goals, and actions were conceived, developed, nurtured, and grown.

Abe sent a letter, saying: "I was reminded what a lucky break it was for the center that you and Henry came along. I have a feeling of deep personal gratitude. You took a job far, far tougher than the one I undertook, and I complicated it with some of my lacks of insight and foresight. So if you carry it off, you will make a small piece of history."

As the end of 1964 approached, we were exhausted but energized—our spirits boosted by Abe's letter. Puppydog was still with us. So great with the kids, he seemed to know more people than either Henry or I did, although our knowledge was constantly expanding. The quiet was amazing, kind of eerie. I held my breath waiting, but the building remained standing.

And then it was 1965.

Their Stories: Reverend Jesse James Russell

Reverend Russell was describing to me the actions of the First Fourteen: "The guards of Christ went to the government after Christ was resurrected and rose. When they told the government what had happened, the governors decided to explain it to all the people by deceit. They said some of the disciples had come and released Christ and taken him. He hadn't risen alone. . . . Just like when Turnbow's house was bombed, Sheriff Smith let it out and the Citizens Council's newspaper said that Turnbow himself had set his own house on fire.

"The coming of the movement to Holmes was much like the coming of Christ. The movement was certainly prophesized: there would be wars and struggles and deaths. And deaths certainly did come. Reverend Lee in Belzoni [in adjoining Humphreys County] gave his life [in 1955] after he registered and was going around organizing his people. He was shot while he was driving his car in Belzoni. He and others from Belzoni registered and were told to take their names off the book, but Reverend Lee refused and then he was killed.

"That kept the other pastors back because they was organizing then and had been holding meetings, talking about registering. The meetings were held in folks' houses. One preacher was holding meetings around the Mileston area in his house and in churches that they didn't just outright name as Freedom Meetings, but that's what they were about. After Lee got killed, things went under a bit and there weren't so many meetings. Things slowed up and the ministers were held back.

"When the movement finally came to Mileston and they had meetings and were getting ready to go to the courthouse, they came to me and asked me to come up with them. They said, 'Come with us, Reverend. We need a pastor with us.' And I said, 'Why don't you get some of those bigger men to go on up with you?' But I knew they probably wouldn't likely to be going up there, and so I went.

"There were one hundred that said they would go, but when it got down to the day there were only twenty on that first day. And then some didn't go back on the second day so it was down to just us fourteen."

Part 2

Working with the People

5

The Congressional Challenge and Marching for Freedom

January–July 1965

On January 1, 1965, a busload of thirty-eight Holmes people left for Washington, D.C., to participate in the Mississippi Freedom Democratic Party's Congressional Challenge, the culmination of the local and state FDP strategy that had begun in 1963. The Freedom Election during the November 1963 gubernatorial race had demonstrated that blacks would vote if the white system allowed it.

The MFDP was challenging the legality of seating the "regular" (white) sixty-eight-member Mississippi delegation to the August 1964 Democratic National Convention. Spearheading the strategy for the Congressional Challenge effort were both Bob Moses, a SNCC and COFO organizer and the designer-director of the Freedom Summer Project, and Guyot, a SNCC and MFDP organizer and leader. Holmes County's movement had been among the earliest local movements to support the development of both the state and the local FDPs. Guyot, who directed the 1964 Freedom Summer Project in Hattiesburg, Mississippi, had been unable to attend the Democratic National Convention because he had been jailed for registering black voters.

Fired up and enthused about the 1965 Washington trip, the local people were able to raise more than six hundred dollars from inside the county to help pay trip expenses, an incredible accomplishment given the poverty-level wages of most residents of the county. A matching amount was sent in by a group of Milwaukeeans interested in helping fund the Holmes trip.

An astute political analyst, Fannie Lou Hamer was a moving speaker who used her powerful face, body, and voice to rally her audience.

While in D.C., our people spoke with U.S. congressmen to gain their support, asking for their votes for the Challenge in the Credentials Committee and on the House floor. They also met with top administration officials—Agriculture Secretary Orville Freeman, Interior Secretary Stewart Udall, and Health, Education, and Welfare Secretary Anthony Celebrezze—to give them a true picture of how those agencies administered their federal programs in Mississippi.

At the January 4 opening ceremony of the 1965 congressional session, the MFDP tried, as it had tried with the August convention delegates, to halt the seating of the entire Mississippi delegation elected in November 1964. The MFDP argued that the Mississippi elections were illegal because blacks had not been allowed to vote and that the white victors should not be seated. The group asked for the seating, instead, of the three MFDP congressional candidates, Mrs. Hamer of Mississippi's Second Congressional District, Mrs. Devine of the Fourth, and Mrs. Gray of the Fifth. The women had run in the fall statewide Freedom

Elections in which nearly eighty thousand voted. At the exact same time of the voting on the floor of Congress, just outside the building, more than five hundred Mississippi Negroes, including the thirty-eight from Holmes County, were demonstrating. In the end, the MFDP Challenge resolution was defeated, with 246 members of Congress voting against it. Many people were encouraged, however, by the 149 northern members who supported the Challenge with their votes.

Bob Moses pointed to the irony that the MFDP "holds mock elections, while the state of Mississippi holds 'mockeries of elections.'" The formal January 4 Challenge wasn't over. The U.S. House Committee on Election Procedures was legally bound to examine the voting conditions in Mississippi. Following official protocol, legal teams from each side were allowed forty days to begin the next steps to gather evidence, take depositions, give testimony, and make attacks and counterattacks. The purpose of the MFDP Challenge was also to work toward the passage of a voting rights bill with provisions for new, free elections in the Deep South.

Fannie Lou Hamer with Holmes movement leaders. Mrs. Hamer was the best-known and most-respected MFDP leader. Her courageous acts of civil disobedience to promote voting rights were often met by violent responses from angry whites. Here she speaks at a rally in Holmes County Courthouse.

On January 14, the Holmes travelers returned home to continue registration attempts and also to work with some of the one hundred out-of-state lawyers who came to help the MFDP take depositions throughout the state. The depositions were evidence in testimony form to be presented, up to forty days after the Challenge vote, to the U.S. House Committee on Election Procedures. On January 23, two San Francisco lawyers and a court reporter arrived at the Mileston center to begin preliminary interviewing of local Negroes who had attempted to register. The lawyers had the right to subpoena witnesses for the hearings in Greenwood up until adjournment on January 29.

A Holmes schoolteacher was subpoenaed and testified about inadequate curriculum, especially in civics, in the Negro schools and the intimidation faced by black teachers wanting to register. On the first deposition day, the opposition lawyers cross-examined at length, so only four MFDP witnesses could be heard.

At one point, the opposition tried to cast Hartman Turnbow's moral character in a bad light. One of our witnesses explained that Turnbow wasn't present in Greenwood because he had remained in Washington at President Johnson's invitation to the Inaugural and was spending an extra week there talking with members of Congress about the Challenge and attending the Supreme Court proceedings on the *U.S. v. Mississippi* case.

Although the *U.S. v. Mississippi* case had been initiated years earlier, it tied into the Congressional Challenge. In 1962 the U.S. Government had brought an action against the state of Mississippi, state election commissioners, and six county registrars, because "the voting rights of African American citizens had been violated." The U.S. District Court for the Southern District of Mississippi dismissed the complaint, but the suit went to the Supreme Court on appeal. Turnbow was able to listen to the Supreme Court hearings.

Back in Holmes, the issues of the Greenwood depositions for the Congressional Challenge covered the difficulties blacks faced in Mississippi when they attempted to exercise their right to vote between 1890 and 1963. The Congressional Challenge case pointed out that Mississippi's school system fed the problem by providing segregated schools where whites received quality teachers and facilities and blacks were provided inadequate schools or often no school at all.

In Greenwood, the lawyers for the state pushed on, arguing many of the same issues found in the *U.S. v. Mississippi* case. They heard testimony about inadequate schools. Negroes had been given new brick school-houses—their answer to the MFDP charges that public education for Negroes was so lacking in civics and civil rights that most children and adults didn't even know they should have the right to vote. The state's lawyers claimed it was irrelevant to the Challenge that Negroes in Holmes were not allowed to pay the poll tax, which meant they weren't eligible to vote. The state argued it was irrelevant that blacks were intimidated and misled by the sheriff and the registrar throughout the 1950s and early 1960s and that since 1963 their homes had been bombed and they were threatened with physical harm while attempting to register. After the MFDP deposed all their testimony, the opposition was given its own forty days to gather depositions about the fairness and legitimacy of the 1964 elections. During their forty days, there was silence. At the end of summer, the depositions and arguments were sent to the House for a vote. SNCC joined in the Challenge support by recruiting two thousand students to go to Washington to pressure legislators to take voting rights seriously.

At the same time in Mississippi, Negroes were quietly attempting to register without holding public demonstrations; twenty went together to the courthouse in Lexington in early January and told the registrar they wanted to "fill out the form." More than 130 registration attempts were made during the month, showing both courage and support for the Challenge. A grand total of ten passed the "registration test" in January, nearly the same number as were "on the books" before the movement.

Henry and I clearly saw two realities—despite the fear of economic or physical harm, blacks in Mississippi demanded the right to vote. And the regular Mississippi Democratic Party neither was democratic nor cared about equality.

The local FDP was gathering strength. Northern donations lifted spirits that same month when a New England group heard of our need for transportation and donated a 1957 Chevrolet to our movement. When Henry and I traveled north to drive it down to Holmes, we stayed with SNCC historian Howard Zinn. That year, while teaching at Boston University, he had published *SNCC: The New Abolitionists*. The car was stationed at the Lexington FDP office and loaned out to communities to carry folks to the courthouse and for other movement trips and business.

In February, on the national front, Malcolm X, the advocate for black self-determination and self-defense, was assassinated. His violent death hardly made a ripple in Holmes County. However, northern news coverage of our movement brought in more unexpected interest and donations. Unannounced, Mel Wax, a columnist for the *San Francisco Chronicle*, stopped in at the Holmes County Community Center while touring the state. Several weeks later, when checks began flowing in from California, we learned that he had written and published a feature on our center. The warmth of the more than one hundred *Chronicle* readers who expressed their compassionate interest in the center was welcome in those midwinter darkest days. The interest and donations were especially helpful because, at the time, only a handful of black people in Holmes County were registered to vote and the local movement efforts were consumed with problems of immediate survival, including harassment from the state patrol, local businesses, and individual whites.

Later in February, Elaine Howmiller of the *Nashville Tennessean* came to Holmes to visit Mary Brumder, who was staying longer to work in the county. When Howmiller discovered I had Nashville connections and relatives who lived there, she turned her social occasion into a full-page feature story with photos. The Nashville community's reaction to her story contrasted dramatically with San Francisco's sympathetic outpouring. No checks came in from Nashville—I first heard of the article's publication when I opened an anonymous envelope containing the ripped-up pages of the article with a scrawled message saying I was a disgrace to the memory of my beloved, deceased uncle and I should never again set foot in the town.

In spite of the positive news coverage, harassment reared its ugly head at about four o'clock in the afternoon of March 29. Five of us were returning from a week-long speaking visit in Linn County, Iowa. Mr. Turnbow, Mrs. Epps, Mrs. Sanders, Henry, and I had been welcomed there. We were helping to organize a Holmes County civil rights support project. While in Iowa, our group appeared on several radio and television broadcasts and met with the Cedar Rapids Junior Chamber of Commerce, the Council on Human Relations, and other interested Iowans.

Mrs. Epps talked about the poor health conditions and facilities of the Holmes County black population and how she had worked to establish a medical clinic in the community center building. Mrs. Sanders spoke about holding voter registration classes in her home in Goodman. For two years, she had been the only one who was successful in organizing civil rights meetings in that community.

We had driven for twenty hours. No police tailed our integrated movement car. But only fifteen miles from home, a flat tire, our fourth on the trip, stopped us down the road from a white man's café near Vaiden in Carroll County, Mississippi. Henry jacked up the car, and because the lug wrench had not worked for the previous flat, he started walking toward the café to inquire about borrowing one. Then he saw a white man aiming a rifle at him from the rear yard of the café. At the same time, Turnbow got out of the car to help with the tire. More white Mississippians gathered in front of the café. They were clustered around a second man with a rifle. He shouted profanities aimed at Negroes and the civil rights workers. He raised his rifle and threatened to shoot. A white woman near the gunman grabbed his arm and begged for restraint. The traffic was heavy, but no one stopped. It was broad daylight.

Before Henry and I could react, our three traveling companions, all people in their sixties and seventies, started to flee. Mrs. Epps and Mrs. Sanders jumped from the car and, along with Turnbow, started running down the highway away from the café. Seeing the blacks run didn't calm the whites at the café. The angered Mississippians continued to shout vulgarities and threatened to shoot as Henry and I returned to the car. The jack was still on the car, and we drove over it with the flat tire and away from Vaiden as fast as we could travel. I don't know what saved us from being shot. Maybe it was the one white woman in the crowd who shouted at the gunman not to shoot. Maybe it was seeing the blacks run like Mississippi whites believed they were supposed to.

When we got home, we called the FBI first. Two days later, two FBI agents arrived. It was an aggravating experience. Our lives were threatened with firearms in broad daylight, a felony crime, but the FBI treated it as a routine incident. We filed a complaint with the sheriff, but the FBI made it clear nothing would be done. The local police, the Mississippi Highway patrol, and the FBI would not protect us.

The movement had first taken root in the county among the nonprofessionals, primarily farmers. Their ownership of land, despite its low acreage and often heavy erosion, made them the most independent element of the black community. As the movement spread, the base of strength continued to be the farmers, followed by poor townspeople, small subsistence businesspeople, and some plantation workers. The black professionals in Holmes were not doctors, dentists, lawyers, or engineers, but mostly schoolteachers, preachers, and the few successful businesspeople, particularly funeral directors. Though less directly shackled by the white power structure, the ministers and the few prosperous businesses owners had stayed back.

The more formally educated teachers had not tried to register in 1963 or before and throughout 1964 had continued to keep their distance, not attending movement meetings or becoming active. As the traditional leaders of the black community, the professionals were at once respected by and aloof from the grassroots community. It seemed that the professionals couldn't comprehend the worthiness of a movement built by the uneducated grassroots. As employees of the county school superintendent, the teachers had a real fear that "moving" would lead to job loss.

Teacher Bernice Patton Montgomery was an exception. She and her farmer husband, Eugene, began to attend the Mileston meetings soon after the 1963 courthouse attempts. Later they were key leaders, along with midwife Willie Mae Wright and George, her farmer husband, to set up a movement meeting in their home community of Sunnymount–Poplar Springs, thirty-five miles into the hill section of the county. In 1964 they opened their homes to Freedom Summer volunteers. Bernice Montgomery showed everyone that her early involvement with the movement hadn't caused a firing. To some extent, her actions disproved the legitimacy of her fellow teachers' fears.

In early 1965, two COFO workers opened an FDP office in the south Lexington black neighborhood of Pecan Grove. The office became the center of the FDP's political work, and while it was noticed by the neighbors, especially the children, no overt reprisals came from Lexington whites. The action of opening the office led to another bold public action, a peaceful march.

In early June 1965, the Mississippi FDP proclaimed a "Freedom Day"

These children, sitting on a tire, lived in Lexington's Pecan Grove neighborhood.

for Tuesday, June 8, the official statewide white municipal Election Day. Our Holmes FDP's press release stated, "Citizens of Holmes County will stage a mass demonstration in Lexington . . . the county seat, on that day . . . [to] support both the Congressional Challenge and the right to full voting privileges." It noted that people would not only peacefully march that day, but also attempt to register.

The Challenge was to call attention to the illegality of seating the present Mississippi representatives: "Since Negroes in Mississippi are systematically discouraged from registering and voting by intimidation, harassment, terror, and confusing and complicated literacy tests, the five men who are now in Congress do not represent the whole of Mississippi, but only the white vote." The U.S. Congress was scheduled to vote on the issue later in the summer.

On Freedom Day the movement came out into the open to make a show of its strength, to build confidence in those who still feared joining, and to prove that movement people were more than just a small bunch of troublemakers, more than what some black folks called "a handful

Children, like this group with a bike, noticed the activity of the FDP movement workers, and their curiosity caused them to play around the office and come as close to us as possible.

of mess." Two years after the first courthouse attempts, Lexington was still predominantly closed to civil rights and its black community still had no movement meetings. In the previous year, more had managed to get in the "book," but registration was still hard, painful, and slow. This Freedom Day at the Holmes County Courthouse on Election Day demonstrated how disenfranchised blacks were. For a large number of blacks to turn out for an Election Day "action" to demand their rights would dramatically say they were no longer afraid to join the movement fight. A large and peaceful march would encourage more to come in and get organized.

Local leaders and organizers focused on convincing their neighbors, friends, and fellow church members that it was the right time to make our voices heard. They talked with the civil rights lawyers in Jackson about what could be done for legal protection. Many leaders had high hopes, although some admitted they'd be surprised if as many as one hundred showed; one said no more than twenty would. Still, our efforts continued. Having few active FDP members in the town itself made Lexington a scary place, still too early in the organizing process for people to have faith that many would come out to face their fears.

On the morning of the march, the white folks were getting ready to vote while the movement folks were getting set to march. Ralthus Hayes and other county FDP leaders decided it would be best to go up to the sheriff's office in the courthouse before the march to let him know what they were planning for the day. They didn't ask him for his permission but they sought protection for the demonstrators. Mainly, they wanted to tell him they were planning to be peaceful and they hoped he could maintain the peace.

One of Holmes County's First Fourteen, Hayes was that morning's primary leader. In the 1940s and 1950s, he had acted on his own, journeying to other counties around the state to attend the meetings for change in those times. As people continued to gather at the FDP office, he and a couple of other leaders wound their way north up Beale to Courthouse Square to find the sheriff.

When I drove up over the hill to the square that morning, my stomach felt a tugging. I wondered if anyone else would show up—and if the few who did show would land in jail or get their heads bloodied on the streets and the lawn. Then, after driving around the square, I turned right, toward the FDP office, to wait for more people. As each car pulled up to the office and each truck let out a new load, the tugging lessened. I looked around and could see the smiles that showed our hearts were growing big and brave. So many cars came. The space at the office was filled with cars parked all up and down the roads of the five streets of Lexington's shantytown. Cars parked in yards, jammed together on the gravel, and still more came. From nearby and from miles away, all kinds came—active workers and folks who'd never before been to a meeting, old and young, people with canes and in rolling chairs, people with babies in their arms, and others with children at their sides. Men came and women came.

Finally we started lining up. The line moved down the road to the highway that led up to the square. Still more came. The line of people stretched for blocks. When we got to the courthouse, we were so numerous we joined hands and make a ring of people all the way around the lawn. People surrounded the big red brick, white-columned courthouse building with its grass, shrubs, and walks, its Confederate monument and trees. We marched, and each was strengthened by the hundreds in front and behind. Relieved, we marched with quick steps and high heads under a bright shining sun.

The marchers saw some of their own people still holding back, just looking on, some talking and pointing but not joining in. Yet we were more than five hundred marching together, feeling good to show we weren't afraid. After several hours, we stopped circling, stood in our places, and joined in prayer and thanksgiving for the peacefulness, success, and strengthening that came from being able to march together. We encircled the clock-towered building and the big old tree where, just two years earlier, the First Fourteen had stood. We shouted songs of love, prayer, conviction, and freedom and then walked away, proud and happy.

The White Citizens Council's *Holmes County Herald* reported the event in an article entitled "Negroes March Here." Editor Paul Tardy wrote that the march was "apparently protesting voter registration procedures in the county." Describing the marchers, Tardy wrote, "Three white females and four white males were mixed in with the Negroes. . . . Almost half the marchers appeared to be school age, others appearing to be quite aged, apparently varying from eighty-odd down to about ten years old. . . . Many carried . . . signs which read . . . 'We don't recognize your congressmen because you won't let us vote,' 'One Man, One Vote,' and other such slogans." The article tended toward objective reporting until the final sentence. Ending as a continuation on a separate page, the last sentence stood alone: "The marching about Tuesday morning was a farce, a nuisance, and a disgrace to the Negro citizenry of the county."

With no arrests and no injuries, Freedom Day was a huge success. Six days later, boosted by their incredible accomplishment, the Holmes FDP joined the statewide Challenge demonstrations that the MFDP organized in Jackson at the same time the state legislature was meeting there.

Jackson's protests turned out to be far different from Lexington's. On the morning of June 14, Guyot, who was the MFDP chair, led five hundred demonstrators out of a Baptist church to begin a mile-long, silent protest march to the state capital. Nearly half of the marchers were in their teens. About seventy-five were white summer workers who had been in the state less than a week. Halfway to the Capitol, Jackson police halted the march and began arresting participants for parading without a permit.

That day Josephine Disparti was driving the Medical Center van when an officer stopped her and told her not to go any further. She was worried about the marchers, and when she drove closer to them, the officer returned and arrested her.

The forceful reaction by Jackson's police served to increase our numbers and extend the protest. Over the next few weeks, hundreds of Holmes adults and teenagers joined others from other counties as demonstrators. The state protests made the same points as the national Congressional Challenge and the Holmes County Freedom Day: black residents were denied the opportunity to vote for representation in Jackson as well as in Washington.

Back in Mileston, Ralthus Hayes, Henry, and I had a serious conversation. We agreed that after encouraging so many others to demonstrate, at least one of the three of us also needed to demonstrate and go to jail. Obviously the prime local leader needed to participate in the action; Hayes was the logical choice. I also volunteered to go so Henry could remain in the county, working to bring more people into the protests and helping get others out of jail.

When our morning arrived, Hayes marched wearing a neat, clean, good-quality suit with his ever-present gold watch chain hanging from his belt loop into his trouser pocket. He wore his wing-tipped dress shoes with the little decorative holes, like the ones my father always wore. He stuffed two fresh packs of Kools into each of his nylon socks. Never careless, especially regarding his own self and well-being, in his well-ordered, methodical way, he had arranged beforehand for his own bail. Being a farm and property owner, he needed any jail stay to be short in order to keep his affairs running smoothly.

Our group of adults and many teenagers from Holmes and adjoining Leflore and Attala counties demonstrated at the old Mississippi State Capitol, which had been made into the Old Capitol Museum when the new capitol was built in 1903. I marched with five teenaged girls from Mileston, including Hayes's youngest daughter, Sandra Faith. To bolster our spirits, we sang and shouted together, "We shall not, we shall not be moved. . . . We shall not, we shall not be moved. . . . We're fighting for our Freedom; we shall not be moved. . . . Just like a tree standing by the water, we shall not be moved."

We knew we'd be arrested. And like Hayes, I had stashed several packs of cigarettes for my stay in jail, not in my socks but with their visible bulges under the waistband of my skirt and in my bra. We marched for no more than ten or fifteen minutes when the paddy wagons arrived, taking all the whites and the black leaders to the city jail, where they put us in cells with bunk beds and mattresses. All the other black adults and young people were put into the cattle pens at the state fairgrounds.

About a dozen other women were in the jail cell with me. On June 21, we spent the day remembering and commemorating Chaney, Schwerner, and Goodman on the first anniversary of their disappearance in Neshoba County. Using pens, markers, and whatever we could scrounge, we created a mural on the tile walls of our cell honoring the memory of those who had worked before us and died in the struggle. Our words and images lasted less than a half day before the guards scrubbed them away. Surprisingly, they didn't punish us for our art-graffiti. We continued filling our time singing, building the camaraderie that comes with strong convictions and jail time. When I was in jail, I felt I knew better how to help others than when I was on the outside.

My jail experience with white protesters, black leaders, and black organizers was different from that of those arrested in the same demonstrations and taken to the fairgrounds. We had beds and were relatively uncrowded. They were held in livestock pens. Mrs. Alma Mitchell Carnegie and her husband Charlie were the oldest of Mileston's First Fourteen; she was in a fairgrounds pen where she had no cell or bed or mattress. The stress of being forced to spend eight nights trying to sleep on the concrete floor of a crowded pen had to have drained her, especially amid the continuing arrests and beatings. In addition, she maintained a complete fast during her entire lockup. She ate not even one bite of their food—more from her deep fear of being poisoned than from political and philosophical resistance. I'm sure her own extensive knowledge of Christian scripture and deep faith buttressed her through that and her many other struggles. Particularly fearful regarding food, even under normal home conditions, she had told me how someone had killed her chickens and poisoned her hogs. She didn't trust the meat sold at the white supermarket or even at Mileston's store.

Still, Carnegie's example lent weight to our experience of protest and punishment. She touched something in me, just as I saw others being touched by her. Along with her palpable and fervent connection to the good, the just, and the right came her vision of the bad, the unjust, and the wrong. Her beliefs sometimes evoked amused and affectionate chuckles at meetings of the movement and the church. She was respected, however, for herself, her life, and especially her willingness to go where her spirit led her. Informed by the spirit, she walked squarely down the freedom-fighting road, inspiring others around and behind her.

Hayes's bonding plans got him out of jail after only a few nights, before most of the rest of us. Nevertheless, he wore the badge of marching, getting arrested, and serving jail time. As a leader, he was the epitome of moderator, mediator, and reconciler of factions. To those who were more emotional or passionately expressive, his patience was almost unbearable. When working out details of actions, Hayes could see all sides of an argument. He would calmly invite each side to speak. Then, listening intently to the first side, he'd respond with "Yes, yes, thank you very much for that fine statement. I'm sure we all agree with your point that such-and-such is true." In the same polite, sweet-smiling manner, he would allow the second side to speak and also would agree with that side. It was as though he couldn't allow a disagreement to exist. Yet he was neither naive nor unrealistic. That spring and summer, in his quiet way, Hayes displayed brilliance in allowing decisions to be made. His strength came from the calm rationality that stopped factions and breaks from exploding. Radicals and conservatives recognized his strength and cool courage. He faced the same angered sheriff again and again and firmly stood for what he knew were his rights.

During the Congressional Challenge actions, Hayes had more sophistication and experience with the complex subtleties of the local, state, and national civil rights organization than any comparably self-educated person. Every day, despite very poor eyesight, he kept up with many newspapers, the above-average *Memphis Commercial Appeal*, a Jackson daily, and the county's weeklies. His actual reading process was slow and laborious, since he had to hold the paper an inch from his eyeglasses to view it through his very thick lenses. But, of all the county leaders, Hayes was probably the most informed on national and movement issues.

While the rest of us were in jail, Henry split his time between Jackson and Holmes, talking with the lawyers and helping the people who needed to get out and also organizing more people from Holmes to join the demonstrations. He worked primarily with Marian Wright and Henry Aronson, the two NAACP *Legal Defense* and Educational *Fund Inc.* (LDF) attorneys, who at the time were among the most active in the state. Henry also worked with Al Bronstein's office at the Lawyers' Constitutional Defense Committee, an affiliate of the American Civil Liberties Union (ACLU). All of the civil rights workers I knew, including the lawyers, called the LDF the Inc. Fund.

Local lawyers active before 1965 included black attorneys Carsie Hall, R. Jess Brown, and Jack Young, who received some aid and assistance from the Inc. Fund and individual civil rights lawyers. In 1964 the Washington, D.C.–based Lawyers' Committee for Civil Rights under Law, commonly referred to as the President's Committee, were the new guys on the civil rights legal block. They felt it was unsuitable to work in the same arena as the ACLU and other groups who were considered radical or "leftie." The President's Committee refused to take part in the efforts of the Freedom Summer Project, although by early 1965 they had set up an office in Jackson. Clearly more corporate and conservative than the seasoned movement groups, the President's Committee lawyers sometimes worked at cross purposes with our strategies and goals, which they seemed unable to grasp. In June 1965 they jumped in to get immediate releases for all those jailed, while the movement was just as fervently trying to fill the jails to create massive disruption.

By the time the Jackson protest was over, more than two hundred people from Holmes County and almost eight hundred others had been jailed in Jackson.

After I got out of jail, I wrote to the mainly northern supporters of the community center, trying to arouse interest and funds for the Challenge. "The Big Response has still not come," my letter proclaimed,

> but a continuous series of smaller marching "forays" staged by local people still enrage and engage Jackson. Negroes from all over the state continue to support the Jackson Marches and daily decide to join in the protest—to march into jail.
>
> Since June 14th, the first day Paul Johnson's legislature convened, over two hundred Holmes County local people have been jailed. Mr. Ralthus Hayes . . . and several members of the center staff have spent many days in jail. Just today, nineteen more [from] Holmes went to Jackson and were . . . jailed. . . . [The] Jackson marches are considered by us here and now to be the most important Mississippi Movement endeavor. . . .
>
> All . . . in the heat of the most crucial work time for the Holmes County cotton farmers. Yet over two hundred have sacrificed.

The letter ends with a plea for funds for bail and transportation back and forth to Jackson.

We printed a flier about the Jackson actions showing our spirited enthusiasm that summer. Around the flier's borders, encircling the text, are the words of the marching song "We're gonna' march in Jackson in the mornin', Lord. We're gonna' march, my Lord. We're getting ready for the Freedom Day, my Lord. Are you ready for the journey? Oh yeah, we're ready to go." The text read, "We have won our first victory. We can march in Jackson without getting arrested!! A federal court has told Mayor Thompson that, until there is a full hearing, Jackson officials cannot arrest FDP Negroes for marching peacefully in Jackson! The FDP is calling all Negroes to join in the March in Jackson on Friday, July 2. All of us who went to jail did not go in vain. . . . All of us shall come marching in Jackson to celebrate our first victory."

Our work was getting results. The number of blacks registered was climbing slowly, and our enthusiasm grew as the increasing engagement of local leaders in the planning and execution of movement actions and campaigns created enormous development benefits. The movement philosophy for outside workers to step back allowed leaders and followers to step forward and take on voting rights and the Congressional Challenge during those months of 1965.

Their Stories: Alma Mitchell Carnegie

When Mrs. Carnegie went to the Greenwood meetings in 1963, it was just another step in a long march extending back to the 1920s, when she sent letters about her plantation's conditions to Herbert Hoover, who was then the director of the Red Cross. Back then, she had to hide copies of the black *Chicago Defender* newspaper in her home. The paper, seditious to the ruling powers, was almost as sacred to her as her Bible. In the 1930s, she hid the tenant farm worker organizers, and in the 1960s, she hid SNCC workers. Like Hayes and a few other 1960s leaders, in the 1940s and 1950s she had attended semiclandestine movement meetings around the state.

Her birth family had contributed a measure of Cherokee blood that showed handsomely in both her and her brother's high, broad cheekbones. Her skin was deep golden brown and soft. The smile wrinkles made marks around her eyes; her face was not rutted or wrinkled, but smooth and soft like a child's. She kept her hair, a natural gray mass of tiny curl-kinks, sometimes knotted into little plaits but usually combed back and unprocessed. The warmth of her smile and shining eyes made those who were near to her feel her seemingly uncontainable inner light.

Once I stayed overnight at the Carnegie home. That night, Mrs. Carnegie was sleeping on a cot in the back room, where she kept her

Alma Mitchell Carnegie in her kitchen. Mrs. Carnegie was a feisty lady with a long record as an activist. She hid farmworker organizers in the 1930s and traveled to clandestine movement meetings in the 1940s and 1950s. In the 1960s she was one of the First Fourteen. She was jailed in a cattle pen at the state fairgrounds for participating in the 1965 Congressional Challenge march and tear gassed during the 1966 Meredith March. Her spirit was a unique combination of drive and serenity.

refrigerator. She said she just loved it so—to lie down and sleep alone in her own bed. When she got up, she would spray her nightgown lightly with perfume, then roll it up to keep the scent in and leave it on her bed. She said, "I just love to have sweet smelling fragrances around me." Her perfumes were an expensive kind she got from the Avon lady who lived up by Sidon. She had perfume in a spray bottle, perfumed talc, and two different kinds of creme sachets.

Mr. Carnegie was sitting still in his big armchair, a black outline with shaggy eyebrows. They were watching Johnny Carson on the *Tonight Show*, who to me seemed so far away—as did New York City. My life and thoughts and being and spirit had been alien to the phenomenon of him. Yet Mrs. Carnegie bounced in, dove in, and swam in the new element seemingly with no tugs or pulls. She lived and breathed it, accepted it and more—hugged it to herself.

She chuckled and was excited to realize that the crowd of girls Johnny had alongside him were the ones that would be in Atlantic City on Saturday night. She knew that, too. "Oh, that scamp! Always stirring up some mess of something," she glowed, readily admitting that she loved Johnny. She glowed every time he came on the screen and sometimes just sat with her beatific smile. She dismissed as just some of his foolishness anything that could be unacceptable that he might do. She excused him of everything and loved to watch and live with him and his banter with his bandleader.

She was in on all the program's "family jokes," and she watched the high jinks with spirit. As with everything she did, she entered in and became part of it. I never saw her bored. Sometimes she acted tired and slowed down, but she never became distracted from being vital and alive. She spoke to Johnny and his guests, "What you talking about? Hey, there, what you mean? Yes, that's the way it be." And she worried about each one that appeared.

Seeing a young singer, blond, willowy, sophisticated, seemingly foreign, she commented on her sunken eyes and how she worked too hard, poor thing, and led a fast life working in the night and not getting enough sleep. The girl was going to Las Vegas to open a nightclub act, and Mrs. Carnegie carried the burden of her sleeplessness, fastness, and running around.

A sugar blues group came on. It was an all-white band with horn, sax, clarinet, and other instruments. "They say the white is always asking why it is the Negroes is always getting so emotional with playing music. And the Negro say, 'Well, what you folks get so emotional over a ball game for?' But now, look, there them whites are with their music and just like us."

Then looking at the girl singer again with her short hair, of which Mrs. Carnegie did not approve, she said, "Looks like they all want to get rid of their feminine. . . . Why she want to chop her nice feminine hair all off like that? So mannish, like a boy." She enjoyed the girl's miniskirt, which reminded her of the hippies, "They aren't no harm, you know. They just want to have fun and enjoy life, and they do and there's nothing wrong in that."

I asked her when they had first gotten a TV. "Way back," she said. "Before you went to the courthouse? Before Kennedy got elected?" "No, it must have been after that. We went to Richard Ferguson's. He stay on the projects over there by Edie Hoskins and then the Boyds and then the Ferguson's house. It's that big house, the one that the head man used to have. Anyway, he had a TV before most people, and was good about letting people come and see it.

"When Kennedy and Nixon was running, I was hoping for Nixon to get it. I didn't know nothing about Kennedy then. I hadn't heard of him. I thought Nixon would be best because Eisenhower and him had worked a good foundation up, and he would be a good man to carry it on. But then I didn't know. And I prayed in earnest to the Lord for to let the best man win. So when Kennedy won, it must have been the best. The first time I saw him on the TV, the skin on his face looked rough. But he was the man. I prayed for the best to win, and he came through and it worked out like that. I came to know him and love him. . . . We must have got our television after that.

"Before we had the television, we had that radio from way back. But it got struck by lightning and it broke. I never got the money together to take it up to Greenwood to get it fixed. There used to be a good man in Tchula for fixing things, but he died and my radio has never got fixed. But when we got the television, we was able to start getting all the news on what was going on right here at home."

"They just showed on the TV . . . a white Catholic priest in Milwaukee and the others marching and going to jail again. Had a boy on there that favored Jean [her grandson Jeanie Boy]. But I don't imagine it was none of our Jean. He's not in Milwaukee, I don't expect. That priest is the same one, I think, that led us into Philadelphia [in Neshoba County]."

I slept late and found both Carnegies up and around. It was chilly and there was a small wood fire in the living room stove and a small one also in the kitchen stove. Eggs seemed the most plentiful—a bowl of about ten or twelve of them were on the table in the back room. Mrs. Carnegie had saved me one piece of her salt pork that she had gotten from Mrs. Beddingfield, where "maybe things is getting better. I may start trading there again. . . . The meats looked fine the other day, and Mrs. Beddingfield said something about a new man bringing her things. I believe Eva

Berryman was telling tales on Mrs. Beddingfield when she say the other day that she bought a cream cone there and found a roach in under the cream at the bottom of the cone. I just don't believe Mrs. Beddingfield would do that. She looks in them cones real good before she fills them with cream. I jes' don't believe she'd have that. That Mrs. Berryman is just lying and telling tales."

Mrs. Carnegie was a mite low on food. She showed me what she had gotten from a relative in Greenwood—two packages of home-frozen tomatoes and one package of corn. The only other things in her refrigerator were one small package wrapped in white paper, perhaps the salt pork from Beddingfield's, and a small dish with the leavings of some bacon. She insisted on making me a piece. I tasted the bacon and gave the rest to her. My breakfast was one egg fried in the inch of grease she poured and the piece of salt pork she made. I gave her most of the fat because she said she couldn't chew the lean because of her teeth—actually her lack of teeth. Also I had one flat biscuit that she had made that morning; she forgot to put in the powder, so the biscuits didn't rise. There was a small bit of sweet apples, something between sauce and preserves, that was delicious. She wanted some coffee but had none. We drank water. She told me that she boils up some Grape Nuts and tea for a stimulant, "It's like being a baby and it's good. Not weak like coffee makes you, but strong and healthy like being a child again. Refreshing and wholesome, and it gives strength, strength."

She told me about the night Roosevelt got elected. "You know Roosevelt was the president for twenty years, and he was up there against Tom Dewey, I believe. We stayed up late listening to who would be president, and it was well after midnight when we heard. Then we came into the kitchen and heated up the stove and lights and all and ate cakes and cookies and bread."

I was sorry to find I had fallen asleep with the light on in the bedroom I was using. I felt very sensitive about the Carnegies and where I might be impinging on them. I felt bad that I had left the light on all night, wasting electricity, and in the morning I told Mrs. Carnegie how sorry I was. She said, "That's all right, child. I saw it there this morning and I let it alone. I thought likely you left it on for the heat. A light can give you some heat."

6

School Desegregation, Head Start, and the Medical Committee

Spring 1965 to Early 1966

Along with our Congressional Challenge and voter registration projects, we also worked on school desegregation. The 1964 Civil Rights Act was clear in proclaiming that all schools in the United States would be desegregated. But you wouldn't have known it was coming, judging from the activity of the school board and administration in Holmes County.

We knew that when it came, it wasn't going to be easy. The Head Start teachers assisted in preparing the students. Zelma Williams said, "We helped the parents decide which of the children were the strongest. We sat each child down and told them all we could, so they would know what was ahead." Still, we were afraid to see how the first black children would be dealt with in the desegregated schools.

Indeed, when desegregation finally came to Holmes, children were treated with unnerving cruelty. For example, on September 9, 1965, Aaron Malone told us about the experience of his children, which I wrote out by hand as an affidavit to present to our lawyers Marian Wright and Henry Aronson. Mr. Malone told me, "My children—Marie, Linda, and William—have been riding the school bus, which mainly carries white children. . . . On the way in, a white boy kept meddling, calling my children 'niggers.' . . . When my children got off, a white boy held a rope across to try to trip them up. Another white boy hit Marie in the face with his hand and spat on her. When Linda, my youngest and in the first grade, started to get off, the Upsey boy shoved her and she fell on her face. The bus driver said nothing.

"[The next day,] one of the Upsey boys hit Marie on the legs with a

103

rope. When they came to get out, the flag boy tripped William and he fell out of the bus on his stomach. I was there and saw him fall out. The bus driver never made the slightest effort to stop this continual harassment and assault. It's been going on now for four days. . . . I called School Superintendent Mr. Thompson about it, but apparently he has done nothing. The bus driver let the Upsey boy get off the bus, even though it's nobody's stop except my children's. Then after the boy kicked Marie, [the bus driver] let the boy back on and drove away."

The suffering the children endured was hard to bear.

When we started working on school desegregation in spring 1965, we hoped it would be easier on the children. We spent months of hard yet hopeful movement efforts to make the difficult and courageous steps of the children successful. For weeks in spring 1965, leaders and workers held meetings and traveled the back roads carrying petition forms and explanations to parents all over the county. Nearly five hundred signed the petitions, even though the simple act of signing endangered entire families. Then on April 1, 1965, the petitions signed by the 467 parents were carried to the superintendent by movement leaders. Ralthus Hayes brought petitions from Choctaw, Norman Clark brought petitions from Marcella, Howard Taft Bailey brought petitions from Old Pilgrims Rest, and Earvin Gibson brought petitions from his south-of-Lexington grocery store. The petitions asked Superintendent Thompson to "use his influence with the school board members" to get them to sign the Federal Compliance Oath by May 5, 1965. The oath dictated that the school board would comply with federal desegregation laws. On April 6, the parents' committee received a disappointing letter from the school board stating that it would not sign the Compliance Oath.

Not to be stopped, the parents carried a second petition to Thompson, this one on May 4, requesting that racial desegregation of the Holmes public schools be initiated and asking to meet with the school board within seven days to begin desegregation planning. Again, Norman Clark was on the petition-delivery committee; he was joined by Ozell Mitchell, Dearies Williams from Tchula, and William Sims. Thompson said he would present the petition to the board, but the parents' committee received no answer. The two petitions were powerful, however, in helping to give our movement lawyers in Jackson the needed ammunition to force the school district to desegregate. The NAACP Legal Defense and Education Fund was among the earliest legal teams to serve the Mississippi civil rights movement. They filed suit against the Holmes County Board of Education, and on July 28 U.S. District Court Judge Harold Cox granted a temporary injunction to desegregate any four grades of the Holmes County schools. The ruling declared that the Holmes County Board of Education was "temporarily restrained and enjoined from requiring segregation of the races in any school under their supervision. . . . with all deliberate speed, as required in 1954 by the Supreme Court in Brown v. Board of Education of Topeka."

The ruling meant that the superintendent had to submit to the court, no later than August 14, 1965, a plan to make an immediate start in the desegregation of at least four grades during the school year commencing in August 1965 and at least four additional grades each school year thereafter.

One might have thought a court order would change things, but that wasn't the case, even as late as August 2. That's when a committee of thirteen movement leaders, again from all parts of the county—Ralthus Hayes, Daisey Lewis, John Henry Malone, Earvin Gibson, Ozell Mitchell, Alma Carnegie, Norman Clark, Willie J. Burns, Robert Head, Lucinda Matthews, Minnie Williams, Lee Henry Lewis, and Robert Howard—met with the superintendent to discuss his desegregation plans for September so they could prepare their people for that first school year. Astonishingly, Thompson denied all knowledge of such plans. He stated that, to his knowledge, neither he nor the school board had submitted any plans for desegregation to anyone. He even denied knowing of Francis Keppel, the commissioner of education in the U.S. Office of Education, in whose office the federal funds to help to support the Holmes schools were approved.

As in so many other movement activities, black community members put themselves in jeopardy by supporting desegregation. Many faced retribution for taking a stand, especially the parents who signed petitions and met with the superintendent and the school board. In July 1965, West Henderson Sr. of Lexington tried to buy groceries at the Howard plantation store, the only place he ever shopped for groceries and clothes. He said, "This time Mr. Brock's son, Gary Brock, he's about twenty or thirty years old and works clerking there most of the time, he told me, 'I can't give you any more credit. My dad told me to tell you that I couldn't give you any more credit 'til he saw you.' The only reason he would have done that to me," Henderson said, "was because he saw my name in the paper." Lexington's *Holmes County Herald* had listed all the people who signed their names to a petition asking for desegregated schools.

The highest court in Mississippi had ordered all schools desegregated. The weekly *Herald* was full of disbelief. An August 5, 1965, *Herald*'s editorial, titled "We Take Issue," stated:

> Holmes County schools at this time face a court order to submit a plan of desegregation for four grades in all schools in the county. In the suit which has been filed in behalf of 338 Negro children of Holmes County we find the Negro Schools referred to as sub-standard, poorly taught, poorly equipped, and gravely inferior to the white schools in a number of . . . ways.
>
> With this we take issue.
>
> We think we have fine schools in Holmes County. Fine Negro schools and fine white schools, and we think we have good and qualified teachers of both races who are dedicated in their work of educating our children. We think the men and women who teach, both Negro and white, are a very special segment of society, and we do not think any of them operate, or teach in, a sub-standard school.
>
> We believe that the Negro parents of Holmes County, who are sincerely concerned with giving their children an education and providing for their future by taking advantage of those opportunities that are available, seek education rather than integration.
>
> We think those who would label our Negro schools as inferior are those who are themselves inferior in their way of life and in their standards of behavior.

As the September 1, 1965, school registration day approached for most schools, movement leaders and workers and the volunteer law students held numerous meetings with parents. At the kindergartens, parents talked with leaders about their children going into desegregated first grades.

Young people canvassed the county to locate the hundreds of first, second, third, and fourth graders. All the canvassing, meetings, and talk served to let the parents know that the white schools had advantages. They were the only accredited schools, with more formally educated teachers, newer textbooks, and science labs with more equipment than the single test tube in their own children's schools. The white schools had libraries filled with books, running hot and cold water, and indoor toilets, and the school board spent twice as much on each child in the white schools as they spent on each child in the black schools. The canvassing spread the word that the lawyers for the Holmes movement had beaten the school board in court, and the court had ordered the school board to let children go to any school they wanted.

In the Holmes County case, the U.S. District Court said exactly what the U.S. Supreme Court had ruled for the nation eleven years earlier, that it was unconstitutional to have separate schools—some only for white children and others only for blacks. The court specifically declared that right there in Holmes, the school board must begin doing right by desegregating its schools that very year. It must let all children in the first four grades go to whatever public school they wanted.

By July 1965, some of the dangers had eased up in registering to vote and some of the fears had settled down a bit. Many more folks had taken steps toward standing up for their rights, and hundreds were standing where only fourteen had stood only two years earlier. However, even with all the greater strength, enrolling in newly integrated schools was a tremendously hard test. The parents were asked to make big, fearful decisions. They had to decide if giving their children the county's best possible education was going to be worth letting their children suffer.

At the Freedom Democratic Party movement office in Lexington, I and other volunteers wrote and mimeographed fliers for local people to distribute. The text of one said:

Choose the Best, Choose integrated schools. You will soon get a letter from the school board. You will get a Choice Form for each of your kids. The form lists all the schools in the county—Negro and white. You have a free choice. You must pick and then mark whatever school you want your child to go to. To get your child into the white school, make a mark beside the white school nearest your home. Buses will go to the integrated schools. Our Negro kids can take part in all sports and band activities right away. Fill in your child's choice form. Get it to the school board within thirty days. But don't rush. Think about it. Talk to your friends. Choose integrated schools because they are accredited, use better books, better labs, more educated teachers.

The flier ended with this sentence, "The School Board Spends Twice as Much on Each White Child than They Spend on Each Child in our Negro Schools."

While movement leaders and parents were planning to put their children in the white schools, white families were making their own plans. They were setting up private schools for white children only. They weren't guarded about it. On August 5—after the court order—an article appeared in the *Lexington Advertiser*, headlined, "Holmes County Schools Ordered Desegregated; Private School Tentatively Planned; Report Given on Injunction Order."

The article started out, "As negotiations are being made as to whether the Holmes County School System will be desegregated or not, a large group of citizens attended a meeting to discuss forming a private school system in the county." The idea was to form a Cruger-Tchula Academy, west of Lexington, where members of the group would pay fifty dollars each for organizing, building, repairing, and other expenses. Tuition was approximately $325 per student, per year. Private schools were also established in Lexington and to the east in Durant.

When our FDP fliers went out, some black folks said, "It isn't time yet" and "It's just a mess that will cause nothing but trouble." Brainwashed words and ideas were spoken about how black people weren't fit to mix into white schools. But real dangers did have to be considered by the locals. Southern whites were tough about their schools and became especially dangerous when they did things in the name of protecting their white children. The Holmes movement worked to face and overcome the dangers and to discount fears.

The movement people supported and reaffirmed one another at this critical time. They knew their children deserved the best schools. They wanted their children to have opportunities denied the older generation so they could grow, learn, and become more than cotton choppers, cotton pickers, and day laborers. They agreed it would be dangerous for small numbers of children to transfer to any of the white schools. The children would be safest transferring in large numbers. The best situation would be for five to ten children to transfer together to each of the all-white schools.

Movement strength in 1965 was greater than ever before. Many felt it was the time to act. They encouraged nonmovement and movement parents to get groups of children together to transfer to the white schools. In the movement we learned firsthand that the people with established power never announce to the less powerful, "Okay, now is the time for change." The seasoned movement people explained to frightened parents that we had to seize the time ourselves to make the school opening a success or the time would never come.

Right before September 1, in meetings all over the county, parents agreed to transfer their youngest children, first through fourth graders, to the white schools. These children were the hardest to part with, being the most defenseless and innocent. But these very qualities made the protesting whites sound ridiculous when they said the white children needed protection from such babes.

Just like the First Fourteen, the desegregating parents agreed to take action, but when the time came, they too wondered if the others would stand up to the agreement.

The morning of September 1 dawned cold and overcast. Children were combed and scrubbed until they shined; dresses and pants were pressed. One poor family with five children in the lower grades had to borrow, make over, and make do—and they did. Their children looked as beautiful as the rest.

Parents loaded themselves and their children into cars and pickups and headed to school in town. Some stopped to give rides to other families and were relieved to find them ready. Together they went to face the schools. At some places they found that parents who had previously agreed to participate had gotten up even earlier that morning and taken their children to be enrolled in their old black schools. They didn't want to transfer with the others. Movement people understood. Each person could only do what felt right. Even without the few who didn't show, many were ready to transfer their children.

The Lexington-area parents met at the FDP movement office; in another town parents met in an old supply house; two other towns also chose meeting places. But the school in Goodman was so intimidating that no one stepped forward to try to transfer. At these four meeting places, workers took down the names of the parents and children in order to make a record.

I was working at the movement office in Lexington. We stood outside as parents arrived to check in. Finally a parent said, "Well, I guess we'd better be going. Come on, boy. Get in, girl!" and they piled back into their car. One girl smiled wanly at me—a smile that couldn't cover the worried excitement running through her. Seeing her parents, grim but determined, made me feel safer, and I knew the little girl was learning much about courage. The car drove off amid shouts of "Good luck" and "Be careful," and the parents were again alone with their children and their determination, driving toward the school. We pushed back the horrors of earlier desegregations that we had seen on the television news. We knew the parents were transferring their children to break the chains that kept them down.

Later we heard what happened in Lexington when they turned the corner and drove onto the school campus. First, relief flooded over them to see that all was quiet. No crowds stood around. No bats, or clubs, or rocks, or guns—no shouts or curses met them. They got out and walked toward the school. The police stopped them, asked where they thought they were going. The parents spoke up, stood their ground, and showed birth certificates and school papers. The police finally let them through, so they entered the building with less trouble than any had expected. They walked in the unfamiliar halls and found the principal's office and started the process of filling out forms, meeting the teachers, and learning about the costs of lunch and new textbooks.

In Tchula, registration had begun a few days earlier, and there were similar issues. Dorothy Jean Head was stopped by two policemen before she could get into the school. Like many others, after trying to enroll her child, she spoke to us so we could write up an affidavit for our lawyers. That way, irregularities would be recorded. She told about the police wanting to know if Luther was her son. "I told him 'yes' and then he asked if I had a birth certificate for him and I told him 'I don't have one with me but I have sent to Jackson for one.' He said I would have to have a birth certificate to register." They weren't unpleasant and they smiled nicely, but they turned her away.

Lucinda Matthews also had problems in Tchula. "I had the 'birth record notebook' of . . . Elmira P. Ydyke," the midwife who had delivered her daughter Irma Forte. It was her record book for the year 1957 and it had her "official entry of my child's birth on August 10, 1957. I had already sent away for the certified copy of Irma's birth certificate and . . . had tried unsuccessfully to get a non-certified copy of her certificate at the Lexington Board of Health Department." The policemen wouldn't let her register and tried to confuse her. She was told she had to have a birth certificate because it was the law. She was told she was only filing an application. Then policemen told her a rumor that they had closed the schools. Finally she gave up. "I never did get through the gate," she said.

School officials tried to intimidate Flora Howard of Mileston, whose children had always attended the Negro school—the Tchula Attendance Center. But she didn't back down. When a woman administrator asked her why she was transferring her son, she answered, "I am transferring him so that he can get a better education." As Mrs. Howard worked on registering her son, the administrator sat behind her. "Whenever I happened to glance over at her," Flora Howard said, "she seemed to be grinning at the man who was talking with me. It gave me the feeling she was making fun at me."

Even with these problems, enrollment ran more smoothly and quietly than expected. In fact, the school officials and teachers appeared more nervous and upset than the parents. Although many suffered stares, waiting, and discomfort, the parents felt relief and joy at their own strength.

During those first few days, the parents continued going to the previously all-white schools to transfer their children. The white officials began to be less courteous, more difficult, and openly angry after the first day, possibly because they were worried about the large turnout of Holmes County blacks who had the determination and bravery to enroll their children.

School officials weren't the only problem. J. T. Sutton of Tchula was fired because, as his wife, Rosie Bell Sutton, said, "we took our children and enrolled them into the school we have a right to enroll them in." J. T.'s employer said, "I guess J.T. can stay at home and see his precious children going to the white schools." That left J. T. and Rosie Bell in serious financial trouble.

The *Herald* reported that the white enrollment in public schools had gone down in 1965. In Lexington only 172 white children registered in the first four grades, down from 223 the previous year. By contrast, more than 225 black children—more than in any other Mississippi county—had tried to enroll in white schools. In the end, many were kept out because of minor rules and roadblocks put up by officials. Even so, 187 black children in all successfully attended the four previously all-white schools, their own new desegregated schools. All of us in the movement recognized the enrollment, without incidences of violence, as a courageous victory.

As the days passed, issues arose. We wrote up affidavit after affidavit.

The teacher of Ruthie B. Marshall's children wanted to "give back [their] money." Mrs. Marshall reported, "[She] said that my children would be happier with their 'own kind,' because the children and the teachers know that they are not supposed to be in this school." Mrs. Marshall didn't back down: "I just said that I wanted them in that school so that they could learn something."

The bus ride to school was often a source of trouble. Mrs. Elsie Williams of Goodman called the principal to make the bus driver stop for her daughter Annie. When Annie came home the first evening after riding the bus, she told her mother she was called "nigger" and that the flag boy said, "I's going to stick this flag up your buddie." Annie was so frightened she caught the bus that took children to the black schools. The harassment on the white buses led to overcrowding on the black ones. One Tchula bus took three loads of black students. In many buses, more than twenty kids stood, often up against the driver and in the stairwell. Children waited for hours at school before it started and after it closed.

In Tchula, the first-grade white teacher quit on the day school started. The principal didn't handle it well, didn't even tell the parents.

In Durant the discrimination was open and widespread, taking the form of subtle intimidation as well as physical abuse. Sarah Ruth Hill said her son Aaron's teacher, Mrs. Clement, "gave each person in the class a note asking for $4.45 for three workbooks and a *Weekly Reader* subscription. She told Aaron's class that if they did not have the money, they should not come back to school. . . . I will send Aaron to school anyway," Mrs. Clement vowed.

Pearlie C. Carter found her first-grader Shirley crying. Shirley's teacher had "snatched the desk out from under her and threw her on the floor. I asked her what she had done," said Mrs. Carter, "but she said she did not do anything." Mrs. Carter's son, Jessie Lee, who was also in the class, said "the teacher came over to [his] . . . desk, grabbed . . . and threw him on the floor also. . . . After he fell, the teacher picked him up and bumped his head against the wall."

The black and white students were separated at lunch. "White children are allowed to take trays and plates and get served in a cafeteria line, Negroes come in and sit at tables which have filled plates on them already," said Mary T. Wade of Durant.

According to Mildred Coffey of Durant, "At lunchtime, children who bring their lunches must stand—not sit—in the hall when they eat. Colored children . . . are too poor to buy [lunch.] Thus, only colored children are made to stand in the halls and eat."

"Discrimination is very evident on the part of the teachers in the classroom," said Mary Alice Hill. Her daughter Willie Mae was in the Durant second-grade classroom.

When the class goes out . . . to go to the bathroom or to get a drink of water, the white children line up first and the colored children must wait until they are finished. At recess time, the white children play inside and the colored children play outside. . . . In the class everyone sits in assigned seats—all the colored children sit together in a group and all the whites must sit together in a group. But worst of all, Willie Mae says that the teacher favors the white children in classroom discussions for she calls on them more than she does the colored children.

In Tchula, the third- and fourth-grade black students had to use the restrooms outside and in the gymnasium building rather than the ones inside the school building.

The white reaction to desegregation was overt and even violent. At Aaron Malone's house, a violent attack frightened us all. His children enrolled in the formerly all-white school, and that apparently angered an unidentified man so strongly that the man walked up to Malone's home and approached Malone's wife as she stood in the doorway holding one baby in her arms and comforting the rest of the children around her. The man shot her in the knee, crippling her.

When Jesse Williams of Durant was going through town and stopped to get a haircut, he saw fliers posted, listing the names of thirty-two parents who had children in the white school. The signs worked both to add more fear in the black community and to tell white business people just who was breaking "the rules" and thus who was fair game for retaliation.

Sammie Lee Hightower of Durant told how a highway patrolman stopped him in December. "[He] asked for my driver's license . . . cursin' so much and then . . . talkin' about the family I came from. He . . . made a threat . . . started playing with his gun and holster . . . said if I ever stepped out of line he would shoot me right between my so-and-so eyes. . . . He also said that he heard that 'you all Hightowers was trying to be smart.' My younger brother, Nathan, goes to the integrated school in Durant."

At the same time, the private schools were surging at the expense of the public schools. The school board played fast and loose with public property. Public school buses had been either sold or leased as surplus property to the private schools. Reportedly, white children were being transported to private schools on the public school buses. Further reports came from children who said they were made to load desks and other public school property into trucks to be taken to the private schools.

Many whites attempted to force whites to boycott two of the formerly all-white public schools in Lexington and Tchula. Pressure was exerted on whites as well as blacks: job firings and threats of firings, welfare cutoffs, loss of credit, and other more subtle economic and social pressures.

For several months arsonists attempted to burn black churches, houses, and community centers. In August it was the Second Pilgrims Rest Church. On September 4, gunfire was exchanged at a community center near Durant. A truckload of white men drove by the center and fired. Armed guards at the center returned the fire. The truck sped off.

White men in capes like those of Ku Klux Klansmen rode in a parade at night throughout the county with lights on inside their cars and trucks to frighten blacks and sympathetic whites. Two weeks later, an eight-foot flaming cross caused damage to a cleaning business owned by Durant's white mayor, C. H. Blanton Jr., who had been active in trying to encourage white parents to let their children attend desegregated classes at Durant Public School.

The courts were busy. Judge Harold Cox refused to give Henry Aronson, Marian Wright, and other NAACP lawyers a restraining order against schools that charged up to four hundred dollars in tuition to attend a public school. He sent the case to a three-judge panel. In the meantime about seven thousand poor black and white children in the state couldn't attend school. Another part of the lawsuit dealt with the issue of guardianship. In Holmes County alone, an estimated five hundred black children couldn't attend school because they didn't live with legal guardians. Even some children whose parents had died were kept out of school because of complicated laws and a baffling court system. The Holmes County Board of Education officials were named as defendants in the suit, along with state officials.

During the entire first year, the children who desegregated the schools endured physical and mental harm from white children, parents, and teachers. They were beaten, chased, and verbally abused by whites and also by some blacks who were afraid of desegregation. But these students bravely returned day after day, achieving a victory of discipline and endurance.

The progress on school desegregation would not have occurred if it hadn't been for the kindergarten and Head Start. Success in teaching the little ones made people recognize the importance of a good education. Head Start made a huge difference to the Holmes movement. The kindergarten at the Holmes County Community Center opened in 1964, just as the center was completed. Center programs for children, a morning kindergarten, and a story time in the library were held each day. Zelma Williams and her aunt Clemma Williams from Tchula volunteered to come every morning to help. There was fear, but parents bravely sent their children. Every night, armed guards watched the Holmes County Community Center.

The kindergarteners used the tables Henry built for them in the community center at Mileston. The first teachers in the program were Rosie Head, Alice Mae Epps, and Zelma Williams.

The children were taught their ABCs and their numbers. They learned songs and dances and learned to socialize. Personal hygiene was taught, and the center's running water was also put to good use. The kindergarten and later the Head Start teachers made sure all the children were clean before lessons began. Many of the plantation children enjoyed their first bath at the center.

The children in these programs, like children everywhere, brought presents for the teachers. Zelma Williams said, "One little girl from one of the plantations brought me a snuff tin filled with rocks and dried corn. It was her toy and it made noise when you shook it. I thanked her, but when she ran off to play with the other children, I had to sit down. I held that snuff tin and cried. It broke my heart to see how little those children had."

After six months of operating the unfunded, shoestring kindergarten in our Holmes County Community Center, antipoverty funding became available through the federal Office of Economic Opportunity (OEO). The funds didn't come directly to Holmes. We had to become affiliated with CDGM, the Child Development Group of Mississippi, and that group was quick to draw down the money.

The antipoverty funding forcefully boosted our efforts. The money came via one of President Johnson's War on Poverty initiatives. He had gathered a committee of sociologists, psychologists, and pediatricians, led by Sargent Shriver and Johns Hopkins University pediatrician Dr. Robert Cooke, to look at ways of helping children overcome the obstacles to learning caused by poverty. By the summer of 1965, the new OEO budget had established an eight-week Head Start program for children from low-income communities going into public school in the fall. It served more than 560,000 children across the United States that first summer. The program provided preschool classes, medical care, dental care, and mental health services.

In Holmes, other new preschools followed our lead and became CDGM Head Start centers, including the ones in Tchula, Old Pilgrims Rest, Sunnymount–Poplar Springs, Second Pilgrims Rest, Lexington, and Durant. The staff of our kindergarten—Rosie Head, Zelma Williams, Elease Gallion, Mary Helen Kohn, and other volunteers—were the first Holmes County Head Start teachers in 1965.

The Holmes County Head Starts grew to more than one hundred students, but growing took work. The new funds brought money for busing and food, making the program accessible to the poorest families and those residing in the most remote areas. The Head Start teachers traveled through the countryside to sign up students. They walked right up to the plantation owners' houses to get permission for plantation children to attend. This time—because transportation and free breakfast and lunch were provided—the plantation owners let "their children" attend.

"When plantation owners said the children were 'his kids,' it was often literally true. Men in the 'big house' fathered children with their workers," said Zelma. "The day the first group of children arrived from one of the plantations, a light-skinned, blue-eyed boy came with them. One of the children, who had been with the Mileston kindergarten from the beginning, took me aside. He nodded toward the boy and told me our school was integrated too. I didn't argue, I just gave him a big smile and agreed with him."

The center was able to hire many additional staff members. The gigantic funding boost from CDGM provided training resources and greater advancement for staff, children, parents, and the community. Rosie Head and Elease Gallion had been the first two center staff workers. Alice Mae Epps became a center kindergarten teacher and worked beside Zelma Williams and Elease Gallion. Before and after Head Start, Mary Helen Kohn and Thelma "Nutchie" Head came in to drop off and pick up the children. Catherine McLaurin and Rosebud Clark were involved during that same time, too. All of the staff were aggressive, bold, and eager to learn; and learn they did.

CDGM was based in Jackson and had been created by several outside whites, particularly Tom Levin, a New York doctor and psychoanalyst. Levin, who had worked during the summer of 1964 with the Medical Committee for Human Rights, and Polly Greenberg, a fervently inspired Head Start program proponent, along with other movement leaders, created the proposal for OEO funding. They were successful and received funding for a Mississippi statewide Head Start program for six thousand preschool children in more than sixty centers to operate during the summer of 1965. Many of the centers were very active in civil rights issues. CDGM became the nation's largest Head Start program, feeding and

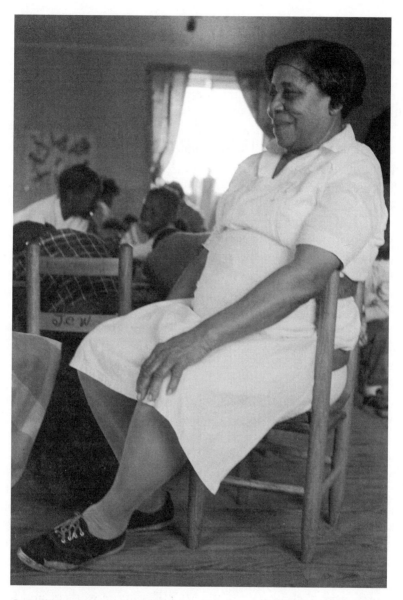

C. Bell Turnbow, wife of Hartman Turnbow, rests in one of the children's chairs. She became the cook when Head Start replaced the kindergarten at the center. Head Start funding brought living wages to the staff.

caring for Mississippi children and creating eleven hundred jobs that were much higher paying than the rate of two dollars per day for chopping cotton. Knowing that the trust of the local people was essential for CDGM's success, Levin recruited the support of civil rights activists, and thirteen of the CDGM's fifteen top administrative positions were filled by people with movement credentials.

Very soon after the Head Start centers opened, Mississippi's white power structure attacked CDGM, calling it "Communist" and "fiscally irresponsible." The Head Start staff, the CDGM administrators and board, community members, and others responded by lobbying. They contacted Martin Luther King Jr., the National Council of Churches (NCC), and the AFL-CIO's Crusade against Poverty. They turned to the national media, to early childhood leaders, and to elected officials.

Later, when funding from Washington dried up, Holmes County took a significant step. In February 1966, we hired a bus and took forty-five children to Washington, D.C., to dramatize the need for federal refunding of Head Start. The children made the national news when they sat on the floor during Congressman Adam Clayton Powell's Education and Labor Committee meeting. Zelma Williams and the preschoolers were pictured in the March 3 issue of *Jet Magazine*.

By fall 1965 Josephine Disparti was growing increasingly frustrated in Holmes County. From the beginning she had resisted the efforts by the Medical Committee for Human Rights (MCHR) to dictate policy in Holmes. The committee wanted Disparti to use its medical van in Holmes County. But the van was met with resistance when leaders worried that it was so highly visible that it would antagonize the Board of Health and jeopardize the clinic at Mileston. Because the local whites viewed movement workers as upstarts masquerading as health professionals, the leaders thought the van might push the Board of Health into doing something like closing down the clinic.

Josephine also worried that the presence of the van would exacerbate the turf battles she saw among the MCHR, outside workers, and some leaders in Holmes. More than one local leader was uncomfortable with the idea of a nurse alone in a mobile unit. Josephine wanted initiatives on such issues to come from the grassroots people, but she struggled to get agreement from the MCHR. It wasn't long after this dispute that she decided to leave Mississippi.

Dr. Alvin Poussaint, a black born in East Harlem, was the supervisor of the growing team of MCHR public health nurses. He was trained as a psychiatrist and had been in the South only a short time. He had visited the Mileston Clinic many times that year, assisting with examinations. He also helped Josephine with purchasing equipment for the clinic with Health Committee funds that were provided by the MCHR. To commemorate the activist work of a D.C. physician involved with left-wing health organizations, the MCHR named the Mileston Clinic for Dr. Irving W. Winik. Josephine trained two new black nurses, Helene Richardson and Patricia Weatherly, who were warmly welcomed by Holmes County black people. The clinic set up a three-dollar annual fee for participating families, with a goal of diagnosing and screening women and children for health problems. Helene and Pat immediately began to carefully document the segregation they observed in the Holmes County hospitals.

Their Stories: Kids Racing the Bug Sprayer

About a dozen children, ranging in age from five to ten years, often hung around the FDP office. They lived in Pecan Grove and were too young to get involved in Holmes movement actions. None came from families that attended movement meetings. But they were excited by the activity around the office and constantly curious about what we were doing.

Their presence was a source of amusement, aggravation, and relaxation for the FDP workers and leaders alike. We couldn't help but fall for them. The children were a reality that was hard to avoid. They weren't an abstraction for Henry, me, or the movement. Our goals were the same for those kids as for the movement. We knew they were the movement's future, and it was for them that we were creating the movement.

Dino, an impish five-year-old, had a special hold on my heart. His spirit had a certain determination. An incident that I observed between Dino and the pesticide truck captured something of his bold resolve and mischievous energy:

A tired sun was leaving the gray sky, descending behind the last tar-papered roof, engulfed by the thick cloud of pesticide now spewing from

The children in Pecan Grove were often underfoot outside the office, providing the staff with headaches and laughter.

the rear of the slow, rumbling truck. The street and the dirt yards emptied of all grownups; porch doors banged and little ones were pulled from the weeds, called from their worlds of rusting, deserted car bodies. The adults sought shelter from the choking fumes.

But the boys continued rolling old tires and spinning wheel rims in the gravel until the last possible moment. Otha rolled his silvery prize rim treacherously close to the orange nose of the lumbering giant. And then he followed the rim as it nicked and skittered and came to rest in the trash-filled gutter.

Shiny, tough Bee-do and slow, sleepy Tom kept up a prancing pace, lurching in and out beside the spray truck like pups. The younger Dwight Dee tested his wings from a safer distance but still boldly imitated his brothers. Even the big guys like Steve and Fat Walter were roused from their toe-writing in the oiled dust beside McGee's gas pumps. They bent to gather gravel pieces to hurl at the huge moving machine.

The child squatting in the center, Otha Lee, was mimicking me as I took the picture.

At the sight of the truck and the boys, Bad Funt, tall for his nine years, straddled his bike for a long moment, immobilized by indecision. Finally he hoisted up into his fake-fur saddle and raced like the younger Squeaky and Rooster over McGee's open drive to the road's edge, where he deftly skidded a shower of stones toward the oncoming fenders. He pulled on the bars and raised his spinning front wheel high off the ground.

Dino's spindly black frame stretched in the center of the graveled road. Taut, he waited for the chugging roar of the monster just turning from the dust trail of Avenue A onto the last strip of "street." His damp sticky donut, carefully placed but untouched, waited on the gravel beside him.

Blind to the antics, the truck continued on. The ground rumbled, and all eyes—from bike-riding Rooster, Squeaky, and Funt to the still bounding and darting Dwight Dee, Tom, Bee-do, and Otha—watched intently as the orange chug ate up the inches remaining. Just as the breath from the truck's grill was almost upon him, Dino bent; he rolled over to clutch his donut, then rose. In haughty slow motion Dino marched from the path.

The hooting chased him into the dense fog that blanketed the path. Dino had won this week's episode. Shouting, laughing, barking, the children ran, greedily gulping the bug-poisoning air. They drifted to the cool cement patch of porch made even tinier by the crowding of their restless little-boy bodies. Dino gobbled his dust-glazed donut almost immediately, although he allowed Timmy and Otha bites. Then he huddled against the screen door, slightly apart from the rest, absently picking at the ragged screen wires as his dark eyes watched the road.

Dino West (*left*) and Steve Ellis were neighbors. They lived in houses close to the FDP office in Pecan Grove.

7

Voter Registration
December 1964–December 1965

The increasingly intense work on school desegregation occurred at the same time as Washington was making strides toward greater equity in voting rights.

In December 1964, eight months before the passage of the Voting Rights Act, Sunnymount activists Bernice and Eugene Montgomery attempted to register. Their daughter Zelpha Montgomery-Whatley, of Galilee, recalled: "My dad, Mr. Eugene, went into the voter registration office first. He asked to register to vote. He was told it was against the law, but if he insisted, he would have to do two things—pay a special tax, called a poll tax, and tell Mr. McClellan how many bubbles were on a bar of soap. He refused to pay the voting tax and certainly couldn't count the bubbles on a bar of soap." He wasn't allowed to register. Zelpha's mother, Bernice, was a science and math teacher at the all-black Mount Olive Elementary and High School. She stepped up to the counter next and asked to register to vote. She was told it was against the law, but if she insisted, she would have to first pay a poll tax. "Secondly," Zelpha said, "she was told that since she had the reputation of being a 'smart nigger' she had to recite the Constitution of the United States of America. If she did so, she could register to vote." She wasn't allowed to register that day, and so she left, but was determined to try again.

On January 28, 1965, Mrs. Montgomery returned to the Holmes County Courthouse to register. "She was mocked and told that the same question applied—she still had to recite the U.S. Constitution," Zelpha recounted. "That was when Miss Bernice handed a United States history book to the registrar . . . [and] began to recite the Constitution word by

Bernice Patton Montgomery, an essential county leader from the hills, was the first black schoolteacher in Holmes to try to register at the courthouse. After being turned away, she finally forced the county clerk to "pass" her by taking him up on his demand and successfully reciting the entire U.S. Constitution.

word, not stammering or missing a single word." Courthouse employees gathered in the doorway. "When she finished, the registrar, in absolute amazement, granted Bernice Patton Montgomery her constitutional right to register and vote," Zelpha said. "Bernice Montgomery became the first black woman to register to vote in Holmes County, Mississippi."

Many demonstrations for civil and voting rights in 1964 and 1965 erupted in violence. The "Bloody Sunday" attack in Selma, Alabama, in March 1965 was televised. State troopers attacked six hundred peaceful demonstrators with billy clubs and tear gas.

The Voting Rights Act passed and then was signed into law by President Lyndon B. Johnson on August 6, 1965. The act suspended poll taxes, literacy tests, and other voter requirements. It also provided for the appointment of federal examiners, who were granted the power to register qualified citizens to vote. Specific problem jurisdictions were required by the act to get "pre-clearance" from either the D.C. District Court or the U.S. attorney general for any new voting practices or procedures. The legislation included a nationwide prohibition of denying the right to vote on account of race or color. It strengthened the ban on the use of poll taxes.

Despite the passage of the new Voting Rights Act, the white governments in many of Mississippi's eighty-two counties dug in their heels more strongly than ever. They were determined not to let blacks vote. In Holmes County, McClellan, the registrar at the courthouse in Lexington, refused to acknowledge that the act had even passed. He slackened his already slow registration pace and refused to register people who needed assistance. He continued to use his own made-up registration tests with absurd questions and requirements, continuing to ask Negro applicants to recite sections from the Mississippi state constitution. He created his own residency requirements and continued publishing registrants' names in the local newspapers to facilitate white retaliation. He wasn't alone. Registrars in other Mississippi counties employed discriminatory devices of disenfranchisement such as tests of good moral character.

But the movement leaders, workers, and volunteers persisted. People were inspired by the actions of the First Fourteen, and the movement spread. The first step to opening up new communities was talking with the strong, curious folks—like Austin Wiley, Bernice and Eugene Montgomery, George and Willie Mae Wright, Howard Taft Bailey, Vanderbilt and Cora Roby, and Link Williams—who dared to venture to the Mileston meetings from eastern hill communities and the Moores, Louies, Quinns, Williamses, and Suttons from other delta areas. Like the original Mileston freedom-seekers who had ventured to Greenwood, these folks wanted help in organizing their own communities, setting up their own meetings, and getting Mileston movement leaders, especially Hartman Turnbow, to speak to their communities' people so they could start trying to register.

After more than two years of struggle, few Holmes County blacks were registered, even though the county had eighty-seven hundred eligible black adults. The percentage was only slightly higher than the rest of the state. In Mississippi before the Voting Rights Act was enacted, less than 7 percent of Mississippi's nonwhites were registered to vote. In the days after President Johnson signed the Voting Rights Act, McClellan summarily turned Holmes County residents away.

More movement folks took action against McClellan and began to systematically document his violations of the act. The Holmes County FDP had a plan. The new law authorized the U.S. attorney general to send federal examiners to assist or even replace local registrars who refused to abide by the 1965 act. We wanted federal examiners to be sent to Holmes County.

On August 24, 1965, I wrote notes updating the Holmes movement's registration attempts for the mimeographed newsletter I mailed to mainly northern supporters: "Several hundred are attempting to register each week. . . . some few more than before are getting registered. . . . nothing to write home about. . . . should write to Washington about it. . . . the voting bill passes. . . . Registrar McClellan slows from eight to two at a time in his office."

As people were turned away from the courthouse, they told their civil rights workers or leaders what had happened; the workers then wrote the testimony into affidavit form, and witnesses verified the authenticity. Napoleon Boyd's affidavit said, "I read and write, but not too well. . . . I filled out several questions but then I had trouble with one and I asked the registrar, Henry McClellan, for help. He said, 'I can't help you. You've got to go back and learn yourself.'" Reverend Johnny B. Williams and Irene Ellis signed it as witnesses.

Norman Clark of Mileston had a similar experience, and I wrote out the affidavit and signed as the witness. He had driven Charlie Brown and James Malone to the courthouse on August 9 to help them get registered. Neither man could read or write. The clerk's wife was there, and as Mr. Clark described it, "Mrs. McClellan, she got very angry, sounding and talking real loud. 'Why do you have to speak for them. They got mouths.' She was shouting and Mr. McClellan came in from the back." Mr. McClellan wouldn't help, saying, as related by Mr. Clark, "The law says a person should read and write before he fills out the form. . . . Anybody that can't read and write is just wasting time coming in here."

McClellan disqualified applicants on technicalities, as Dan Malone of Pickens reported: "I spelled "Holmes" without the "l," and he told me he couldn't pass me because I didn't spell it right." He disqualified Marie

Fisher for not meeting the residency requirement, even though she had lived in the town of Lexington for two years and in Old Pilgrims Rest her entire life before that.

Ralthus Hayes gathered dozens of affidavits like these and, on August 11, sent them to U.S. Attorney General Nicholas Katzenbach, noting that "Mr. McClellan has given evidence . . . to show that, even with the 1965 Act, he plans to make it difficult for our Negro citizens to register to vote." Indeed, Holmes badly needed federal intervention. "I earnestly petition the government of the United States to appoint federal examiners," Hayes went on, "in order tö secure Holmes County Negroes the right to vote."

No response came. The Holmes County FDP sent another letter to the attorney general on September 10: "We come to you from Holmes County, Mississippi to keep on with our complaining and our asking. We bring this letter with twenty-three more statements of petition to add to the fifty-three complaints and requests we have already sent from our county since the new Voting Rights Act has passed." The letter ended with "We would like you to review all you have received from Holmes County with the new evidences we are bringing now, and do something so that the government of the United States will appoint federal examiners to Holmes County, Mississippi so that we and all the other Negroes of Holmes County may get the right to vote."

Within those twenty-three affidavits, many people noted that McClellan had administered his own literacy tests. Even if they had filled out the form correctly, with every word spelled right, McClellan would hand them a newspaper or a magazine to read. If they had trouble pronouncing a name or if they stumbled on a technical word, McClellan would deny their registration application.

Finally, in late October 1965, Holmes County got good news from Washington—Attorney General Katzenbach had assigned federal voting examiners to twelve counties in Louisiana, Alabama, South Carolina, and Mississippi. Half of the examiners were designated for Mississippi, for Holmes County and Jefferson, Neshoba, Hinds, Desoto, and Walthall counties. Katzenbach noted that his action occurred because local registrars were either using unlawful literacy tests or causing unreasonable delay in processing applications.

Edith Quinn, along with her neighbors the Louies and the Moores, was a movement leader from the Howard area.

On November 8, 1965, federal examiners arrived and set up registration offices in the Lexington post office, keeping them open eight hours a day, six days a week. They registered voters at a rapid pace—2,100 were registered by December 30, contrasting sharply with McClellan's record of only 690 blacks registered between January and October 1965. In the fifteen months since Henry and I had arrived in Holmes, the number of black registered voters had quadrupled to 2,800 as a result of the federal registration.

The voting rights law had an immediate impact on U.S. blacks. By December 1965, a quarter of a million new black voters had been registered, one-third of them by federal examiners.

The long-demanded federal registrar arrived right in the midst of our second year of work on the federal Agricultural Stabilization and Conservation Service County Allotment Board Elections.

Sam Howze, a black movement worker from Pittsburgh, took a leading role. Sam, who arrived in Mississippi in 1965, became the SNCC project director for Holmes. He was a great help on many fronts, including voter registration. For the County Allotment Board Elections, he helped to change the way the ASCS unfairly assigned cotton allotments. Each farmer was allowed to farm a certain number of acres in the profitable cotton. Blacks were given far fewer acres than whites, causing the whites to prosper, while the blacks would make so much less money that they would sometimes go bankrupt or end up working for the whites.

Every farmer could vote, whether a registered voter or not, and 1964, the year Henry and I arrived, was the first year when Negroes participated in an ASCS election. They protested the irregularities in the election procedures. In 1964 ASCS officials had carried guns and demanded to see the "secret" ballots—among other irregularities—so in 1965 farmers were able to vote by mail. Of the eligible ASC voters in the county, 59 percent were black. All fall we worked on education and getting nominations by petition. All of our work to win black seats on the board produced results: thirty-seven black candidates got on the ballot, ten were elected, and the process forced a month-long federal investigation of the county office.

Our group was feeling its strength. We ran an ad, "An Open Letter to the White Business Men and Leaders," in the *Lexington Advertiser,* calling for a store boycott.

Jobs were crucial to real equality. Some grassroots attempts at setting up a farmer's cooperative had gained interest, and a small group of people started a leather workshop. Six unskilled Mileston people, most of whom were unemployed or had been kicked off of plantations because of their movement activity, managed to borrow four hundred dollars from the new Poor Peoples Corporation for the start-up. They received training and moved into an active workshop across from the community center, where they were making purses and belts for the northern market and making and repairing shoes for local people.

The most exciting developments were the changes at the Holmes County Community Center at Mileston. When we arrived, it was big and modern but had no money, no resources, and only volunteer staff. As the months passed, Anthony "Tony" Leonard Jones and Edgar Love appeared and worked out in the county, canvassing, attending community mass meetings, and spreading information about the movement.

Henry and I moved away from Mileston in August. Because we were by then the only outside workers in Holmes County, more than ever the staff looked to the two of us for problem solving. We realized that our mere presence hindered them from making decisions. We moved to a small house less than a mile from Pecan Grove, just outside Lexington. The name of the settlement was Balance Due, an apt description of the financial condition of its residents. Our place wasn't so much a house as a shack. Rent was ten dollars a month, and our new home had electricity and an outside pump for water. There was a yard with a place to grow vegetables. People came to help me garden. I even planted a row of cotton.

In his early thirties, Henry was older than the average outside volunteer civil rights worker. His age, along with his quiet patience and careful organizing skill, brought him more than the usual amount of respect from the local leaders, both the grassroots leaders and the professionals. Indeed, other outside workers from SNCC, COFO, and other groups sometimes viewed Henry's position in the Holmes community with suspicion, since he looked like he could have been building a personal power base. Had his motives or inclinations been different—had he thought he could best help the community by running for office or heading up groups—his power in the movement might have allowed such personal elevation, although with costs.

Given his unique position, Henry was aware of his role and was sensitive to the "stifling" effect his presence had on local leadership. Quite consciously, he would avoid serving in a leadership capacity, refusing membership on committees, boards, and in any nonorganizer positions. We tried never to do anything that could be done just as well or better by the local people.

By the end of 1965, we were able to turn over the center almost completely to the local people. The director, the board of trustees, and the staff took over the management of the center and performed extremely well. Our job in Holmes County had drastically changed in just one year. We were proud that the center was on its feet with local leaders engaged in the planning and execution of movement activities and campaigns. Our position also changed as we moved on to county movement organization. For us, the work in Mississippi continued to be stimulating and creative. In spite of the fear, shootings, and worry about tactics and decisions, there was grit, conviction, hope, and the friendship of local people.

Their Stories: McGee's Café

The COFO workers helped set up the FDP office in Lexington's Pecan Grove because Lexington was the geographical and political center of the county. Much movement work continued in Mileston, but the FDP office attracted additional county leaders, staff, and volunteers. Most of the buildings in Pecan Grove were small one-story shotgun shacks. There was no church and no school. The only public building was McGee's Café and Gas Station, which was located two blocks from the new FDP office.

I entered the café, pushing on its sturdy wooden white-painted front door. The flimsier screen door flapped painlessly against my back. It was winter, and since there were only two small windows, the deep hues of the counter made the room seem dark. Even the various checkered and printed oilcloths covering the five rickety tables failed to brighten the room. Way up on a shelf, above the adding machine on the counter, a tiny color TV flickered.

Boys often would hang out in McGee's Café, the only business in Pecan Grove.

The place was especially dull and cheerless when it was empty, as it was on that day, occupied only by tiny Dino, the wandering mascot of Pecan Grove. He was rolling in the dust on the worn wooden floor, in his raggedy, two-sizes-too-large cheap trousers and his three-sizes-too-large cut-down boy's sports jacket. He crawled under the tables and then around each of the high and low counter stools. He was chasing after a grimy nickel. Immediately upon catching it, he rolled it away again. "Nickel" might be the first word Dino ever learned to say. It was one of only a few words the five-year-old pronounced loudly and clearly. When a customer ventured inside, Dino strained his big head on his thin neck way back, as he did to every being on two legs who walked in, and said his word, "nickel."

On crowded nights the drabness of the room was forgotten, replaced by the heat of moving, talking, sometimes laughing, pushing bodies and the bright lights and glass from the semimodern, overworked jukebox, whose bulky frame sat next to the side door.

The adjoining oblong room was neat and clean. It was well worn, but not stifling or dilapidated. There was dust but not greasy grime, and only seldom did lean red roaches scurry along the clean counter or among the nickel bags of potato chips and barbecue-flavored pork skins. When there were customers, the perpetually tired, vacant-seeming Nanny McGee and her sullen, shiny-black granddaughter Penny moved quickly, taking away the remains of candy wrappers, empty quarts of beer, or half-drunk soda pop bottles. The newspaper was usually folded neatly on the stool near the cash register or on top of the ice cream and beer chests. They kept the daily paper whole; it was not just the scraps of last Thursday's edition.

The stock filled the shelves in precise order and tidiness with some room to spare. The red-papered, nickel portions of Zesta crackers were stacked evenly next to the twenty-three-cent Hardens bread. At waist level, near the register, were twenty-four five-stick packs of Doublemint, Spearmint, and sometimes Juicy Fruit gum. The store sold small cartons of pocket tins of Prince Albert Crimp Cut Long Burning Pipe and Cigarette Tobacco, Prince Albert rolling papers, some old CB rolling papers, Cannon Ball chewing tobacco, and tiny shiny casks of snuff. Also close at hand were penny balls of orange and grape bubblegum. The medicines

Penny McGee, the young granddaughter of café owners Nanny and Bob McGee, worked behind the counter and operated the cash register.

were well separated from the food, the candy from the canned goods. The only open food was two-for-a-penny Tom's cookies in a large, clear, plastic see-through drum; the gallon jar in which floated ten-cent cold franks; and the five-gallon jug of briny-smelling, white-knuckled, pink pickled pigs feet. All the other food was packaged in bags, jars, bottles, and cans. The containers were all tiny, such as two-ounce cans of cooked Vienna sausages and five-ounce boxes of Cheer washing powder. They were so small, the average supermarket shopper may have thought they were toy replicas of the real thing.

The last room was separated from the common room by the kitchen and a swinging gate. Only schoolteachers and the more substantial, matching-wardrobe type people seemed to frequent it. I never ventured inside. Permission wasn't asked; it seemed to be a long-established, well-accepted pattern, in which people knew their place.

8

The Greenville Air Base Demonstration and the Community Action Program

January–December 1966

In February 1966, several Holmes County FDP leaders drove nearly one hundred miles northwest of Holmes to Greenville, in Washington County, for a three-day Poor Peoples Conference. Almost nine hundred poor blacks from many parts of the state were gathering there with movement organizers to figure out what actions they might take to change the abysmal conditions they were struggling under.

Before we left Holmes for the meeting, Mrs. Carnegie had told Henry and me that she would go to the meeting, but she certainly did not want to go to jail again. She insisted she was just going to listen.

When we arrived, it was apparent that most of those gathered lived in dire conditions. Many of them had been thrown off the fertile delta land that, as sharecroppers and plantation workers, they labored on but didn't own. They had no homes or farms or jobs of their own. They were hungrier and much poorer than most people in the Holmes movement. Hundreds had set up tents and makeshift structures for shelters for a demonstration of unknown duration that they were calling "Freedom City." The national media called it "Strike City." These people were suffering from multiple issues that included federal cutbacks in cotton acreage and increased automation that caused layoffs. For plantation workers, striking for higher wages entailed many risks, especially the risk of being evicted from the land and their homes.

At the meeting, talk centered on housing, land, jobs, and especially food. The state of Mississippi was sitting on the opportunity to receive $1.6 million worth of food from the federal Office of Economic Oppor-

Alma Mitchell Carnegie, though at first determined not to get involved, joined a group of homeless and jobless people as they occupied the empty Greenville Air Base. The group successfully pressured the state of Mississippi to accept and distribute federal funding for low-income people.

tunity to distribute to needy Mississippians. The state officials refused to set up the discrimination-free administrative board that was a requirement for getting the food into Mississippi.

The OEO food distribution was generated by Lyndon Johnson's War on Poverty legislation initiated in January 1964. When the U.S. poverty rate hit 19 percent, Johnson created programs to address poverty, including such social welfare programs as the Job Corps, the Community Action Program, and Volunteers in Service to America. These programs combined with civil rights initiatives, forming Johnson's ideal of the "Great Society." In Mississippi in early 1966, the War on Poverty had barely made a dent. Efforts to assist the poor brought negative reactions from powerful white politicians, and the White House was flooded with reports of near starvation in many counties.

All sorts of people at the Poor Peoples Conference suggested plans to keep the pressure high, from going back home to begin organized letter-writing, to breaking into supermarkets or chopping down national forests. One group really wanted to do something to get immediate media attention. A leader stood up and said, "Okay, everybody who wants to actually plan and do something now, come into the other room and we'll decide." When people stood up to go into the other room, Henry noticed Mrs. Carnegie going with them. He ran up to her and said, "Mrs. Carnegie, what are you doing? You said you didn't want to go to jail again." "I'm sorry, Henry," she said. "I just can't help it. I just have to go in there."

Mrs. Carnegie's group decided to demonstrate to force some changes. They wanted the federal government to take action, the state to give out the food, and the people with power to help poor people solve some of their problems. The next day, Mrs. Carnegie and a group of about thirty-five from that meeting marched onto the closed and empty Greenville Air Base. Others from the conference went back to their counties to have meetings and spread the word, to get help to support the air base group. The federal military base's unused land and buildings were serving as a symbol of the waste of resources that could be used to help homeless, landless people with housing, jobs, and training programs. Mrs. Carnegie was the only Holmes leader to join in the air base protest. Having often railed against, and taken actions to change, suffering and injustices in

Holmes County, she could not resist joining the struggle of the people who were homeless and freezing.

Back in Holmes County on that same day, a big meeting was held and the story of the conference and the air base group was told. Because the air base was federal property, the state and local police didn't quite know what to do with the protesters. The demonstration leaders told the air force officer on the base, "We are here because we are hungry and cold and we have no jobs and no land." Snow covered the ground. The weather was bitterly cold and the group carried in blankets and clothing. They moved into an unheated building near the main gate. Later in the day, about fifteen more people, including women with small children, brought in wood-burning stoves and joined the first group. One mother, with her three children, told newspaper reporters, "It's a whole lot warmer in here."

Calling themselves the Poor Peoples Conference, they issued a statement saying, "It is federal property and there are hundreds of empty houses and buildings. We need those houses and we need the land. We could be trained for jobs in the buildings." Food distribution was a big issue. The group stated that the dried food provided in the current federal program was "full of bugs and weevils" and that fresh vegetables, fruit, and meat were not included. They wanted the state to set up food distribution by the OEO, in the new federal antipoverty program.

The workers helping to organize the group consisted of volunteers, staff, and leaders from the Delta Ministry of the National Council of Churches as well as the Mississippi Freedom Democratic Party. They called for removing antipoverty programs from the hands of county supervisors. "They don't represent us," the statement continued.

The Delta Ministry was formed by the NCC in 1964 to hold grassroots training sessions for sharecroppers on the importance of voting, political activism, and community discussions. It fought for Head Start, increased health care, and affordable housing. To appease white religious leaders, the Delta Ministry was not to participate in movement struggles across the South but rather was to be a "ministry of reconciliation" that would provide direct services to relieve suffering. Even though there was white southern opposition, the Delta Ministry grew. Within a year it was one of the most active movement organizations in the state, staffing community centers, freedom schools, health projects, and organizing efforts. In 1965 it was a crucial leader in founding the Child Development Group of Mississippi, one of the most effective Head Start programs. In the tradition of SNCC and CORE, the Delta Ministry used its large field staff to develop economic and political power for the poorest and most disadvantaged. Despite the Delta Ministry's support, the day after the protesters moved into the air base, the police kicked them out. Although forced to leave, the group wasn't jailed, and Mrs. Carnegie went back to her farmhouse in Holmes County. The other protesters gathered back at Freedom City. Some Holmes FDP farmers came to the frigid tents, bringing the demonstrators food gathered from Holmes farms. They tried to learn about what was going on.

The demonstration brought some changes. Soon after the protesters moved onto the base, the state of Mississippi set up a discrimination-free administrative board, which allowed Mississippi to finally qualify for OEO's distribution of $1.6 million in food throughout the state. Holmes's new commodities program was important in helping thousands more than ever before to get help from the county welfare department. Also, Holmes FDP leaders and members came to see that they were part of a wider struggle. Although many took part in the conference and later donated food, only Mrs. Carnegie joined the direct action in the occupation of the air base.

Because so few from Holmes actively participated, some people from other counties regarded the Holmes movement as too conservative, saying its people were too scared and that most were not really poor or suffering enough to see themselves as part of that fight. Despite Holmes leaders' experience with successfully organizing a movement at home, the people in the air base action felt Holmes should have been more active. When people don't identify with a struggle and feel it as their own, they cannot take it on as fully as those who do. Although the people in Holmes were in sympathy with the landless, jobless, homeless, and hungry—even saw the rightness and need for action and demonstrations—they didn't completely see it as their own fight. The experience showed us in Holmes that when people join a difficult, dangerous effort, the world may hear and listen. Action, indeed, creates change.

In the midst of the Poor Peoples' actions, Henry and I began con-

Curtis "Ollie" Hoover, from a rural area south of Lexington, was a steady
movement worker.

ducting workshops throughout the county to build and strengthen grass-roots movement structures. We aimed our work at helping the county FDP to stand on its own, with leaders increasingly taking over more planning and strategizing. At that time, at least ten communities were organized. Because they were meeting regularly, we had places where the special workshops could meet. The meeting notices got out by word of mouth. Only two or three movement homes had phones, so the facts of the meetings were communicated individually.

The workshops were usually held in the evening after everyone's mealtime, almost always in a church. Ten or twelve people would attend, though sometimes only four or five; some folks arrived early and others straggled in late. Usually a preacher would open with a prayer and turn the workshop over to the local leader and Henry. In the eastern hill region, for example, Austin Wiley was the leader in Mount Olive, Willie Mae Wright and her husband George were the strong Sunnymount leaders, and Vanderbilt Roby, aided by his wife Cora, were the Old Pilgrims Rest pillars.

The Holmes County FDP was one of the strongest FDP organizations in the state, having a very good working relationship with the state MFDP. When a state-level campaign, action, or response was needed or planned, MFDP chairman Guyot or other state-level workers would communicate with Henry and with Ralthus Hayes. By 1966 Guyot and other FDP workers also had contact with Howard Taft Bailey from Old Pilgrims Rest and Walter Bruce from Durant, who had both developed into strong local leaders. The Holmes leaders in turn might inform Guyot of Holmes plans and needs and get advice and suggestions. Because he had access to the office phone and sometimes attended Jackson meetings, Henry was in touch with Guyot more regularly than the Holmes leaders were, although they too had their own connections with Guyot and the state movement.

Because much more work was under way, we hoped the county's FDP could soon stand on its own, increasingly taking over more planning and strategizing. The many activities centered around the antipoverty programs of late 1965 and early 1966 added complexity to our already not-so-simple life. With regular weekly meetings in fifteen different communities and a monthly countywide meeting that met each third Sunday in a different one of those communities, the Holmes FDP clearly was developing into an extremely active and well-organized movement.

At the same time we were seriously planning for 1967, when local elections would be held for offices in the county and its five election districts or "beats." These elections were the first in which new black voters could have a real chance to meaningfully participate. If enough blacks could get registered by then, our hope—indeed our dream—was to elect some black officials.

Blacks had been given the vote through the duration of the 1867–1877 Reconstruction Act and then completely lost the right to vote at the 1890 Mississippi Constitutional Convention. Through our work, blacks could now, in effect, be elected to take office in Mississippi for the first time in seventy-seven years. Movement people were taking leadership roles at their weekly meetings, in the schools, in the communities, and in the churches. They were raising money. Although modest, the funds collected at meetings and "plate dinners" helped pay for the FDP office's phone, rent, lights, some supplies, and gasoline. Because the Holmes FDP emphasized organizing rather than confrontational politics, it became a force in developing the new federally funded antipoverty programs.

We had already proved that our Head Starts were successful, but that shook the white racist power structure. Within a short time they attempted a power grab. Across the country, funding had been routed through local agencies called Community Action Programs (CAPs). In our region, Central Mississippi Incorporated (CMI) was an umbrella group for CAPs in six Mississippi counties, including ours. There was a huge ruckus about the area CAPs and CMI. The white power structure tried to elect whites to the CMI board of directors and gain control over the Head Start centers we had built. The CDGM's influence was fading. Mrs. Lewis described the moves of the six-county CMI, saying, "CAP came into Holmes County unexpected, before the poor Negro and poor white had the chance to take part in it or decide if it would help our county or not." It wasn't long before the Holmes FDP got involved.

OEO funding, aimed at training, employing, and empowering the poor, was available to each state, including Mississippi. The Holmes FDP knew that unless everything was carefully watched, the whites in power would give as little as possible to the poor. We had a group of leaders who fought to keep our Head Start program independent of CMI. Canny and vigilant with the new programs, they were ready when the white politicians tried to take control. Our leaders started watchdogging and protesting whenever anything seemed wrong. They called meetings to help people understand their rights under the law.

In March 1966, white leaders held a planning meeting to coordinate efforts. They expected to be able to ram things down our throats. FDP leaders quickly spread the word, and that night five hundred blacks and thirty whites crowded into the courthouse courtroom, where most had never before attended an official meeting. Once again, the setting was symbolic. The movement members let the whites know that they knew the laws as well as, if not better than, the white officials and would be watching the officials' every move. We let them know we would not be satisfied with crumbs.

The meeting dragged on. Movement activists brought a series of demands, and we ultimately won, electing a thirty-one-member permanent advisory committee that would elect a CAP board of directors. In addition, each Head Start center would elect a separate advisory committee. The Holmes movement thus restructured the organization of poverty programs during the course of a single meeting. Movement members were able to elect a majority to the committees and influence key policy decisions of the Holmes and CMI CAP. And Holmes movement people remained watchful.

A lot was happening with the community workshops on voters' rights and election education at that time, and that's where I was putting my energy. I was aware that local leaders were active with CAP and CMI. They chaired meetings and made major decisions. If funding resources for poor blacks were threatened, the black leadership didn't hesitate to call a group of people to protest. It was a time of learning and gaining strength.

Another interesting development in the county occurred in the summer of 1966: the possibility of establishing a revolving fund to help people who needed loans. Constance Curry, the southern field person from the American Friends Service Committee (AFSC) Southern Office, based in Atlanta, was in contact with Daisey Lewis. Mrs. Lewis, working with Howard Taft Bailey and others, settled on a grant of one thousand dollars from the AFSC to start the fund. A list of loan procedures was set up to "help people that are involved in Civil Rights work and have financial pressures put upon them because of their involvement." Eleanor Eaton from the national AFSC office and Curry both made several trips to Holmes and met with me, Henry, Mrs. Lewis, Mr. Bailey, and other local leaders. Strict rules were set up for the loans, and it took some time to see about a bonding company for the fund. But in January of 1967, the one-thousand-dollar grant was sent to the "Holmes County Service Fund." The loans, each one $250 or less, made to people in crisis were very helpful in that time of need.

With this small safety cushion from AFSC and the significant CAP and Head Start programs to offer, Holmes leaders gained entrance into several local communities that had kept their doors shut to Freedom Democratic Party organizing. Because the people of the movement had experience and information about the antipoverty programs, they were allowed in. Their organizing grew. The people in the newly opened communities joined in and participated in activities they had never before approached.

Their Stories: Rosie Head's Birthday Party

Rosie Head's birthday party was to begin sometime in the late evening. We left Lexington about seven-thirty, with Henry insisting that the party might be over by the time we got there. He really didn't want to go, since attending such functions was basically against his principles and philosophy and concept of his role in the community. Henry wasn't a highly social person. He played with children and ideas, but social events didn't attract him. Henry also felt that he was a worker and an organizer, that he wasn't in Holmes County to play. He made friends with local people on an individual basis but stayed in the background at large gatherings, political meetings, and parties. On this night, he went to the party with me.

Lights were on in the main room of the community center, but it was totally empty. Everyone was crowded into the much smaller library room. The many books, packed into the totally shelf-lined walls and spilling over into cardboard boxes stacked high along the sides, were being ignored. I wondered if anyone gave them a thought or was intimidated by them.

Young women took on leadership roles in the movement. Rosie Head (*right*) and Elease Gallion (*behind Rosie*) were both living with their parents when the movement sparked them to action at the Greenwood meetings. They worked with the 1964 Summer Project volunteers and later ran the kindergarten and center programs for health, welfare, voter registration, and legal issues. On the left are Lula Turner Erwin and Catherine McLaurin.

No one reached up to leaf through any of the books. At a party of people with more formal education, such a roomful of books would have been a boon for any wallflower or bored, uncomfortable, or out-of-tune guest. Here, anyone not engaged in a spirited game of whist, selecting records, shouting for the record to be played, joking spiritedly, or drinking with a small group was simply sitting quietly watching all the action. Several men and women were in that category.

The thirty-odd people were cramped into the bright, well-lit room that was crowded by the extra-large upright Coke machine, the four desks, a small couch, and numerous chairs. There were also the coats, hats, sweaters, and purses piled on the boxes, tables, and extra spaces.

The room was yellow-bright and warm from all the people and motion. The tiny transistor phonograph blared at full volume. American-Japanese ingenuity had developed something so small that yielded a big sound. Although the 45-rpm records were worn and scratched with continual use, most were the latest current hits in soul music—Aretha Franklin with her "Chain of Fools," Joe Tex and his "lady with the skinny legs" and man "with the raggedy clothes," Wilson Pickett, Marvin Gaye, and Tammie Turrell.

No one was dancing and no one was singing along, but the music was a part of the experience. Most were listening and responding to it. One man, in the middle of making a whist lead, said, "That's right, baby, tell it like it is."

Their Stories: Reverend Joseph McChriston

"There you are. There you are," he said, with a nodding cheerful smile. The phrase pervaded the conversation we held one day and became indistinguishable in content from the more stereotyped "Yassuh, yassuh," "Boss," "Capt'n," and "Tha's right."

"There you are. There you are." He said it without head-scratching or hat-tipping. His back was straight, uncringing, and his arms hung loosely. But he did say it continuously, and in the end you knew little more of Joseph McChriston's real thoughts or feelings than you did at the beginning.

He was involved and active at the Holmes County Community Cen-

Reverend Joseph McChriston, a pastor and a hill farmer, was one of the men who guarded the community center at Mileston during the first dangerous years.

ter in 1964 and 1965. In the pitch-black night he stood guard, protecting us from the gun-shooting, firebombing night riders.

In spring 1966, when the whites were organizing the CAP, we were counterorganizing to protest their faults and violations, to prevent their wrongdoing, and to fight for a real voice for blacks. He was at that first meeting at the courthouse and was elected as one of the six whom the movement added to the supervisor-appointed board. He came into the premeetings in the old FDP office, boning up, getting caught up on the issues in preparation for meeting with the twelve-person integrated committee. He seemed to make a special effort, arriving in midafternoon, perhaps from work, for sometimes he wore the thin-striped blue-on-white coveralls of the carpenter. He came more than fifteen miles from his tumbling, weathered one-story house to the office in Lexington. He listened carefully, and he had the air and spark of one you could depend on to stand firm and speak.

For most formal meetings, he appeared dressed in a stiff-pressed black preaching suit and a white shirt and tie, crisp, neat, nearly dapper. His body was hard, not large but strong, and he was still young; he looked about thirty-five years old. His face was not lined or aged, although tiredness sometimes showed in his eyes. His features were narrow, almost delicate when compared with the more common broad Negroid features, making him handsome by Caucasian standards. He had one jutting front top tooth, which gave his grin a dash, not really a smirk. His eyes sometimes sparked with an amused twinkle. He had an air of confidence and strength, and when he spoke it seemed he was respected.

He voted in the final integrated meeting to decide whether Holmes County should become part of Central Mississippi Incorporated. Standing by the decision determined earlier at a meeting of blacks, in the face of obvious opposition he voted "No," not to enter CMI. He stood firm.

Part 3

Building Political Strategies

9

Political Organizing

January–June 1966

In early 1966 we had already begun our long march to the November 1967 elections. Those local elections were unlike any other project yet undertaken in Holmes. In a way, the effort had begun years before. The first act toward voter registration in 1963 was actually the beginning of work on the 1967 elections.

As early as fall 1964, Larry Stevens, one of the white outside volunteers who stayed in Holmes for several months after Freedom Summer, started looking at maps. He spent hours poring over maps of the county, figuring out the lines of the beats, the electoral subdivisions of Mississippi counties. He studied the maps and mumbled about the 1967 local elections. He and Ed Brown, who was the SNCC project director in Holmes for a few months that fall, were the most politically advanced and theoretical of the outside workers.

In late 1964 and early 1965 they were using those political maps to organize the county FDP along the five Holmes beat lines: Lexington, Beat 1; Durant, Beat 2; Ebenezer, Beat 3; the areas around Thornton, including Mileston, Beat 4; and Tchula, Beat 5. They were election-planning this way at a time when very few blacks in the county and throughout the state were actually registered—only ten were registered in Holmes in 1963. Two years later, by November 1965, when the federal registrar arrived in Holmes, McClellan had added only 690 blacks on his books. So you can imagine how crazy the plotting for any elections seemed in 1964 and 1965.

The 1967 elections were tantalizing because they included important local offices that were up for election only every four years. If we could

157

The Freedom Democratic Party office in Lexington. Leaders often met at this "shotgun shack" office in Pecan Grove, which functioned as the movement hub. Lexington was a predominantly white community, much more risky than the black rural area where the movement started. *Left to right:* Reverend Seymour and Henry Lorenzi.

get enough blacks registered before then, we would be able to elect black supervisors, justices of the peace, and constables at the beat level as well as such county officials as sheriff, circuit clerk, and state representative.

Our work in 1966 on the Special Beat 5 Election, the June Primary, and the November general election were all undertaken in the spirit of giving locals new experiences that built their ability to vote as a bloc when their registered numbers warranted the possibility of winning. All were steps in developing a grassroots structure. The crucial part wasn't electing candidates as much as developing an election "machine." The process was a teaching device for the leaders and organizers.

In 1965 and 1966, people ran for office and voted in preparation and practice for creating black successes in the local races of 1967. Because we didn't have enough registered voters to affect an election outcome, our main movement involvement was voter education and political organizing for ultimate election victories.

The MFDP led the political process to add candidates to the June 7 state Democratic primary ballot. By April 1966 we were ready to publicly announce the six candidates who had successfully filed to run in the state Democratic Party primary:

- Reverend Clifton R. Whitley, age thirty-two, chaplain and professor at Rust College in Holly Springs, Marshall County, was running for the U.S. Senate. Educated at Gammon Theological Seminary in Atlanta, Whitley had been an MFDP delegate to the 1964 Democratic National Convention. He was opposing James O. Eastland, the four-term incumbent, who was a vociferous opponent of civil rights and a supporter of Jim Crow laws.
- Dock Drummond, age seventy-six, a retired plumber from Kosciusko, Attala County, was running for the U.S. House of Representatives from Mississippi's First Congressional District, the seat that had been held by Rep. Tom Abernethy for twenty years.
- Holmes County's own FDP chairman, Ralthus Hayes, age fifty, a project landowner and farmer from Choctaw, Mileston, in the Tchula beat, was running for U.S. Representative from Mississippi's Second Congressional District. He opposed eleven-term incumbent Rep. Jamie Whitten, a very conservative segregationist.
- Ed King, the white Mississippian with whom Henry and I stayed during our 1964 COFO orientation, was a thirty-year-old chaplain at Tougaloo College. He was running for U.S. Representative from Mississippi's Third Congressional District; the seat had been held for nine terms by John Bell Williams, a staunch states'-rights segregationist. Tougaloo was the campus where many early SNCC workers, including Guyot and Hollis Watkins, had developed their activism. In the 1963 Freedom Vote, Ed King ran for lieutenant governor along with the Mississippi NAACP state president, while Aaron Henry of Clarksdale, Coahoma County, ran for governor. In

1964, King was an MFDP delegate to the Atlantic City Convention and an MFDP national committeeman.

- Reverend Clinton Collier, age fifty-six, of Neshoba County, was seeking the seat being vacated by Prentiss Walker, U.S. Representative from Mississippi's Fourth Congressional District. Collier had been a public school teacher until he lost his job because of civil rights activity.
- Lawrence Guyot, age twenty-six, of Pass Christian, Harrison County, was running for U.S. Representative from Mississippi's Fifth Congressional District. Guyot, the MFDP chairman, sought the seat held by thirty-year incumbent William Colmer.

Mississippi had a significant number of blacks openly engaged in an election for the first time in a century. The movement was gravely concerned about violent reactions against the candidates. The day before the group filed to run for office, a fifteen-year-old youth was shot in the hip on the way to an election rally for Ed King. That same day, a highway patrolman beat an MFDP committee member who was traveling to Jackson. In many parts of Mississippi, the Klan reorganized, warning blacks to stay away from the polls. Collier was repeatedly arrested and harassed.

The candidates developed their election platforms in a series of meetings with state FDP leaders, organizers, and staff. The MFDP presented issues it felt the state should know about. The candidates designed the platforms to be empowering, indigenous, educational, and clearly directed at creating political power for those without power. Many of the issues came from Greenwood, where movement politics had developed in the early 1960s. These candidates for state-level offices needed platforms that covered wider issues than a candidate for local office would. Each candidate developed his own platform in his own way.

Ralthus Hayes's draft plank on voting stated that a "federal registrar should be sent to every Mississippi county, and they should be mobile and readily available to all the people, whether it means reaching them by going out to commodity lines, plantations, or churches. Registrars should stay open at least a few nights a week so as to register daytime workers." In the category of welfare, he called for a "HEW (Health, Education, and Welfare) department investigation of the inadequacy of its programs

These Pecan Grove neighbors weren't active in the movement, but their presence showed us that the movement was for all families as much as it was for the activists.

in the Second Congressional District, the exclusion of Negroes from HEW jobs in many of the district's counties, and the fact that the white officials in some of the counties had not accepted any HEW welfare program at all."

The platforms of all the candidates were very similar. Poor people were to be significantly represented in running all federal programs, including the new antipoverty program. The impact of living wages had created a new awareness. Head Start was run by the poor, and for the first time people had well-paid jobs as drivers, teachers, cooks, and cleaners. The candidates called for CDGM Head Starts in every county.

Other planks stated that the money spent to expand the war in Vietnam should be used instead to fight poverty at home and that Medicare should be extended to all ages, along with an end to segregated hospitals. Washington needed to start a massive public works program that would provide jobs and improve communities by hiring workers to build roads, sewers, and dams and to clear forests. The candidates argued that new industries that hired fairly and paid a higher minimum wage would improve the everyday lives of the people.

They wanted voting rights protected and wanted people to enroll their children in desegregated schools and to protest unfair conditions without retaliation. All schools needed to be improved by better books, labs, and more parent involvement. All grades through graduate and law schools must become desegregated and scholarships made available.

Vast acres of federal land were unused. The candidates wanted it transferred to landless people. They wanted free legal counsel for the poor, both white and black, and assurance of integrated juries. And there were more ideas and visions.

The six MFDP candidates launched their campaigns, speaking their platform messages to citizens' groups across the state. On the second anniversary of the founding of the MFDP, all the candidates and many guest speakers made presentations at its monthly convention in Jackson.

The candidates knocked on doors, attended meetings, and handed out their honest and heartfelt campaign literature. In one of his fliers, Reverend Collier wrote:

I was born on August 24, 1910, in Neshoba County, fourteen miles from Philadelphia. My mother is from the same county, and my father came from Leake County. Three of my grandparents were slaves. Papa started me off counting his money from cotton and seed sales when I was eight years old. I found that sometimes he got his money and sometimes he didn't. I did about any labor job to get through college. My father and I ditched and cleared land, and the little children picked cotton.

I went north to the big cities, and during 1943–45 served in the Navy. This was followed by a period at Howard University and employment by the government and in factories. In 1956, I came home and obtained a teaching license and job in the public school system. This lasted until the civil rights struggle came to the state, when I was put out of the school system. Also when I returned home, I entered the Methodist church and took up farming again.

Politics is about the bread we eat. It is about Head Starts. It is about the right of certain men to make slaves of others. It is about some men being rich, and others poor. It is about war and it is about peace.

Ralthus Hayes's campaign was the most difficult, because just after passage of the 1965 Voting Rights Act, the Mississippi legislature had carefully and ruthlessly carved up his Second Congressional District, the only black-majority congressional district in the state for most of the previous one hundred years. Almost 60 percent black in the early 1960s, the district had been diluted by distributing a portion of it to three other districts, thus allowing no black majority in any of the five districts. The new district extended two hundred miles from Hayes's home. But Hayes took it in stride, didn't slow down, and was proud to campaign for such a high office.

He wrote hundreds of letters and invited himself to speak in towns he had never set foot in before. As a full-time working farmer, he was able to travel only one day a week. One of his letters said:

Dear friends: So that those working on the Second Congressional District campaign and myself can know more about your county, we wondered if the civil rights workers could please send us a report on the Movement there: what has been organized, what issues people are working on, what kind of jobs people hold, and if your county is getting more or fewer jobs, what big problems there are.

Also, since I've been the FDP chairman here in Holmes County for a time and have been working actively in this Movement, perhaps I can help people out from other counties, to some extent, with their problems of getting the wrong yields and of parents losing their jobs over school integration.

He also wrote of the success of one group that came to see him:

Perhaps other people in the Movement would like to do what the DeSoto FDP people did—a carload of people came Saturday and talked with me and one of the civil rights workers about the problems of farmers and townspeople . . . organizing the people in their county. We told them of how the FDP is trying to help farmers and townspeople in Holmes County, and is working on problems from FHA loans to community action programs to job discrimination. It was good to meet together and learn from each other. . . . Now I have a better idea of what is wrong in their district.

Hayes's goal was finding a campaign manager and establishing a finance committee in each county. He also wanted to get each county to endorse his platform or help change it. The long distances made letters especially important. Hayes and his campaign team wrote letters to every person they could think of to ask for advice and support.

In response to Hayes's letter, Stokely Carmichael offered, "Let the people make up the platform." Julian Bond was trying to make room in his schedule to come and speak at a rally for Hayes. Hunter Morey, a Head Start representative, sent a list of state CDGM office addresses. Bernice Montgomery's niece made up a list of the churches. Victoria Gray offered to run a workshop. A movement worker in Sunflower offered to do political education. Annie Devine and her husband George were thinking big: they wanted to hold a county redistricting meeting.

A statewide rally was planned for April 30–May 1, 1966, with sing-ing, outdoor cooking, baseball, a dance, and an opportunity to fundraise. The informal rally committee included Rosie Head, Alice Mae Epps, Lela Mae Walden, and Bernice and Eugene Montgomery.

Collier, Whitley, and Hayes worked together as much as they could. Collier got a "regular" phone in the Philadelphia office that people could use to call out collect. In Neshoba County, as in Holmes, the FDP had no campaign funds from movement organizations. With the redistricting, Collier became a candidate for Holmes, and he joined Hayes in shaking hands and going to churches, meetings, and rallies. Hayes and Whitley traveled to DeSoto County and met with more than two hundred enthu-siastic people who were especially interested in the Community Action Programs and school desegregation.

As practice for the 1967 election, still eighteen months away, we held dozens of trainings on poll watching and gathering solid voting data. The MFDP office in Jackson produced a booklet that spelled out the concerns and explained the legal issues involved in poll watching, noting that it was a legal right to watch the polls and that rules had to be followed.

The booklet also encouraged voting: "The Polls open at 7 in the morning. You should try and vote as early as you can. Don't wait until it's too late. The polls close at 6 in the evening. If you live a good distance from the polling place and have a car, stop along the way and pick up your friends and neighbors."

On June 7, in addition to the ballot to vote for a senator and a congressman, voters received a second ballot to vote on the constitu-tional amendment regarding how justices of the peace should be paid. At that time, the justices were getting paid from a portion of the fines imposed when they found somebody guilty. The legislature proposed that a straight salary be paid instead. The MFDP agreed, because the existing plan allowed a justice of the peace to find someone guilty just to be paid more.

In May 1966, with extensive involvement from Henry and me, the FDP held a month of community workshops, where several hundreds of the grassroots people from many areas of the county gathered to discuss what lay ahead with the election. We covered how we had gotten to that point and the role the FDP had played. The workshops gave people information about the politics and the election process one month ahead of the primary election and several months ahead of the fall general election. Because most of the people had never before voted, they had few images or concepts about how a campaign was organized. We introduced our plan of creating a block captain and precinct leader system for each of the five beats in the county, and local leaders in each community were chosen or volunteered to be precinct leaders and block captains. Like previous workshops we had held, the meetings took place in movement churches in the organized communities.

In Mississippi, the white Democratic Party did not support any black candidates. When some movement blacks tried to attend county and state Democratic conventions, the party wouldn't even allow them to enter the meeting areas.

By June 1966, only one year after the passage of the Voting Rights Act, five thousand Holmes blacks had been registered by the federal registrars at the post office. However, the dramatic spurt of black registration that came with the arrival of those registrars had already begun to wane. Approximately four thousand blacks were still unregistered. Then, just as the new voters were about to show their strength at the polls, two events occurred.

On June 4, a recently activated Holmes Ku Klux Klan tried to scare blacks from voting. They held a nighttime rally at which they erected a twenty-five-foot flaming cross and the Grand Dragon of the State of Mississippi gave a speech. And—making the national news—James Meredith surprised everyone by starting his March against Fear on June 5 and getting shot on June 6, his first day into Mississippi. The eyes of the world turned to the violence and hatred directed by whites against blacks.

Some stayed away from the polls because of the threats of violence. Efforts were made to poll-watch, but in many precincts the poll watchers received poor treatment from election officials. The elections couldn't be stopped. The results were good, but not as good as we had privately hoped they could be. The Democratic primary held only one victory for the MFDP. Reverend Clifton Whitley, who was running for the U.S. Senate, won majorities in two predominately black river counties, Claiborne and Jefferson. Hayes lost his race.

Their Stories: Mr. and Mrs. Burrell Tate

Big, dark red-brown and shiny, Mrs. Tate was smooth-skinned with almost delicate features in her full face. When Henry and I stopped by to visit the Tates, she was the first to respond to our horn toot and had come out on the porch, recognized us, and begun to shout loudly in the same kind of over-enthusiastic welcome that greeted us everywhere in the county. Dressed in a brightly printed Sunday dress, she laughed with her whole body, warmly shouting her surprise and glee to us to "Come on in" and to Mr. Tate to "Come on out and see Henry and Sue."

Their small house wasn't raggedy, and neither was it big—only two rooms, though big ones, and a kitchen. There might have been more in the back, but its total image and feel was of a poor, small dwelling. The house sat in the middle of flat, barren land, not planted in lawn or pasture or trees—just bare dusty flatness, with woods way off.

The inside was spotlessly clean, neat, and comfortable. The TV blared out the football game as we sat in the sitting room–bedroom on rockers and straight-back chairs. Mrs. Tate sat down on the bench in front of a sturdy old vanity chest. The big four-poster double bed was behind us, and the room was bright and refreshing. Although there were no images of Jesus on the wall, the straight honest being of Burrell let you know that Jesus was a presence there. A lit, gold-plated framed picture of Dr. Martin Luther King Jr. hung on one wall, connected by an extension cord to the one light socket in the ceiling.

Mr. Tate was a short, solidly built man, sturdy though crippled. He limped on a heavy left shoe that had two inches of sole to match his shorter leg up with his right one. He was light-skinned, with gray hair and features more white than Negroid. Tan freckles spotted the ridge of his broad nose and wide, wrinkled forehead. He laughed a high rising cackle, nearly a whinny. It was bright and cheerful but verged on nervousness. An unsure, hopeful, laugh-interruption was but a small part of his conversation, which burst with the many things that involved him. Words tripped over words to get all his meaning out. He was busy with a newfound freedom to speak about his pride, concerns, hardships, and the injustices he'd seen. Although his rapid words and thoughts spilled out, bumping each other, his natural rhythm was a slow, even-pitched flat drawl.

Burrell Tate, a careful, astute leader from the hill community of Ebenezer, was a remarkable teller of his own stories.

Mr. Tate talked of many things during the three hours we shared in his front bedroom. Mrs. Tate interrupted once or twice to say in a rather embarrassed tone that Burrell should quit talking for a while and let Henry say a thing or two. But Henry and I passed, and Tate went on enthusiastically. Several other times she verified that what he said was true.

He talked about a white nurse who worked in the primarily black CAP Head Start. "Not long ago," Mr. Tate said, "I was telling that white lady, T. J. Brown's wife, about how it is, going over parts of the Bible and pointing out how we're all God's children. I told her that the Negro is just like any other man. He has a mind and a heart. He loves his family and children and wants the best for them. He has feelings just like any other man, feelings that can be hurt and hurt him. Negroes got to be treated right. In the past, they has beat and burned and mobbed Negroes just on the count of their being Negroes. The Bible shows you're not supposed to treat people like that, and Negroes is people just like any others with a mind and feelings that can be hurt just like white people.

"I told it out for her about how in the past it's been the whites that kill Negroes, how it was the white women that was the cause of killing Negro mens. A white lady could go off and tell their men that I was talking to her, and the men would go out and mob me. I didn't have no protection. They could just take me out and beat me and cut out my tongue and burn me slow. Hang me up in a tree, and my brother could come to get me and the whites would stop him, say you can't cut that nigger down 'til we say to. That's how it was. That's the history of the Negro 'round these parts, and in America. But it's past that time now, and things has got to start getting right, because that's no way to treat another man."

Mr. Tate went on about his land, "We've been on this land here about twenty years or more. It was around '45, I bought this piece of land [a piece of the Clark family's land]. . . . My mother didn't want nothing to do with it. It was too far in, too far off from the road. They didn't have no roads back in here then. She didn't like it down in here. The old folks called it Buzzards' Roost, and she didn't want to be living in no buzzards' place.

"I got my loan through the Federal Land Bank. . . . Yes, that must have been around the time of the Mileston projects with the FHA. I was thinking about going on over and trying to get a project place [through the Roosevelt-era program], but my wife wouldn't go over into the delta."

"I just didn't know no better, I guess," said Mrs. Tate. "If we had done that, we would have had a nice house now probably."

"She was afraid of the malaria swamps over in the delta," Mr. Tate explained, "and she didn't want to move down into the delta. It's true. If we had gone over there, we probably would have had a nice project house, better than this old piece of house that we have here. But I don't regret that. Let me tell you, I do believe and I have faith. And I am where God intended me to be. We all are where God intends. . . .

"Let me tell you what I mean about this faith. I haven't never lived on no white man's place where I had to be dependent. Before I moved onto this land of mine, I rented for twelve years from a white man. I ain't never worked on shares. I worked straight cash rent from the man, and I was the only man on the place that didn't get furnish from the man. I paid him straight cash rent—two bales of cotton. I took my cows and stock down to that place in Yazoo where I was renting, and folks said, 'You ain't never gonna take your stock off that Mr. Thomas' place. Nobody ever leave old Mister Thomas' place able to take their things off.'"

But I said, 'Nobody's going to keep me from taking my things. Nobody is going to make me leave my things at Thomas'. I won't get indebted to him with my things. I won't put my livestock under a note to him.' Oh, no, Thomas didn't like that. He kept taking from my government check when he wasn't supposed to, and he didn't like that I wasn't getting furnish from him.

"I don't want to be dependent on no man. The white never has wanted the Negro to stand on his two feet. Always wanted him to be underneath the white and keep him depending on the white for everything. That's one trouble with the Negro—so many don't know how to stand up alone.

"It's true that in past years, before Negroes started demanding things, the white man would let a Negro buy land and do things to set them up and help. They would pile up a Negro so that he had too much—a house and land and then a car too, and the load was too much. It would keep him dependent on the white. And in the end, they'd work it out so the white got it all anyway. . . .

"When I got this piece of land, I had to scuffle and scrape to get up the notes for it. Right about that time, when I was first getting on here, my wife, she took sick, and I had to carry her to the hospital for an operation. Then she came home, but six months later she was sick still, and I had to take her on back to the hospital.

"My two girls was little then and, when my wife come home, then one of the girls took sick. The medicine and the doctor bills was taking all what little I had to pay on the land, meet the note. Then my leg started getting worse. I always has been crippled since I was around fourteen, but at this same time my leg started getting all swoll up so I couldn't walk on it, couldn't walk behind a mule. So I was sick. And my wife and children and I was just getting the land cleared but I couldn't walk no plow behind a mule to make no crop.

"I needed to buy a tractor to do the work, but I didn't want to put up the land and get dependent on that. It was a dark time, and I didn't know what I should do. I had to have a tractor to do my work, but I just didn't like the idea of getting so far under on a tractor that I would lose what I already had scraped and scuffled so hard for. Here is where the faith come in.

"I asked the Lord what must I do. One day I was sitting out on the porch worrying about the tractor and going into the hole for it, and then I fell back into a dream like. There was this great big wide hole in the ground, the side slanting like a spinning top to the point way down in the bottom. Now you may think this is all foolishness and nonsense, but I know this is facts. I fell into that big hole and I was in the bottom of it. I started scratching and climbing trying to dig my way up to the top. I scratched and scratched and I took off my shoes and dug with my toes into the sides and clawed with my hands and fingers trying to make it up that side and get out of that hole. I'd fall back and then I'd scrape some more, and little by little, scraping and scratching and clawing and grabbing and hanging on, I was making it up the side of that hole. I was so tired I didn't think I was going to make it. Finally, when I just was getting up near the top where I could see over, I was holding on real tight with my feet and hands and I was almost out of the hole and looking over the edge when I was so tired that I woke up.

"I woke up out of that dream and then this was the interpretation I made out of it. God was telling me that I would get the loan on a tractor and it would be a hard struggle. I would have to scrape and scuffle the whole way over the whole four years. But I would make it. Yes, I would. So I got the loan and told my wife it would be hard going all the way, but the Lord intends it that way. I was scraping and scuffling for every dime, grabbing here and there, and it looked like I wasn't going to make it some time. But at the end of the four years, we did make it out. And it got better, where I was making ten, fifteen bales of cotton, which is not a lot but enough to provide for a family."

10

The Meredith March

June–July 1966

James Meredith's 220-mile Memphis-to-Jackson March against Fear started at a bad time for ongoing voter registration and election organizing in Mississippi. He began the march on Sunday, June 5, 1966, two days before the June 7 Mississippi primary elections, which we referred to as the white Democratic primary. The march interrupted the Holmes and state FDP's intense push. Many of us were upset because his one-man effort diverted attention away from the election efforts.

The movement reality of needing to respond to Meredith and participate in the march frustrated, even angered, many of us. Then, surprisingly, the march ultimately enhanced and strengthened our plans for more registration drives in Holmes and around the state.

A native of Kosciusko in Attala County, James Meredith started his walk from Memphis, fewer than thirty miles from the Tennessee-Mississippi border. He had not consulted or coordinated his effort with any local, regional, or national movement group. Only a few friends and supporters joined him. A handful of TV, newspaper, and radio media came to observe and record. Four years earlier, in 1962, he had become a civil rights celebrity when he tried to attend the University of Mississippi–Oxford. That was also a solitary action unaffiliated with the organized movement. It took John Kennedy's three thousand national guardsmen to restore order to the Ole Miss campus and allow Meredith to register as a third-year student. He successfully graduated in 1963.

On the second day of the march, June 6, Meredith crossed into Mississippi. Just inside the state at Hernando in DeSoto County, his walk was cut short. In front of his supporters, the media, FBI agents, and the

Mississippi Highway Patrol, shotgun pellets riddled his head, shoulder, and leg. "Oh my God!" he cried out as he fell. He was injured badly and taken to the hospital.

Almost immediately, Guyot, in his role as SNCC organizer and the MFDP chairman, was called by national leaders to come to Memphis for an emergency June 7 planning meeting at the Lorraine Motel, where Martin Luther King Jr.'s Southern Christian Leadership Conference (SCLC) people often stayed. In addition to the principals of MFDP and SCLC, Floyd McKissick of CORE, Roy Wilkins of the NAACP, and Stokely Carmichael, Cleve Sellers, and Stanley Wise of SNCC attended.

Holmes had direct working contact only with Stokely, who was appointed SNCC field director in Holmes soon after Henry and I arrived. Later, in 1965, he went into Lowndes County, Alabama, as a key SNCC activist working on voter registration aimed at the 1966 local elections. The Lowndes County Freedom Organization was formed under his leadership.

Back in Lexington, while waiting for election results, we watched the TV reports of the Memphis meeting. The leaders announced that they would continue James Meredith's march. They invited anyone from any part of America who loved freedom, to join in. A small planning meeting was called for June 8. Ralthus Hayes, the astute chairman of the Holmes FDP, who had just been defeated in the primary, was invited, and Henry and I drove him to Memphis.

King, McKissick, and the other "higher-ups" wanted to hear what we Mississippians needed from the march. In the motel room, a group of only ten or fifteen people sat on the beds, chairs, and floor. At one table Fannie Lou Hamer, of Ruleville in Sunflower County, the impassioned speaker and singer who gave us much to arouse our courage, and the steadfast Annie Devine of Canton in Madison County were present. Hamer and Devine spoke for the MFDP. They succeeded in getting our point across. We needed to engage in actual voter registration drives rather than simply marching. Within the tenets of grassroots organizing, especially those of MFDP, SNCC, and COFO, the local people were essential to defining the needs and the organizing actions, whether in a rural area, a town, a county, a city, or the entire state. The opinions of the Mississippi leaders were indispensable to any planning for actions in their state, and we all wanted a unified response to the shooting.

As northern white workers, Henry and I said little. We had worked only in one county, not on the state level. We agreed wholeheartedly that we needed a march focused on our priorities and efforts. Mr. Hayes spoke up a few times. He didn't seem as awestruck as we were to be in the same realm as these national leaders.

The group accepted the goal of registering blacks to vote, and the march resumed the next day. Most Holmes movement people came together to support Meredith's march and fight back whatever fears were rising in them. They talked in their meetings about what they could do. Some, like Mrs. Carnegie, immediately traveled the seventy miles north to meet the march at the closest place to Mileston. She continued marching for more than 125 miles. Others from Holmes marched shorter distances for just one or two days.

Holmes was originally on the march route, so some in our fifteen-odd communities with weekly movement meetings opened up their land, houses, communities, and kitchens to the marchers. They had sent messages and committees to the march leaders, letting them know how welcome the marchers would be. But to make the march more relevant to the Mississippi registration and election efforts, the march route bypassed Holmes to hit counties of greater need—counties that were without voter registration drives or federal registrars.

The Holmes FDP encouraged its people to march and raise consciousness around registration in the less organized counties. Mr. Hayes joined the march for many days and spent full evenings knocking on doors, trying to turn people out to register at the courthouse in the counties the march was approaching. He and others spoke at the rallies and meetings held nightly at the march and surrounding areas. Henry traveled back and forth to the march several times.

Many people from Holmes helped feed the marchers, including Zelma Williams and Elease Gallion. One day, Zelma witnessed a horrible event. "We had dropped off supplies and were returning to the car when we came upon a group of white men and one black man dressed in coveralls," Zelma said. "The white men were shouting at him, 'Eat it.' They were making him eat his hat because he had registered to vote. That poor man stood there, ripped some fabric off his hat with his teeth and chewed. I'll never forget his face or how helpless I felt."

The Holmes County Courthouse in Lexington played a strong role in the Holmes County civil rights movement. The First Fourteen tried to "redish" (register) at this courthouse in April 1963. More than five hundred people marched for civil rights here in 1965, and Willie Ricks from SNCC gave a rousing speech here during the 1966 Meredith March.

The Holmes FDP invited a speaker from the march to come into the county seat and speak to the local people at a freedom rally. It was held at Courthouse Square in the middle of Lexington. That building had come to mean so much in their struggle that the movement used it at every possible opportunity. Willie Ricks, a SNCC field secretary from Atlanta, spoke to several hundred people gathered around the square. Soon they moved onto the courthouse lawn to better hear Ricks, who was the first at the Meredith March demonstrations to introduce the Black Power concept. Stokely had taken up the Black Power chant during the march, calling attention to the differences in philosophy between those in older organizations focused on nonviolent change and those with the need for a more forceful rhetoric and action.

In Lexington, when the Holmes people moved in to hear Ricks, they stood where they had marched the year before and where the determined First Fourteen had stood in 1963. That day in 1966, hundreds heard Ricks publicly speak for equality. He addressed the sheriff and other white officials, who stood in the doorways and poked their heads out of their offices.

Ricks began. He told of trying to register. He told of the past and how badly blacks had been oppressed. One lady cried out to the Lord that she never thought she'd see the day when such truth would be told aloud with powerful whites standing right there to bear witness to all the wrongs they had caused. Ricks spoke on and on, and the people said, "That's right, brother!" and "Tell it like it is!" and "Amen." Ricks urged them to work, struggle, and organize more, so when the 1967 elections came, they could elect their own people. He boldly shouted out the vision.

He pointed at Sheriff Andrew P. Smith, on the very same courthouse steps, not four feet away, and said, "That sheriff can be replaced! Next year you can have your own!" Electric sighs and tension spread through the crowd. I, like others, squirmed with the excitement of standing near something dangerous but breathtaking and beautiful. Just being there in the warm sun among so many, listening to such taboo speech, was a large, victorious change. The rally inspired the group. Many then joined the march.

I don't know whether there were dozens or hundreds of reporters, but it is certain that the world got a twenty-two-day dose of what it was like to be black in Mississippi. The actual shooting of James Meredith was televised at the time and repeated often in describing the march. The white who shot him, Aubrey James Norvell, was caught within minutes of the incident. The nation saw that he showed no shame or remorse for what he had done. In fact, he looked quite proud of himself.

The national media covering the Meredith March took notice of stories from all over the state about the retaliation that blacks experienced when they tried to register. They reported on the common consequences of movement involvement—lights and gas shut off in the homes of "trouble-makers," evictions by landlords, banks calling in loans, houses being shot at, property being destroyed, and bosses firing black workers. Walking down the street, people who had recently tried to register were called names, belittled, beaten, or—if caught outside after dark—shot. The march put all these oppressive, retaliatory tactics into the public eye.

When the march was passing near Holmes, I arranged to take Norman and Rosebud Clark's youngest, their ten-year-old daughter Kayrecia, with me to march to the next planned overnight stop in Canton. Henry drove Kayrecia and me to U.S. Highway 51 to drop us off to join the marchers. Several hundreds of us streamed along in the hot June sun along the rural highway, with few bystanders other than highway patrolmen. My memory of those marching hours is of high-spirited singing and sociability among us marchers; it was fairly peaceful. Mrs. Carnegie was in the group, often walking in the front lines with King, Stokely, and the others.

Since the beginning, the marchers had rarely been attacked on the main route, although many assaults on side roads were reported. Over the whole three weeks of the march, the numbers marching ebbed and flowed from hundreds to a couple thousand.

When we arrived in Canton, things got ugly. Mrs. Devine got permission from the chairman of the all-white county school board to allow the marchers to use the grounds of a public Negro elementary school to set up tents for sleeping. But when we started raising the tents in the designated schoolyard, the Mississippi State Police and other police agencies harassed us. When we persisted in working on the tents, they barraged us with tear gas. They threw a chemical irritant on us. One white marcher received second-degree burns on her legs. The gas-masked troopers charged at us, beating and hitting with rifles and dragging away the troublemakers. We scattered throughout the neighborhood, fleeing the fumes, fumbling to take care of ourselves, the children, and the old. I was frantic to find Kayrecia and Mrs. Carnegie in the chaos and was relieved to find them unharmed.

I'm not sure what I had expected to happen, but I was shocked to see physical danger and pain actually materializing. Many were wounded, some severely. The immediacy was frightening, although I knew "real" bullets would have caused much worse effects. The next day, marchers came back to the school and found men with machine guns on the school's roof and armed troopers surrounding the grounds.

Along the march route, rallies were held in the evenings. Fannie Lou Hamer and Andrew Young joined the other national civil rights leaders on stage. Speeches and songs buoyed the spirits of the crowd. Zelma and Elease attended the final night's concert at Tougaloo College and were entertained by James Brown and other musicians.

The march concluded on June 26, stretching the eight miles from the Tougaloo College campus to the capitol. It culminated with a rally of fifteen thousand people. James Meredith had recovered enough to complete the march. More than one thousand officers in the Mississippi State Highway Patrol, the National Guard, and local law enforcement agencies guarded the capital city, but the damage to the white status quo had been done. Nearly three thousand black Mississippians had registered to vote during the process.

When Stokely shouted "black power" at the Meredith March, much of the media reacted as if it was a new concept, but we had heard rumblings about it for months. Elner Bailey, Howard Taft Bailey's daughter, had attended a conference in Atlanta in April 1966, and when she returned she submitted the following to the Holmes County Community Center newsletter: "On Friday night, I attended a very interesting discussion on politics in the South. Participating in the discussion were two Southern white men, and Stokely, a civil rights worker in Lowndes County, Alabama. Both white men made a few statements; they were concerned about what Stokely had to say.

Stokely talks about 'black power.' He talked about black power until some of the white people said that they felt left out, and the reason that they joined the Movement in the first place was because they were left out of their race."

More than a year earlier, when Stokely arrived in Lowndes County to work on voter registration, Lowndes was 80 percent black, but not a single black citizen was registered to vote.

We were aware that in other parts of the country, especially in Alabama, more militant action was taking place. Also in April 1966, the *Birmingham News* had reported:

> Stokely Carmichael, the twenty-four-year-old civil rights worker who moved into the Black Belt political picture in early 1965, said that the new party will have a slate of candidates for seven county offices in November.
>
> He says Negroes will select their candidates at a mass meeting May 3, the date of the Democratic primary. This procedure is set out by law for a new political party to get on the ballot. Carmichael describes the Democratic Party as the "most treacherous enemy of the Negro." The field secretary for the Student Nonviolent Coordinating Committee (SNCC) said that the goal of the Black Panther Party is to gain power through votes. Carmichael says power, not desegregation, is the answer for the Negro. "When you go for power you just take over."

During and immediately after the Meredith March, we heard from our supporters across the country. They were uneasy about the militant tone of Stokely and the Meredith March. Both Henry and I could tell from their letters and phone calls that some were so uneasy they were going to cut back on their financial help. I felt compelled to write the following message, which I attached to the August newsletter to our donors and friends.

> I don't know what Black Power means to you, though I can imagine how hysterically it has been distorted by the media. To us it has seemed like an especially good, much-needed concept

of cultural pride. True "freedom" cannot come to the black man so long as he has only shame and hatred for his black skin. He cannot be free until he stops trying to be what he isn't and starts accepting with pride what he is.

The barriers that have been built between white and black, most easily seen in this openly racist, segregated area, are not easily set aside—not in a month, a summer, a year, or even our several years. Of course, we are accepted, recognized as "friendly" whites, on some levels even considered black.

The problems of a white organizer in the black community are real—very real. Our power is many times what a black organizer's power is. We have seen it as we worked right beside capable black organizers. Criticisms do not flow naturally toward us—for we are white. Adult leaders over-emphasize our opinions and have great difficulty making decisions in opposition to what they believe our feeling is. Daily, people react, relate, accept, and agree with us, not because we are right, but because we're white. We reinforce, by the mere existence of our white skin, the Negroes' lack of confidence.

At the same time, we are trying to encourage and develop their self-confidence, a belief in their own ability to move and operate with potency. The black organizer can instill a self-pride in the people by the example of his black leadership. The black organizer breaks down those myths, provides positive, concrete evidence of the non-validity of black inferiority, impotence, and inability to do anything alone. The people can positively identify with the black organizer.

We have felt these effects from the very first setting of our feet into the black community. In earlier phases of the Movement, the black-white issue had less importance. Whites were needed in 1964 to break down state-imposed barriers to organizing. The positive values brought by white organizers have many times outweighed those negative effects. Still, the ultimate goal of every outside organizer is complete local control of the local Movement. That's our goal.

Their Stories: Eugene Montgomery

Eugene Montgomery stopped by to visit at our Balance Due house one evening. I heard him at least three or four minutes before I could see him, because, not too far from the highway—I'm sure before he got to the footbridge—he started whistling for the dogs. He whistled and whistled, all the way over the bridge and up the mud path, up the hill, past the front of the house to the gate to our yard. All the way to the front porch he whistled for the confused animals.

"Lorenzah, Lorenzah!" he yelled at the top of his voice, or rather barked in mock anger, even though I was already standing in the door in plain sight, hands on my hips in mock irritation. The yelling was normal for us. We yelled at each other a lot, pushing, shoving, acting foolish much of the time—our way of expressing the real affection we felt for each other.

Eugene was a tall man, solidly and strongly built, lean and lithe with hard, strong muscles and no evidence of fat. He was a rich coppery brown, bright, shiny, with a lot of color but not dark. He acted much younger than his fifty years—lively, spirited, playful, and joking.

That evening, Eugene was pretty far along toward drunkenness. He swayed as he stood, eyes heavy and lids closing, tongue thick and words so slurred they were sometimes unintelligible. Eugene would skip drinking for a good while, but when he did drink, he was known to get pretty nasty. I had been around him when he had too many and it was uncomfortable. That evening I saw no escape. Henry was out and I couldn't think of a good excuse to walk out on my company.

I steadied myself and decided to cope with the situation. I offered him some hot coffee and went into the kitchen to boil some water. Then I took my can of tobacco and cigarette paper and went out to the porch to sit in the darkening evening. Eugene followed, sat in a rocker, used my tobacco, and we began to talk.

I served him piping hot coffee and after it cooled for a while, he took sips and then gulps of it. It began to take effect, and he rested in the rocker, elbows on his knees, head in his palms. He rubbed his scalp, his eyes, the bridge of his nose, and his ears. He reflected, "I don't know why I drink so much all at once and just keep drinking. . . . I carried a

Eugene Montgomery, an energetic worker and the husband of leader Bernice Montgomery, tirelessly drove, attended meetings, and made others see the humor in the movement drama.

pint with me to Kemper County when I left." He paused, and drank some coffee.

"Sue, you just don't know how pitiful it is to see grown men scared to walk into their ASC office." He was excited and enthusiastic about having gone to talk to the group about the Agriculture Stabilization and Conservation Service. It was as if he had suddenly discovered a new role for himself, a need he could fill.

"People in Holmes County should go out and all around into all these other counties. The peoples there are pitiful and they need to be told. I told them there in Kemper, I told them, 'I understand what you're going through exactly. I know what you feel like because I was just like that once, and I know you don't believe what I say. But I'm begging you. When I first learned about ASC, I had it told to me by a white, that Mary Brumder. And that white girl just kept telling me and telling me. But now I'm not here telling you like that. I'm begging you. Believe me. You can go into the ASC office. That man's not going to do nothing to you.'

"Oh, I talked to them people." Eugene's eyes were lighted and bright, and he struggled to contain a smile. Several times he burst into laughter, as when he was telling how pitiful they were. He also talked about how they'd taken him to Kemper by way of Neshoba County, where the 1964 murder of the three civil rights workers took place. He was bubbling with excitement and relief after overcoming his wariness about going to Neshoba County. He had constantly kidded and mocked his own fear before he had left, but he made sure to carry his pistol in his pocket that day.

Eugene was quite full of his Kemper experience and having been a big shot. "Them people fed me a big dinner, fixed it for me at one o'clock. And they gave me a pint of whiskey and six dollars too. . . . They want me to come back another time for a meeting before they go in to hold their county convention. I'm supposed to go back there. I gave them your phone number for them to get in touch with me, and you must remind me."

It had grown darker until it was full night and very black. We sat on the porch rocking, a cooling breeze blowing from off the creek that didn't smell as it sometimes did. We were interrupted only by passing back and forth the can of Prince Albert, the cigarette paper, and the matches. The stillness of the night, with its deep yellow moon low in the sky to the east, was broken only by the lowing of cattle.

"It's Wednesday today, huh?" Eugene asked. I realized that I heard the cows too, so it must be Wednesday, sale day at the auction barn across the field from my house.

Gene told a bit about how as a young boy he used to have to get up at three o'clock in the morning and carry the milk to the dairy. "We didn't have no freezers back then, so we would milk the cows and lower the cans down into the spring and the water would keep it cool. Then I'd get up while it was still dark. And in the dark I'd hitch up the wagon and go around to all the places that I knew we had the cans and lift them up out of the water and load them up into the wagon and carry them on into town. I had to hurry and get up that early so that I could make it into town when the sun would just barely be rising. You had to do that or otherwise the sun would be up and shine on that milk and spoil it.

"One day I was out plowing in the fields. I wasn't a real big fellow then, maybe twelve or fourteen. The cotton must have been up, oh, about knee high, and I was plowing behind two mules. We didn't have tractors then. This old white man, Cap'n Ferdinand Pitchford, he come up to where I was plowing and said we had some mighty fine cotton there. He wanted to know if the cotton was that high or if I had just plowed it so deep that it looked that high. I told him, 'No, no, I ain't plowed this deep at all. These mules ain't no damn good and I can't plow too deep the way these sons-of-bitches plow.' I told him that, just like that.

"Well, he turned to call over to where my daddy, Ben, was in the field. He called, 'Hey, Ben. This boy here says these mules ain't no good. Come on, let's go to town and buy you a mule. And you better carry someone with you to see to the mule getting back.' So that's where I come in. He said, 'Carry Gene here,' and I stopped plowing and jumped on in the truck with them.

"So we rode on in to Lexington in the truck down to the place to buy the mule. It was down round where Weathersby has his showcase now. You know where his cars are. That was a livery stable then. And they bought the mule. He had asked Ben if he wanted to get one or two new mules. Ben had decided to just get one and thought he could mate her with the other one he already had. The mule was a fine mule and cost $125.

"I got up on it and rode it on back to the field. That was a real fine mule, too. A beautiful mule. Oh, I thought it was just fine, just what I wanted. I hitched that new mule up with the other mule and went back to plowing. Oh, she was beautiful, plowed real good. Well, I was in that field just plowing away, thinking that that was just all I wanted. That night Ben asked me how I liked the mule, and I said she was real good. I liked her fine. 'Did you feed her?'

"'Yessir, I fed her and watered her and curried her. I did everything for that mule. She's a good mule.'

"'Well, do you think you want to go out and plow her in the morning?' 'Yes, sir,' I said, 'the first thing!' Well, just say I didn't sleep that night I liked it so fine.

"Ben told me that he'd give me twenty-five cents to plow one of the fields on Saturday. It was a half-day's work and twenty-five cents was doing just fine. On a Saturday too, after I had already worked all the week.

"So that Saturday I went to plowing with that same mule. It was a hot day and I stopped plowing and hitched the mule up to go over to the house. When I got back to where I had hitched it, I found the mule lying dead on the ground. She was killed and I had killed that mule. No, I didn't overwork her. That's not why she died. See when I tied her up, the rope just drawed up tighter and tighter and she fell dead. When I got back, she was laying right there dead. See, I knew better than that. I knew how to hitch a mule. There's some rope you can tie that just won't draw up. I could tie a rope around your neck and swing you around in the air and it won't draw up at all. Then there's another I can tie around your neck and swing you round, and it would squeeze you tighter and tighter. Ben taught me how to tie a rope, how to hitch a mule, and I knowed better than what I did. Oh, that was bad. I felt so bad. I killed that mule.

"What was so bad was I had to face telling my daddy. So when Ben got back, I told him she fell dead when the plow hit a stump. See, when you're plowing along steady in a field and your mule is going along chunk chunk chunk, just steady going. Well, if that plow hit a stump, she'll jerk up. It'll stop her; jerk her back. And that's all he knew 'til this day. I'll have to tell him some time before he die. I haven't yet been forgiven for that lie. You are the only one to this day that know how that mule got killed."

We sat for a while and then Gene said, "Sue, you should have been here about ten years ago, when I bought my first car. I bought a 1948

Ford. It was a demonstrator. I was working at the grocer's up in Greenwood. Bernice and I was already married, had some children too. But the boy I was transferring up to Greenwood with, his car broke. I decided I was going to buy me a car. And I was going to pay cash money for it."

Gene said he went down to Canton to the dealer there. "I went there and I was looking at a Ford he had there. I said, 'How much you get for this?' The man said, 'Eight hundred dollars.'

"Then I asked, 'What about if I pay cash?' So then he said, 'Seven hundred.'

"I said, 'No, that's too much.' So he said, 'Well, I'll have to go see the boss.' And he went and got the boss. That same old bastard is still there today. You go there today and you'll see him standing there, walking on two sticks now.

"I told the boss, 'I'll give you six hundred dollars cash money for it.' The boss said, 'You can have it for $625.'

"I said, 'No, six hundred dollars is all I have.' So then he ask, 'Well, that's okay. When can you pay the other twenty-five dollars?'

"I told him, 'No, I can't ever pay it.' He said, 'Why don't you go over an' crank her up and take a good look at her?'

"I said, 'I don't want to crank her up. I already has cranked her and I won't pay no more than six hundred dollars cash money.' So the boss said I could have it for six hundred dollars and I wrote a check on the First National in Lexington for six hundred dollars. I only had three hundred dollars in the bank, but it was evening time, and I knew the bank was already closed and he couldn't call them.

"After I wrote the check, then I drove to Lexington to see if I could work something up. I stopped at Nathaniel Hooker's—he was the one at the bank. He owned the bank and he was my granddaddy's boss-man. He and Ferdinand Pitchford was big drinking men together. I went in and told him, I said, 'I just wrote a check today that will be coming into your bank tomorrow. It's a check for six hundred dollars. I only have three hundred dollars in there. What can we work out?'

"He say, 'Well, you go get Ben and bring him in with you in the morning and I'll talk to him.' Now I was a man then. I had a horse and a cow. And it looked like he could have dealt straight with me, but I decided I'd go to Ben with it.

"So I went and told Ben. The next morning I just got up and went on up to Greenwood to work. Ben, he went and made a loan for six months for that money, and I paid it back to him and my mama Causey, deposited every week from my pay. Causey put it in the bank."

Gene and Bernice married in the 1940s, when she was nineteen and he was twenty-five. Once, in a dispirited mood, Gene reflected, "I still don't know why Bernice ever married me. Never could figure out why she'd have such a dummy. She went through college, and I only finished the ninth grade. One thing though, I did put her through school."

They met through church work. "I was a real serious church worker then," Gene explained. "It's true. I was so serious, I even felt I was gonna be a preacher. The Sunnymount people all said they'd call for me when I started preaching. But they were Baptist, and I was a Methodist. Still I thought I was gonna be a preacher. You couldn't be no preacher, not when you're married to a pretty young wife and all. I broke away from all that—broke away from the church.

"I had a quartet and was the leader, the manager, and the lead singer," he said. "We was good. We traveled all around and did singing. Bernice was a songster in her church down at Galilee. I was a fine singer then. But the singing then was not nothing like now. If nowadays they heard us, they'd say we weren't any good. But back twenty-five years ago, that was fine singing.

"I dressed real good for the singing. I had me a twenty-one-dollar suit of clothes. In those days you could get a whole suit of clothes—suit, shirt, socks, hat, everything you needed—for twenty-one dollars. All except for shoes. I had my shoes made for me. I used to go to Herman Flowers' daddy's store, right there in the same place it is now up on the square. I'd get me a fine, sharp suit of clothes. That's it! That's why Bernice married me—me and my fine clothes! I wasn't ugly then. I looked good."

Their Stories: A Group Gathers for a Countywide Meeting

The Countywide Meeting was established in late 1963 or early 1964 when local communities began setting up their own regular weekly meetings and Hartman Turnbow and other leaders were riding around the county working to open up communities. The leaders talked among folks

Reverend Willie B. Davis with his granddaughter. A preacher from the hill section of the county, Davis took on the position of Holmes County FDP finance manager in the 1967 election campaign.

they knew, visited churches, and made speeches to encourage people to organize their home people.

When more than two or three communities started meetings, the leaders encouraged scheduling a regular monthly Third Sunday County-wide Meeting to share their progress in what they were learning and doing. When the thirty-five outside Freedom Summer volunteers arrived in 1964, the Third Sunday Meetings had already become a fundamental anchor for movement development. The description below captures the preparatory bustle of a Countywide Meeting; it ends just as the meeting is to begin. It's a glimpse of one of Holmes County's most important movement establishments.

A good number of cars were on the highway on that Sunday afternoon at three o'clock. They weren't rushing past as city or freeway cars might; instead they seemed to be traveling in a social way, as they do from church, or from funerals, or from visiting. People were out and about in Lexington. We passed them in the courthouse square as we drove halfway around in the inner lane. During the previous year or so, the square had been adorned, city fashion, with concrete dividers, making two lanes of one-way traffic.

Within a block of the square we entered the most obvious, all-white section, with blacktopped roads; concrete sidewalks; wide quarter- and half-acre lots; thick, blue-green lawns; and two- and sometimes three-story, white, painted, comfortable homes. Large oak and cedar trees formed a shady maze that the yellow sunlight poked through in spots and patches. No people were out, no porch swingers, no lawn mowers, no car washers, no bike riders, nobody.

We entered a black section. There were paved roads for the first time in the 132 years of this town, thanks to the pressure of blacks who had registered to vote. The pavement narrowed to less than two lanes, so you knew where you were. A one-lane, paved bridge crossed the creek, and the long lawns shrank to patches of green and yellow. The houses became the unpainted shotgun type, railroad huts, which have a room behind a room, behind a room.

We entered Schoolhouse Bottom, and soon the large brick schoolhouse appeared on the left. It was nice looking, of brick-and-mortar construction, built sometime after 1954 when the whites hoped a brick school would help make "separate but equal" more valid. Inside there were no science laboratories, or libraries, or new books to match its exterior promise. In the gravel area of St. John's Church, across from the school, about thirty cars were parked. It was the meeting place for that month's Third Sunday FDP Countywide Meeting.

St. John's Church was only slightly larger than an enlarged shotgun house, long and narrow with windows along the sides and a double front door as an entrance. St. John's was more prosperous than the general run of churches. Outside, it had a white-washed, concrete set of steps. There was a stack of red bricks nearby, signaling that preparations were being made for some improvement.

There were fewer trees in the bottom than in the white section, and the sun shone down fully on the area. Older men and ladies sat in their trucks waiting. Young children played in truck beds, between cars on the gravel, and on the merry-go-round in the playground. Middle-aged and some younger men stood straight or leaned on the sides of trucks and cars, rolling cigarettes, exchanging news of the day. The women were also in their groups, a little more subdued than the men, and a few were smoking. All were talking and laughing. Clusters of folks stood in front of the church, on the walk up to the church, and on the steps. Folks steadily joined in, driving or walking from both directions. All were dressed up, shiny, starchy, and clean in their Sunday clothes. The men wore suits and ties and wide-striped shirts. Their hats were felt or straw skimmers. Some wore newly pressed dark pants and white shirts; others wore khakis. The women wore pinks and lemons, bright greens and oranges, turquoise, lavender, white, and brown. Many wore hats with small bands of flowers or velvet. Some wore tall wide-brimmed frothy giants. All were definitely Sunday-go-to-meeting clothes.

Tom Griffin urged folks to start filing in. He was a tall, dark, dull-black man, one of the rare young men around at the time. Too many young men in the South went to Chicago and Detroit. Tom was no older than thirty-five. He was tall but not broad, solid, yet slightly gangling. He was a bachelor who ran his brother's rural store. He got energetically involved in meetings, taking part, often asking questions, and encouraging the leaders in the group. He held several elected positions and served on most committees.

Tom walked into the church and directly up the one center aisle to the table at the front. Benches seating six to ten people ran against the walls on each side. The walls were white, painted, unadorned boards. One large printed calendar, with no picture, only a few advertising words from a chemical company, hung on the wall. There were chairs at the front, and a raised wooden platform extended out maybe eight feet. On the platform were several tables with vases of orange plastic flowers.

People started filing in, filling first the back rows, several considering themselves leader enough or elder enough to sit in the side-facing benches in the front. That area was reserved for deacons in a normal church meeting. The group of sixty or so came in slowly, even tentatively, heavy on the weak and uneven flooring.

Tom called for a song, and after some hesitation one woman's voice began to drone out a tune. After the first line or so, more of the women joined in. Most men and a good number of the women hummed, mumbled, moaned, and droned to the slow rhythm of the dirge as the hymn went on. Tom raised his arms for us to rise and the body stood. Reverend Pittman began his invocation.

Reverend Pittman was almost dark brown. Bright highlights of gold gleamed on his skin. His hair was gray; he seemed near seventy years old. He moved slowly and unsteadily with a long, gnarled stick of a cane. He looked somewhat dapper in his old-fashioned suit. His voice seemed weak and soft in conversation, but in speaking of the Lord, he was more sure. He started loud and fervent and built to a humming, rhythmic, pulsing chant. Finally, in a rapid, rushing whisper he spoke the formula, "these and in all things we asked in Jesus' name, Amen," and sat down.

Roll was called. "Pickens." No one stood at first, but one slowly raised himself. "Ebenezer." Burrell Tate and several other Ebenezer people stood. "West Grove." Two stood. There was scattered handclapping. "Lexington." Absurdly, no one rose, even though one-third or even half of the group were from Lexington. A repeat of "Lexington" and then a wait, and still no one stood. Other communities were called. "Union Paradise, Long Branch, West, Mileston, Sunnymount, Bowling Green." From each, one or two, or six or seven, stood. "Tchula, Cruger, Goodman, Mount Olive." No one stood. "Old Pilgrims Rest." At least fifteen rose quickly. A ripple of excitement and pleasure flowed over the body.

There were smiles of pleasure and applause. "Durant, Second Pilgrims Rest." Another ten or fifteen people rose. All enjoyed the game. There was murmuring and chatter, some clapping and noisy arrangements of bodies in the seats. More names were called. "Sweet Hope, Gauges Springs, Franklin." One or two rose from each. And then there was silence.

The pace of the meeting was unhurried and leisurely. Except for two or three leaders, no one seemed especially harried, or concerned, or even knowledgeable of the possibilities the business might bring. Most people seemed to be spectators, waiting to see the show.

Mrs. Daisey Lewis, bold, determined, conscientious, organized, knowledgeable, and an immensely active leader, spoke in her clear sharp voice, "Someone should say a word or two on the ASC elections, give us some final words." Someone suggested they needed to talk about poll officials. Someone else suggested selective buying, and someone wanted to talk about boycott planning meetings in Lexington. Mrs. Lewis said she'd like to make an announcement on the community centers.

And so, with the meeting agenda set, the meeting began.

11

The November 1966 Elections and Coalition Building

Fall 1966–January 1967

After the Meredith March excitement calmed down, we got back to work. Sometimes national politics caught our attention, such as the formation of the Black Panther Party in California that October, but for the most part, we were immersed in Holmes County politics. That summer, new outside volunteers came in to do grunt work and planning—whatever the movement leaders needed.

One of the sharpest was Bob Colman, a white Australian who was a quick learner and very energetic. He was well suited to work with local people, Henry, and me. He worked well on his own as well as with a team. Local women began copying the names of the registered voters from the lists in the circuit clerk's books in the courthouse and the federal examiner's records in the post office. The local staff got assistance from the outside workers in typing up and filing the names of voters for the coming election campaigns. Top leaders like Walter Bruce, Ralthus Hayes, and Howard Taft Bailey worked with Henry and Colman to set up a block captain–precinct leader system that covered all the precincts in the five beats of the county.

Grassroots movement people became leaders just by signing on. They volunteered to be block captains or precinct leaders. We were thankful we were working in Mississippi and not Alabama, where general elections were being held in 1966. SNCC was feverishly pushing black turnout in Lowndes and other Alabama counties, while we had another whole year to lay groundwork for our real election test.

195

Setting up the block captains took months of organizing. It affected more than 150 local FDP members. During that same summer, Henry and I, along with Colman, held leadership training workshops for the members of the executive committee to coordinate them with the grass-roots workers at the block-captain level. We wrote and mimeographed an Executive Member's Manual describing the concept of a "political machine." We used the manual as a focus for our discussions and gave a copy of it to everyone who came to the workshops.

Whether or not to run black candidates was not dealt with as publicly as our organizing was. Although outside workers often assumed having a black sheriff candidate and running blacks for as many offices as possible was necessary, many local leaders—even some at the top—had reservations. The outside volunteers often used the term *black sheriff*, but it wasn't brought up for public discussion at meetings. A yes-no question on the Block Captain's Canvass Sheet about a black sheriff candidate in 1967 was aimed at getting the block captains and the people comfortable using the term.

Privately, in conversations with Henry, Hayes and other leaders expressed reservations and fears about a black takeover. At that time, Hayes was respected and regarded as the foremost county FDP leader. He was strong, with a calm courage and greater political sophistication than most in the county, and he had serious misgivings about putting in a black sheriff in 1967. Of course, the actual candidate's qualifications would determine his chances. It was essential that a black sheriff, when elected, needed to do a better job than any white had ever done before. Hayes felt the position of blacks in the county could be hurt much more by a bad black sheriff than by a bad white one. He preferred to have a bad white elected in 1967 rather than a bad black, for that would serve to ready the people for even more resistance. Hayes wanted to give whites enough rope to hang themselves rather than to latch onto a rope that might hang blacks. Many outside workers thought this a conservative position, but the instincts and judgment of a local leader—particularly a key leader or anyone who spoke from a lifetime of Holmes experiences—were difficult to dispute.

Walter Bruce, the dynamic leader in Beat 2, which included Second Pilgrims Rest and Durant, was building a strong, effective grassroots or-

Walter Bruce, a strong leader, spent several dangerous years "opening up" the predominantly white hill towns of Durant, West, and Goodman. As the 1967 Freedom Democratic Party county campaign coordinator, he led training workshops in a different community each night of the week.

ganization. Bruce was a carpenter and a quartet singer who regularly performed on the radio. He had energy. The good black turnout to meetings and the well-organized Election Day system he was creating for the November 1966 general election in his Durant precinct made Bruce sought after as a leader of leaders. He spread his organizing ideas from Durant to West, Long Branch, and Goodman as he planned approaches into other Beat 2 communities. The FDP county executive committee hoped that Bruce would become the county coordinator and spread his viable system to all the county's beats. Finally, Henry was able to secure very minimal funds through the Friends of the Children of Mississippi and the Delta Ministry to cover some of the heavy gas expenses. Bruce accepted the county coordinator position and used the gas money to lead a beat leadership workshop every weeknight, each in a different one of the five beats. For several months in late 1966, Bruce kept up this amazing schedule.

Bruce's grasp of the block captain–precinct leader system was thorough. He refined all sorts of methods for Election Day procedures, such as team poll-watching and using a precinct headquarters like one he set up in a café as a place for volunteers to check in. Also, he instituted ideas about running strict meetings, calling roll, raising money, fining people for not attending, and raking offenders over the coals for their fears, false excuses, and inactivity. And somehow he got away with it all and preached his methods to the leaders of other meetings throughout the county. Some, like E. G. Groves, the "founder" of the Second Pilgrims Rest movement meeting and "discoverer" of Bruce, balked; he bitterly criticized Bruce for trying to make the movement into the church. Groves had chosen Bruce as his "vice" before turning the Second Pilgrims Rest meeting over to him. But it was difficult to deny Bruce's success when his Durant meeting had more people attending, more money raised, and more projects involving more folks than anywhere else in Holmes.

While we were deep into election organizing, the MFDP was also fighting in federal court to get three black candidates onto the November 8 ballot as Independents. Clifton Whitley, who had won the primary race, was running for the U.S. Senate, while Dock Drummond and Mrs. Emma Sanders were running for seats in the U.S. House of Representatives. After the primary elections, the Mississippi legislature had passed a law requiring additional petition signatures for Independent candidates. The MFDP lawyers argued against the increase and prevailed; on October 26, a federal court panel temporarily suspended the new state law and the secretary of state was ordered to add the three candidates' names to the ballot. It was a victory.

The November 1966 general election arrived and gave us the opportunity to practice for the 1967 elections. We initiated a trial run of the block captain, precinct captain, poll-watchers system. Holmes had a good turnout at the November 8 balloting. In many precincts our poll watchers were allowed in. They paid close attention to the counting process, carefully recording every vote as it was read aloud. In other precincts FDP poll watchers were forced out or intimidated. All three black candidates lost, although in Holmes, Whitley lost by the narrowest margin.

Throughout 1964, 1965, and much of 1966, the professionals had shied away from the movement. Most were schoolteachers with the most formal education of any blacks in a county where no black doctors, dentists, lawyers, or engineers lived. A few pastors had some advanced formal education, but, although less directly shackled by the white power structure than the teachers, they too had stayed back. So had most of the few prosperous businessmen.

The professionals may have been too impatient to sit through the nonparliamentary proceedings of the grassroots people. But the organization had proved itself. When it looked as if the movement could succeed at electing some black candidates, the professionals joined in. None except Bernice Patton Montgomery had previously attended meetings or become active movement participants. And although the FDP had managed without the professionals for several years, a large black election campaign needed the acceptance of this element of the community. The professionals were respected by the grassroots people and had a great deal of influence over them. In addition, the local nonprofessionals were getting tired, having labored alone for nearly four years.

While Bruce was serving as county coordinator, he spearheaded a systematic plan to get professionals into the movement. During 1966, a few schoolteachers had attended his Second Pilgrims Rest meeting. Whenever professionals showed up, they were treated with ridicule overlaid with a great deal of respect. Although many of the nonprofessionals spoke bitterly of the teachers, Bruce thought it was important for the movement to have professionals participating with us.

Henry also believed the professionals were necessary to the FDP's success in 1967 and future prospects, so he gave top priority to getting them into the movement. He and Bruce urged movement leaders to consciously undertake special approaches to the professionals. In November 1966, at the same meeting where Bruce was designated county coordinator to grapple with the problems of both beat organization and FDP finance and fund-raising, a committee of county leaders was set up to formally work on the issue of "coalition," as it was then being called. Bruce was an active member of the coalition committee, which included Reverend L. E. Robinson, Daisey Montgomery Lewis, and Ralthus Hayes. No one opposed Bruce's idea. The leadership wanted the professionals in the FDP.

Next on our plate was the ASCS election in December. In that instance the system worked; we were successful in running and electing several ASCS candidates.

It was during this time that we were joined by FDP organizer Alexander "Alec" Shimkin. He left the University of Michigan to join the civil rights movement, and before coming to Holmes, he worked in Marks in Quitman County and for the Freedom Information Service in Jackson. He was arrested at a demonstration in Natchez in October 1965 and detained for three days at Parchman State Prison Farm. Demitri Shimkin, Alec's father, was an anthropology professor at the University of Illinois. When he visited Alec, he also became interested in the movement in Holmes. Alec became an immediate asset to the FDP office.

Then in January 1967, in addition to the regular community and county FDP meetings, the leadership set up an every-other-Friday-night Leadership (or Coalition) Meeting specifically aimed at bringing in the professionals. Schoolteachers, key preachers, and some of the more successful businessmen, including owners of cafés, funeral homes, and the like, began to attend. The coalition meetings were considered safe and respectable. NAACP people like Joe Smith from Tchula and Turnbow, who had earlier moved his main focus from FDP to the NAACP, worked with the coalition in a new coordinated fashion.

The NAACP was the established Mississippi civil rights organization,

In order to win the 1967 elections, the movement needed the black professionals to join the grassroots effort. Reverend L. E. Robinson was one of the members of the coalition committee who successfully brought the two groups together.

with history behind it from the 1940s and 1950s. From the founding of a Holmes chapter of the NAACP in Tchula in December 1965, personality clashes within the chapter had often flared up. Many FDP members in Holmes County had started in the NAACP and stayed on the rolls. There was not much NAACP activity at the county level in Holmes, but information and speeches from the national and state levels filtered through and were a source of motivation. Hayes, Ozell Mitchell, and Alma Mitchell Carnegie had been NAACP members for years. Hayes had gone to Jackson to see Thurgood Marshall speak at an NAACP event in the 1950s.

In the early 1960s, the FDP brought a vibrancy that the older organization was lacking. The FDP became the largest and strongest grassroots civil rights organization in the county. It was also encouraging the drive for greater cooperation and combining forces among blacks.

While officially both the NAACP and the FDP wanted the groups to cooperate, not all members followed the leadership. There were splits between people within the NAACP and between members of the two organizations. Some felt that the FDP was taking a "militant" stance. The NAACP was more "moderate," more likely to back white liberal candidates and candidates who ran as Democrats. At the same time, the personality and style of state NAACP leader Charles Evers was suspect by the FDP leaders and organizers. Charles Evers, brother of the murdered Medgar Evers, along with other state-level NAACP leaders, was inclined to keep working with the main Democratic Party instead of supporting candidates through the separate Freedom Democratic Party. Tchula's NAACP chair, Joe Smith, was regarded by many in the FDP as less than astute, so they feared he would act as an unknowing tool of whatever "evil" the state or national NAACP was hatching. Hayes and others considered these splits troublesome on both the county and the state levels.

In reality, the county FDP didn't have strict executive leadership or control. Instead, the FDP's strength was that hundreds of people identified as members and many more agreed with its message.

The Friday night coalition-leadership meetings were attended not only by the professionals and NAACP people, but also by the grassroots community leaders, mainly FDP people. The FDP people were the majority in attendance. Hayes usually led the meeting, with Bailey sometimes taking over. Still, deference was paid to the preachers and professionals in the audience. They were sought out to speak up and to take leadership roles.

There were very few cities in Mississippi where professionals led the movement. For the most part, they stayed out until they realized how strong the movement had become. In some communities the professionals stayed out until the very end and then came in busloads. When that happened, resentment often followed. Holmes movement members, in contrast to those in some parts of the state, did not, for the most part, see professionals as a threat. In fact, they lobbied for them. Those who might have felt supplanted instead expressed gratitude that qualified candidates were finally stepping forward.

The Holmes Movement had a clear objective and didn't dwell on who got in first. The goal was to get all blacks involved and working together: farmers, renters, landowners, town people, hill people, and professionals. The Holmes movement had broad support for its goal of bringing everyone in regardless of status. The addition of the professionals made the movement so strong that it was able to flex its muscles.

Some issues were not publicly debated but were discussed at length in private. Should we present an all-black slate? Should an uneducated person run? Was the FDP trying to run things? Was the NAACP against a campaign of black candidates? Were the teachers scared and lacking the courage to help in the fight? Theoretical and personality issues were seldom mentioned aloud in public meetings. The business of the meeting was always the immediately pressing practical matter—finding candidates. On the private level, however, there were plenty of rumors and bad feelings. The problem of who was qualified to be a candidate was solved when candidates actually stepped forward. Various leaders approached, on their own, individuals who they thought should run.

But in public gatherings of the county groups, possible candidates were never discussed and then sought out. People rarely spoke up against particular candidates at open meetings. We knew the real test of support would come at the polls. Having too many candidates was never the problem. Beat meetings selected the candidates for beat positions, then the beat-level names were brought to the Countywide Meeting for approval by the county movement.

Contested positions between more than one individual did not arise, because once one had declared, others did not want to cause public splits by making people decide between them. Howard Taft Bailey wanted to run for Beat 1 supervisor, but T. C. Johnson declared before Bailey put his own name forward, so Bailey stayed back. In Beat 4, the names of both Shadrach Davis and Norman Clark were spoken for the supervisor candidacy, but neither officially declared his intentions. It was generally accepted that only one black candidate should run for an office, and it was a struggle to find enough candidates for one per office.

The biggest problem was selecting candidates for county offices, particularly the symbolically loaded office of high sheriff. Although Henry and other leaders were making their own lists of prospects for the various offices, coming up with county candidates, especially for sheriff, was difficult. Privately, Henry was considering Ralthus Hayes, John Henry Malone, and possibly Howard Taft Bailey from among the old movement people. The professionals were still not involved enough to be considered. Willie James Burns never spoke up about becoming a candidate for sheriff, although during the previous three years he had dropped hints that he wanted to be drafted. But no one was being drafted.

John Malone seemed the best choice among the old FDP people. He was young, but not so young that he did not have the respect of the older folks; and he was well enough educated to be acceptable to the professionals. Actually, the educational qualifications turned out to be important to grassroots folks with little formal education, even those who were the most verbal in their bitterness against the educated. Thus Malone's literacy and ability were prime factors making him the most seriously considered and sought-after "old FDP" possibility. However, he was not sure he wanted to run. He openly expressed his fear of getting killed by the whites if he were to seek or win the sheriff post.

Hayes lacked a formal education, and although he was widely accepted as a top leader, he had many enemies. In addition, the Milton Olive Head Start Program was being funded during this time, and Hayes sought the directorship. His lack of finesse opened doors of rumor and talk against him. His qualifications were being disputed, in a move perhaps spearheaded by Bailey. Nor was Bailey himself in the best of positions: several people severely distrusted him, and his hand in downgrading Hayes helped him little. There was an issue about missing loan money at the community center at Mileston; Hayes, Lee and Daisey Lewis, and other members of the center's board of trustees were questioned. Thus, up through December 1966, finding a black sheriff candidate from among the old FDP leaders led to a dead end. Some leaders kept urging Henry to run for sheriff. Although that seemed like a sure victory in some ways, Henry refused, just as he had refused the directorship of the Milton Olive project and any formal leadership role in the campaign.

The dynamics of the movement continued to change. Turnbow was still a force to be reckoned with. He was regarded as a hero. At the same time he was stepping out of prominent leadership of the FDP, and that left a void.

Since early 1966, Henry and I had repeatedly reminded and explained to the local people that we were transitioning out of the FDP. We consciously worked toward changing our role so the county movement could function effectively on its own. We defined success in terms of the whole organizational process and not just in electoral results. If the local movement depended too much upon the work of outsiders to win posts for blacks, then once having won, the officeholders and the movement would still be weak. But if the local leaders and the local organized movement were doing the campaign jobs themselves, then whether or not they were successful at the polls, they would have gained new independence just through the process of having done it themselves. We carefully chose a role of minimal involvement. We remained in the county in order to develop nonpolitical projects and tried to stay out of the political realm. At most, we supported leaders who needed to discuss decisions and strategies.

Their Stories: Five People Comment about Henry Lorenzi

Henry Lorenzi was a mathematician, the most human mathematician that ever existed in the world. He never, ever treated anyone differently, regardless of how they communicated. He was never condescending. Instead of saying "I don't understand," he asked, "Can we talk more about this?"

His goal was to bring as many people into the movement as possible

Henry Lorenzi worked and relaxed in the rough Balance Due shack. We moved to Lexington to staff the county Freedom Democratic Party office, living first in Balance Due and later in Pecan Grove. Behind Henry are SNCC posters: the man and child is by Earl Newman, and the photograph on the top right is by Danny Lyon.

by dealing with their frame of reference. Henry encouraged people to participate from their point of view, from where they stood, from their position, and by paying attention to their own tempo. He listened to people to determine what projects they were most interested in, their abilities, and their capacity to communicate. He recognized the relationship between information and power, and utilized it. He knew who would be the best person to present an issue and who would be the best to conduct a meeting.

There was beauty and skill to the way he was able to get into ticklish spots and not become part of the process. He was a master at communication by silence. He knew what you don't say is just as important as what you do say.

Henry had one objective, building power, not for himself, but for others. It was so much a part of his personality that people could get past his not being black; they could get past all of his credentials to see him as a good man.

—Lawrence Guyot

The day I met Henry and Sue was the day my life changed. I remember Henry asked me to run the community center. I said, "Henry, you got all these people running around here with education, why do you want me to do it." He said to me, "Education don't have nothing to do with it, you have common sense."

After I accepted the position, every morning when I would walk into the center, he would wink his eye and say, "Didn't I tell you, you could do it." He was always trying to encourage me to do more. He tried to help me learn to type. He said, "All you have to do is hunt and peck."

But Henry got it in his mind for you to do something, he would worry you until you tried it at least. He was a lovable person. You always knew exactly where he stood with you because he was always going to be straightforward with you.

The only thing I could never understand is how he could drink black coffee all day. Every day in Mileston, he continued to walk through the building with a cup of black coffee and try and get us to taste it. Good? It tasted like dirt.

—Rosie Head

I was in school at the Tchula Attendance Center and I was working on a math problem and I asked Henry for some help. He said, "Let me look at it" and then said, "I want you to think beyond the box. OK? Just keep working on it. I'm not going to tell you what to do but I am going to help you work through it." I got an "A" on the next test. Whenever I had time with him, he said, "You can do it." And I'd always work through it. As African Americans, we didn't get math in schools like some of the white schools. We'd have to figure it out ourselves. We just would go by the little example they showed us, and that's how we would get the math. So he was one of the persons that taught me to think outside the box, to think beyond and you can do it. I thank him for all the encouragement he gave. He and Sue were both lovely persons that you could always talk to, but Henry was just a listener and he did what needed to be done.

—Gloria Jean Louie, daughter of
First Fourteen leader Jack Louie

You know Henry, whatever he got into, especially academics, he was really smart. There was one thing about Henry and Susan, they could have accomplished much, material wise, but the reason we are all here and the reason we think so highly of them is that, we feel, that we mean more to them than all of the stuff they could have accumulated.

They went to places on vacation that you would be surprised. They went back to New York. We couldn't think of Henry in New York. We were so used to seeing him around the community center. We say, "You going to New York?"

They carried us places. People had gone to Dorchester; some people had been to Atlanta and stuff. I went to pick up a car in Cleveland with Don Madison from Columbus, Ohio. That's when I first left Mississippi. All of these people and Henry and Sue, and all of the workers really exposed us, not just to marching. They lived in our homes and they exposed us to a lifestyle that black people in Mississippi, where I'm from, had never been used to in no kind of way.

We weren't used to being around white people. We thought differently but Henry and Sue gave us a whole new demeanor.

They lived with us. Someone living with you who turns out to be your best friend. When our minds were so focused on picking cotton and chopping cotton and one white man is in charge of so many people, Henry and Sue came in and exposed us to themselves and say, we are just like you. They carried me to Philadelphia, to New Jersey to the Boardwalk, that's something else. They were regular people.

—Sam Epps, son of Nancy Epps,
a local movement leader

I was somewhat impatient with the slow progress of the voter registration and school desegregation efforts until Henry Lorenzi cautioned me that, as someone who would soon leave Mississippi, it was not for me to make decisions for people who would remain to live with the consequences of their decisions and the realities there. It was a humbling lesson and one I never forgot.

—Mike Reiss, white Yale Law School student
and 1966 Summer LDF worker

12

Reading "The Some People" Story and a Trip North

February–April 1967

On a pitch dark and cold, muddy night, February 10, 1967, an elections meeting was held in a large, paint-peeling, wooden church building. I had been asked to write a short piece, something that would take ten or fifteen minutes to read to the group. Its purpose was to set a mood—to call up a feeling in the people gathered—that would help them continue in their work and become more united in their strength. Some of the leaders thought such a piece could help, for this was a meeting that brought together the new coalition committee and the longtime movement members.

The leaders felt that the old movement people were tired of the struggle. They needed something to boost them up, remind them of their accomplishments, and help them feel the way to continue. The new people needed something to give them respect for those who seemed slower, to introduce them to some of the things the movement people had done. And the whole group needed something to remind them that they all needed each other; they had to work together.

The piece I wrote, "The Some People of That Place," grew much longer than I intended. Several leaders who read drafts said, "Just start and read until people get tired." So, on the night of the meeting, I carried my papers into the stark, bare-bulbed, nearly empty church and sat warming myself by the orange flame of the open gas heater while people slowly congregated.

Despite the bitter cold and the forecast for rain, nearly one hundred

Singing was essential to building the movement and inspired people in the struggle. Every meeting, including this Countywide Meeting at the community center
at Mileston, began and ended with song.

people turned out for the meeting. They filled the space on the wooden,
front-facing benches, the side pews usually reserved for church deacons,
and the various straight-backed and folding chairs up on the platform
facing outward toward the congregation. More stood along the bare side
and back walls, and a few sat crowded around the rickety table in the back
corner.

The opening song was followed by a long prayerful invocation that
was followed by another song. Finally, after some announcements and
several incidental remarks, I was presented to the body and began to read.
It grew very quiet in the church, and although the people seemed attentive, there were few of the usual "Amens" and "That's Rights."

I was worried, because my rough narrative was a story about them. I
realized how bold it was to write down recent history and, even more so,
to read it to the main history makers, whom I referred to as "The Some
People." Although I had used no names or specific places and had not

even referred specifically to the black civil rights movement, it was obvious to all what I was describing. I knew that many of them knew better than I what had happened and that each had his or her own version. My darting glances up from the page gave me a view of only a few rows of faces directly in front of me. The silence told me nothing.

Anxiously, I read on for more than an hour. When I finally stopped at the end of the second year of the four-year tale, I looked up slowly into their intense silence. I noticed one deeply wrinkled old man in midcenter with slumped shoulders and head nodding forward and a large woman way on the end of the front row leaning heavily to one side. But I had no time to study on them before a loud voice from the platform behind me broke the silence.

A man jumped to his feet. He was shouting in a clear, booming voice: "That there is no story!" he stated. It was Hartman Turnbow, and his opinion was important. I could envision the violence with which he was capable of tearing the story, or me, apart. He lifted his muscular arms up toward his chest and his broad, farm-hardened fingers wrestled with the air as they usually did when he was beginning to warm to his subject. "No, sir!" he shouted. "That there's no story. That's not a story at all. That's History!"

The rest of the congregation broke its silence with foot thumping, hand clapping, and loud talking. Some of Turnbow's words were lost in the noise of the others shouting that it was fine, just what they wanted for their grandchildren to read. Several questioned my not using any names, suggesting that every person's name and the names of all the places should be written in a history.

I told them I hadn't meant for the story to be the only history written of their movement. I knew much more needed to be written and that many facts had been left out. The full history of those times would come only when some of them would tell their own story. In the end, most agreed with a gray-haired, gentle-spoken man who, in the manner of passing a motion, nearly demanded that, no matter what else got written, what he had heard that night should be bound up in a book and put inside the county public library, and many copies should be made so that each of the people there could keep one on a shelf at home for himself and his children and grands to read.

I was moved by the reception to my words, and I vowed to remember the wishes of the group.

Not long after I read "The Some People" story aloud at the coalition meeting, Henry and I decided to head north for an extended period of time in order to let the leaders take charge of their own movement. We investigated possibilities for our lives outside the FDP, but we also went to raise funds for the coming election effort.

We were gone for well over a month, almost two—by far the longest period we'd been away in the three years since we'd arrived. After weeks in the North, I reached my saturation point and truly yearned to return, to see our house and yard, to see our friends, the local people, to feel the warmth of early spring, to be among those who were active and concerned and working on such monumental changes as electing black candidates to local offices.

In the North we described the movement—boasted and bragged, in fact, over the accomplishments and the spirit of "our people." Set against what seemed to be drab lives, even of those active and concerned northerners, the writers, foundation people, and government servants, the lives and activities of our people grew more real and meaningful.

We headed back to our home in Mississippi on the train. The night before entering the state was a sleepless one for me. I set myself up in the club car armed with wine and cigarettes. I distracted all thoughts by reading an abominable popular woman's magazine from cover to cover—the soap-opera stories, the advice to those with marital problems, the recipes, and the oversimplified explanation of American foreign policy designed to painlessly educate the busy, scatterbrained female—"The Girl's Guide to American Foreign Policy"—which the editors suggested might be read in two or three sittings for better absorption. Finally, as the first light of dawn spread and birds chirruped over the clacking of the tracks, I returned to my seat and resigned myself to finding sleep. We hadn't yet reached the border of our fair state.

At 10:00 a.m. the bright sun and heat forced my eyes and body to waken. I wondered where we were and peered out the window through slit eyes. The train slowed to a halt. A conductor yelled, "Grenada, Grenada, Mississippi, Grenada," and something hit me.

My eyes opened, my ears jerked, and forming between my throat and my heart was a tense, hot, and harassing lump. His voice drawled. As he passed in the aisle in front of me, I saw his thick and wrinkled skin—pink tanned above the blue collar of his uniform and below the band of his conductor's cap. His ears were pink white, and his face was red.

The hot lump spread out and down through my chest and stomach, which was already beginning to knot. My now-open eyes darted around the car, and I could not keep them from staring—first at his middle-aged, middle-height, middle-weight, middle-build form and his leathery, reddish-tan neck. To my left was an old, wrinkled, red-faced man, a peckerwood. In front of him was a young white woman with two towheads and near her a young, dark-haired, square-faced, pudgy-cheeked, pug-nosed, brawny white fellow with close-set eyes. He was kind of a Klan-looking type, like Billie Joe, one of our sheriff's deputies at "home."

I was hit by the whiteness, by that enormous detail of life back here at home. Somehow, in a mysterious, yet much-needed way, I had submerged the Mississippi reality so deeply that I had forgotten what it was like. I wondered how in less than two months, I had so easily forgotten the whites, forgotten the lump, forgotten the fear. With just the drawl and the glimpse of red necks, it came back with a blow. Dazed, numb, and with the lump spreading and crawling inside, I felt tears of indignation at the trickery of my mind, the claustrophobia in the trap I had set for myself. The train pulled out of Grenada and clattered on in the sun and the dry yellows of clay fields toward Winona.

I stared at the whites, forcing my fears to be felt and endured. I tuned my ears to their voices and had to fight to keep control and watch the view whisking past the window. The shades of variegated trees and shrubs passed. The fields with yellow, red, gray soil were already turned and rowed.

We entered Winona. The white paint-peeled sign was trimmed in black—for me, the black was in memory of the beatings of Fannie Lou Hamer. Her story was familiar to many in the movement who had followed the horrors of violence against movement activists. During the 1964 Democratic National Convention, she told the world on national television of her 1963 arrest in Winona. She described the multiple beatings she had suffered at the orders of her jailers in retaliation for attending a voter registration workshop. They forced other prisoners to take turns beating her on her cot in the jail cell . . . in the Winona Jail that I couldn't see from the train but that I could feel wherever I looked.

A black soldier rose from his seat, gathered his bag, stiffened, and walked off the train and toward his home. The depot, which had remained unchanged for forty years, was made of brick, built to last. The iron-wheeled loading carts stood idle at the station. For two blocks, red-framed painted storefronts faced the dusty main street. The signs on the clapboard storefronts dated to the teens or early twenties. J. W. Chalders Hardware, TWL Fashions, Jackson's Grocery, and then big green tractors. Again came the fields of green and dusty gray, orange and red clay, tan and brown. We passed few people in the fields. Here and there was a Jersey cow. One field was filled with black Angus-looking steers.

Soon afterward we halted at Vaiden, marked by another small wooden sign. Inside the once-well-used depot were charts, desks, and a phone. The door on one side led to the dark, dim room where the blacks waited. The other side was for whites, the whites I had forgotten existed. I was now trembling, shivering at the thought. I realized then that right on this very highway, a bit outside this grand town of Vaiden, in the broad daylight of a spring afternoon just two years ago, was the place where whites had terrorized and chased me, Henry, and the three local black leaders.

The train pulled off again to the south, even faster, getting closer and closer to "home." My eyes still stared at the whites around me. Telephone posts and trees swept past the window. A few tin-roofed shacks—tumbling, weathered huts that could have been shelter for hounds—had real living children sitting on the porch. A kerchiefed woman was sweeping with a broom. Later, a man—a poor white this time—walked behind his mule, a big dark beast that dragged the plough.

Highway 51 emerged. It raced beside us, and I thought of the times I'd driven it running scared. I saw the green tin sign with raised white lettering announcing to motorists that they were leaving Carroll County and entering Holmes County. A day earlier I would have expected my heart to leap at those words and my mind to fill with exciting memories, but the congestion in my chest ruled everything. I continued to sit immobile, in horror, full of sick queasiness.

We passed a gin, deserted, not spewing smoke or lint or seed or bustling with anything at this spring planting time. We went in and out of

West, another town where our tracks divided the rich from the poor, the white from the black. Its previously prosperous businesses all faced the trains, once new-fangled contraptions, so all could marvel.

Before it really sunk in that this was home and that the next stop was ours, I felt the train easing up. I saw the silver water tower with the letters D—U—R—A—N—T spelled out. I didn't bother looking any more. Instead I tried to compose my unsettled self, to find my things, to keep my eyes from staring, and to keep my hands from showing their distress.

I could feel the tense tolerance I hadn't needed in the North. Not living with it, I'd forgotten it was needed. I was reacquiring the skills for survival, and I steeled myself for meeting the spits and sneers and stares, arming myself with a thick skin, and learning again to live with uneasy fear. I straightened up, bundled up, loaded up, and walked slowly down the aisle.

Henry was behind me. We waited, then finally moved ahead. I stepped slowly off the train and touched the ground of "home."

Their Stories: Movement Visitors to the Balance Due House

One dusty gravel road wound around the settlement. The only other entry was a path from the highway to a three-board-wide, thirty-foot-long footbridge. That bridge landed on our side of the creek right at our front yard. With our easy bridge access, we didn't relate much to the neighborhood. In the years we lived in Balance Due, we never knew of any movement folks who lived there.

Many movement folks—leaders, staff, and volunteers—did find their way to our house, though, especially in 1967. They didn't come just to seek help or advice, but also to share stories and relax. Some days were quiet, but plenty of them included a full house and lots of activity.

We also gathered with movement folks at meetings and more formal interactions, and we connected in homes—theirs and ours—in ways that were entertaining, intimate, up-close and personal. The exchange was just as educational for the various movement locals as it was for Henry, me, and Alec, the white outside worker who sometimes lived in our Balance Due house.

Life could be chaotic in the Balance Due house. One morning I woke to Eugene Montgomery stamping on the front porch, yelling, "Hey, up there! Get on up from outta there. Get up outten that bed in there! Up, up!" He kept up his shouting until Henry jumped out of bed, stumbled to find his pants and socks, and opened the door. Then Gene just shouted all the more as he came lumbering in smiling and shouting that we were lazybones that should be up and out of bed by this time.

I dressed and came into the living room. Henry lit the heater, put on his socks, found his slippers, rolled a cigarette, and we talked. About nothing, just loud playfulness, gruff, pushy insults and shouts back and forth at each other. "How you doin', boss?" Henry threw at Gene.

"Where you been? What you come back here for? Thought we'd got rid of you white folks for good," Gene threw back at Henry. "That rolling machine—make me one. Go on, show me how it works. I've seen them things before. . . . I was going to Peoria. Hell, you didn't wait for me. I come by here at nine o'clock that night and you weren't here. I woulda gone with . . ." And we talked on and on.

Alec Shimkin got up from the other room, and there was more talk about how cold it was out, and finally Alec and Gene left. By the time I made the bed, Henry had smoked about three home-rolled cigarettes and was on his pipe and fixing his own coffee. I decided to go out for the mail and to buy some cream of wheat. We worked so late in the night that I woke before noon only occasionally, and I never felt fully awake until much after noontime. That day the air felt good. I drove the icy, rutted gravel roads, breaking ice floats that formed over the pothole in the road to the mailbox.

I went to the Sunflower store. They had quick cream of wheat, which takes five minutes, instead of instant, which takes thirty seconds, or instant mix, which takes only ten seconds. Joe Stein, the Sunflower owner, told me cream of wheat was a slow item and that folks who buy it prefer the five-minute kind. He said he might get the other kind in next week, just to try it. I ended up buying four dollars worth of other stuff and stopping at another white store, where I bought the five-minute kind.

At home again, I read the mail and fixed breakfast. We talked about a house going up for rent. It had a heater in every room and running water inside, but the rent was forty dollars a month, more than three times what we paid for our Balance Due place. Henry said he should have the landlord, Fanny Booker, save it for us, as we had become uncomfortably cold in the house and the water from the pump looked sickeningly bad. We were getting soft. It was hard to think of leaving our place, because it was great in the summer with the bridge and its coziness.

I sat down to do some work but then procrastinated about how I should eat some prunes, maybe some fig bars, and how damn cold my hands and feet felt. I ended up back in the front room, eating cookies and reading. Alice Mae Epps came in and we began to talk.

She told of Bailey's coming over Saturday night when she got back from Chicago and telling her she had missed getting the MACE (Mississippi Action for Community Education) job, how Dan Wesley had come over after the MACE workshop and said she should have come a half hour earlier and she would have had the job. Instead he got it. But Alice said she thought Dan looked like he might do a good job. She thought the job would have been just right for her now that she's tired of staying home all the time. Even if she weren't making a lot of money, she'd like to get out and talk with adults about getting things going again. I stopped talking to her and started making dinner for Henry, and her too, because Henry was leaving soon to go see Bernice at the Milton Olive office.

Alice talked of going to Rock Island over Christmas and then going to Chicago to see her sister Jane, but not staying with her because her husband was a "funny man, who didn't allow any smoking or drinking, even beer, in his house." She said, "He had got funny; I didn't know when. But Vietnam does funny things to people." She said she never had too much to do with him. We talked about more of her family—her daddy, whom she had brought to Lexington to Dr. Brumby's because he'd taken sick; and Skeet (Sam), who was married and in Chicago; and Jane, who had come home with Little Man for a week or two; and Fanny Mae, who was in Kosciusko still teaching. She talked more about Mrs. Carnegie and others.

Alec came in while we were talking. Then Mrs. Lela Walden came in. Alec and Henry left. Mrs. Walden and Alice mainly talked, exchanging stories about welfare—"how bad they do folks," what this one said to that white lady, and "how bad the white folks do people." But then also about "how bad some folks takes advantage of welfare, leading an easy life," such as the woman who stays up near Alice Mae who pays only three dollars for food stamps and gets one hundred dollars' worth and though she isn't married, stays with a man who makes a dollar an hour. When Mrs. Walden objected that perhaps the man didn't do anything for her with his money, Alice insisted that the "man do do things for her with his money." Even worse, the woman actually lives in Humphreys County, so she draws commodities from the welfare over there as well. The two exchanged more white-folks-in-the-welfare-office stories—"the big, long-nosed ole woman" and "the funny one rouged up all over her face." Mrs. Walden told how they were "always sneaking up to find out what's going on in your house" and how "Miss Juanita rides by and peeps into your house trying find a man's pants in there." Alice told how they asked her, when she applied for welfare, how much cotton her mother makes and how she told them they'd have to "ask her mama because that weren't none of her cotton. It was her mama's cotton." After a while, Mrs. Walden left to go to a food stamps meeting at the Epworth Church.

Henry came back in, and we talked some more with Alice. She told us Dr. Jackson, the only Negro doctor in Greenwood, was leaving for Iowa to go back to school, which would leave no Negro doctor nearby. Four or five years earlier, a colored woman doctor—Dr. Garner—worked two or three days a week in a Lexington office near Fanny Golden's funeral home. She also had an office in Greenwood. She was in Holmes about two years, not very old, and not married. She had a young son and was a very good doctor. None of her people were in Lexington, but she came because she heard it was a good place where there were no Negro doctors. She had gone to school in Maryland, was very nice, and took care of old people. If her patients didn't have the money, she didn't send them a bill. Aretha Wesley's mother paid for three very expensive treatments, and then the doctor told her she didn't have to pay for any more. She kept going for treatments for free. But the whites ended up running that doctor out of town. She started getting threatening phone calls. One time, vandals had torn everything up in her office, had gone through all the files, desks, and cabinets and pulled everything out. She left.

Mrs. Maroney from across the way came, saying she'd been looking for us two or three times when she had our fifty cents to pay back, but she didn't have it now. Something was wrong up under her house with water running out all over. Henry went over to help her, and Alice got ready to leave. After several phone calls to help Mrs. Maroney find a plumber, I finally settled down to write.

In the front room, I warmed my feet and rolled a cigarette; then it was time to listen to the news on the TV. We fell asleep with the TV blaring and woke only when Alec came over around 7:30 p.m. I dressed in the other room and sat down to write but ended up listening to them talk. Henry was eating pecans, so I decided to make some dinner. By 10:30 p.m., we were finally done eating and I settled back down to work.

Part 4

Developing the Slate of Candidates

13

Selecting the FDP Candidates from Holmes

January–June 1967

In January 1967 Henry and I had announced to the FDP executive board and a county coalition meeting that we were "transitioning out" of the 1967 politics. Many local people expressed disappointment and fears over the prospect of not having us working on the elections. They insisted, perhaps out of politeness, that local people would be unable to do it without Henry.

However, Henry's withdrawal opened the way for professionals to step in and for all leaders to fully embrace their leadership roles. Before this time, Howard Taft Bailey sometimes deferred to Henry at meetings with what seemed to us a slight submerged bitterness. Bailey was an important leader, along with Hartman Turnbow and Ralthus Hayes, and one of the few leaders who worked regularly helping people and solving problems at the FDP office. He and Henry got along. He had the ambition to be more, but he seemed uncomfortable or unsure about taking charge. While discussing issues, he would sometimes seem almost angry but at the same time would defer to Henry on a decision. In these situations, he had a stiff manner of holding himself; he would stammer and flash an occasional look of anger. I'm not sure Bailey felt Henry was holding him down or influencing other leaders against him. Yet, it did seem he wasn't able to fully lead with Henry there. After Henry stepped back from direct election work, Bailey became noticeably more relaxed and confident.

Attendance at the leadership coalition meetings was sporadic, from the usual 35 people to as many as 125. Disagreements were usually hushed up or smoothed over rather than brought out and debated in public meetings. The early meetings served to lay the groundwork for unity. People spoke up and exchanged information about themselves, the movement, and the county. Professionals took the opportunity to declare their willingness to be part of the movement and admit to fears they had held in the past. The meetings were a mechanism for county candidates to declare their intentions.

Leading preachers like C. L. Clark, Jodie Saffold, and Warren Booker, and schoolteachers LePlause Polk and Kelly Walls attended the meetings. Some of the older, respected members of the community also attended, including I. H. Montgomery, Austin Wiley, and Lexington's Jesse Williams, who had past FDP experience.

Beat 2 covered Durant and Goodman and was well organized, as usual. Ironically, it was the beat where white voters were in an absolute majority, and so it was impossible to win without white votes (which meant it was impossible to win). Already in January the local coalition had set up a system for raising campaign money, and at the Second Pilgrims Rest meeting, Ward Montgomery had been approved as the candidate for the Beat 2 supervisor post. Montgomery's early candidacy made a black campaign for the 1967 elections more of a reality, and the excitement in Beat 2 helped to energize the movement in the county and other beats.

The question of who would run for sheriff was a well-worn topic of conversation. Since no sheriff candidate had emerged, at the leadership coalition meeting on the last Friday night in January, Eugene Montgomery threatened to declare his intention to run. Although he may have had some real desire to run, his point was to force the community to come up with an alternative, since he knew they would never accept him.

In attendance was Robert R. "Bob" Smith, a relatively unknown schoolteacher from Lexington. Tom Griffin and T. C. Johnson took credit for urging Smith to come out to the meeting. After Eugene Montgomery's declaration, they introduced Smith, who rose to his lank height to face the body and request support for his candidacy for sheriff of Holmes County. The outside organizers and others from outside Lexington had never seen this bright-skinned, middle-aged math teacher before. He was a dark-horse candidate, yet a welcome surprise. He was of the middle to

Local Freedom Democratic Party leaders Norman Clark (*center*) and Robert Cooper Howard (*right*) discuss strategy with an outside worker in the campaign office.

upper-middle class, a member of the prestigious Asia Baptist Church, and a brother of Percy, one of the powerful deacons at Asia. He recognized the grassroots movement and was asking for its support.

Even though Burrell Tate had been considering running for sheriff himself, he told of how relieved he was to have a person with such high qualifications come forward and lift the burden from his own shoulders. He said he knew Smith had a better chance of success. It was more important for the FDP to get blacks into office than for any one person to get elected. Eugene Montgomery's reaction perhaps indicated the general way Smith was received. He immediately withdrew his own name and with excitement and pride moved to accept and support Smith's candidacy.

Tate, one of the strongest and most "grassroots" of the grassroots county leaders, seemed near tears as he spoke to the group declaring how thrilled he was that a schoolteacher had come forward. He said he felt unburdened now that the weight the people had been carrying would be shared by better-educated people. I knew there was a contradictory mixture of great respect and grave distrust, yet I could almost feel the great relief, awed respect, and joy.

With an actual sheriff candidate, the movement seriously faced the prospects of a real campaign in 1967. Other candidates stepped forward. The county needed candidates even in the weakest and least-organized beats because having local beat candidates would turn out voters for the county-office candidates.

Thomas C. (T.C.) Johnson, who had been kidding for at least six months in his "Top Cat," big-talking way about being sheriff, declared as a candidate for Beat 1 supervisor. Because Beat 1 (Lexington and the surrounding area) was the largest and most disjointed beat, there was no official meeting to validate T. C. Johnson's candidacy. He became the candidate at that same January coalition meeting.

Ralthus Hayes had strong county support and became the supervisor candidate for Beat 5, which covered Tchula and Cruger. Because he lived on the rural Choctaw project in Mileston, he had always attended the nearby Mileston FDP meeting in Beat 4. It was a complex situation because Tchula was the territory of Joe Smith and the NAACP. Except for the little work Smith did, Tchula was disorganized, and it was slightly hostile to Hayes. Even though Hayes was a long-standing NAACP member, as were many other FDP leaders, he wasn't active in the Tchula chapter, partially because of its history. It was the only NAACP chapter in the county and had formed in 1965. Hayes had tried, unsuccessfully, to start a Tchula FDP meeting, so his main support in Beat 5 came from the poorly organized Cruger area north of Tchula. Even though Cruger was in the heart of the delta area, it was dominated by whites; the blacks had few movement meetings. Still, Hayes became the Beat 5 candidate.

The FDP Countywide Meeting accepted all four men—Ward Montgomery, Robert R. "Bob" Smith, T. C. Johnson, and Ralthus Hayes, as the official candidates.

Once others started declaring, John Henry Malone, who had hung back from running for sheriff, agreed to run for Beat 3 supervisor, covering Ebenezer, Pickens, Coxburg, and the surrounding areas. Malone was having family problems and seemed to need money, although he owned and managed a fairly successful farm operation. He was just finishing up a training program in welding with the Manpower Development and Training Administration but was stymied when he discovered that the only jobs for welders were down at the Gulf Coast shipyards or up north. He decided to stay in Holmes, perhaps encouraged by the prospect of gaining a directorship in one of the new education and welfare programs that were proposed for the area.

After four years of intense movement activity, Beat 4, covering Thornton and Mileston, the original movement area, still didn't have a supervisor candidate. It was the one beat where over 80 percent of the registered voters were black, but it too was divided and disorganized. It was split between the landowners and the plantation people. Also the old movement people, mainly landowners, couldn't agree with each other. A slate to fill all three beat positions—supervisor, justice of the peace (JP), and constable—could win in Beat 4, so the important work ahead was to mend the internal splits.

Both Shadrach Davis, the Mileston Head Start committee chairman, and Norman Clark, the Mileston community chairman and executive committee member, would have accepted the supervisor candidacy if drafted, but because neither would declare his intentions, no action was taken. That left Willie James Burns, the most aggressive and in many ways the most sophisticated and militant in dealings with whites. He had been talking for years about wanting to be sheriff, but he never came forward. Instead, he declared and was accepted as the Beat 4 supervisor candidate. John Daniel Wesley became the Beat 4 JP candidate, and no one was settled upon for Beat 4 constable until much later.

On the third Sunday in March, Vernon Tom Griffin of Gages Springs was accepted as the Beat 1 JP candidate at the FDP Countywide Meeting in Bowling Green. Given the disorganization in Beat 1, it was not too surprising that Griffin, who had a controversial and damaging drinking problem, was accepted.

No black attorneys lived in the county, so the office of county attorney was not seriously considered, although some were in favor of supporting a different white lawyer to oppose incumbent Pat Barrett. When it was discovered that the coroner did not have to be a licensed physician and, further, that the coroner was next in line for the sheriff's job, there was talk of finding a coroner candidate, but no black declared. A schoolteacher would have been qualified for the tax assessor's job, but no schoolteacher came forward for that post.

The county circuit clerk position was a serious target because of the abysmal voter-registration record of the long-serving circuit clerk, the incumbent Henry McClellan. After a lot of thought and talk, Mary Lee Hightower, a young but extremely active FDP worker from Durant, decided to run for circuit clerk. Because she was only in her early twenties, there were the expected questions about her age. She was also unfamiliar with most of the county outside of Beat 2, but her energy and personality were strong, and her candidacy was agreed upon in April.

Ed McGaw, a young South Lexington neighbor of T. C. Johnson, declared his intention to be the candidate for constable of Beat 1. Known at meetings mainly as T.C.'s sidekick, McGaw was accepted as the natural "running mate" for T.C., since the positions of supervisor and constable were traditionally seen as team offices. In Alabama in 1966, a black sheriff was elected, but his constables, all white, worked against him; we didn't want to repeat that difficult situation. We knew a decent registration drive to get several hundred more Beat 1 blacks registered would give T.C., McGaw, and Griffin a comfortable black voting majority.

In mid-April the first public notice of the ten black candidates ran in the *Lexington Advertiser*, encouraging more people to consider candidacy. The organizers persisted in reminding Beat 4 that it should run a constable candidate. Mr. Mister Dulaney (yes, his real first name was "Mister"), a key plantation leader and a Masonic high "wishful master," was finally getting more involved in the movement. In his sixties, he agreed to consider the post if no one younger stepped forward. The game of wanting to be drafted was being played out to the end.

The class splits between project farmers and plantation workers were fermenting under the surface of everything, and Mister Dulaney's position increased the difficulties. Finally in the first week of June—the last week for filing nominating petitions before the June 9 deadline—the Mileston meeting accepted the candidacy of Griffin McLaurin Jr. for Beat 4 constable. McLaurin was a young Mileston man in his thirties who had stepped up on his own. His father owned one of the less successful project farms in Mileston, and Griffin cut pulpwood for his living.

Robert G. Clark also took a long time to make up his mind. As the project director of the Migrant Farmer's Education Program and previously a public school teacher and coach, Clark had attended a few of the coalition meetings and talked with several of the FDP and other leaders. Like most schoolteachers, Clark had not been directly active in the early years of the local or county movement. He was a popular young bachelor from Ebenezer, greatly respected by the young people he worked with and the many adults in his current program. When, in 1966, he moved from the public school system to the directorship of the federal program run though Saints, the private Negro junior college in Lexington, Clark gained a good deal more freedom and ability to speak out and work for the people. He was well known and respected by many.

At first, some movement leaders looked on Clark with suspicion. In early 1966 he had been appointed by the whites to represent the Negro community and run for a seat against veteran FDP leader Burrell Tate on the county Community Action Program board. Clark won and was sometimes on the wrong side during the battles that ensued between the movement and the CAP power structure. In both Clark's and Tate's home community of Ebenezer, the people had later elected Tate over Clark to serve as their community CAP representative.

Clark was very, very sharp, and interested in learning. He began attending some of the FDP meetings in his community and talked to leaders like Bernice Montgomery, Ralthus Hayes, and Henry. His experience with the whites on CAP had disillusioned him, and he was beginning to recognize the power of the black movement. Probably the most politically ambitious and sophisticated of all the candidates, Clark kept quiet counsel, took the longest to weigh all the factors, and concluded that there was a good chance to win an office. He declared for the post of state representative from Holmes County and was accepted enthusiastically by many. The black slate had grown to twelve.

In all, there were twenty-two local positions up for election. At the FDP office in Lexington, political education materials were mimeographed, including our own comic-book-style picture book of information on the importance and powers of the county supervisors and other officials. Our book helped get across how crucial it was to have leaders and officers elected at the most local level, the beat level. It was written by FDP organizer Alec Shimkin, and I drew the illustrations. We used materials from the Jackson movement and lawyers' offices as a basis for leadership training.

We also studied picture books on candidates and offices that were used in Lowndes County, Alabama. In 1966 the Lowndes County Freedom Organization had entered several local residents as candidates for county offices. That's when they adopted the emblem of the black panther. The Lowndes movement organized political education classes and registration drives and published a booklet informing citizens of the problems they could face if they registered. Lowndes faced some tough battles. Blacks there formed a new party, Lowndes County African Americans, after the Democratic Party raised its candidate filing fee to five hundred dollars. Each of their seven candidates lost in the November 1966 general election.

One of the biggest decisions our Holmes group faced was whether to run as Independents or as Democrats. The Mississippi Freedom Democratic Party was most amenable to the Independent position. It saw real dangers in running as Democrats, even though in previous years the FDP had run as Democrats when it could and even had sued over the constitutionality of taking an oath of loyalty to the Democratic Party.

The state NAACP, along with state chair Charles Evers, leaned toward running as Democrats. Evers was known for making deals with power structures in "his" counties to run whites for certain offices and not for others, hoping for white support of black candidates. The Holmes FDP strongly doubted that Holmes whites would vote for any black candidates. The FDP, whose aim was building black organizations, favored the Lowndes model because they ran an all-black slate.

County leaders respected Guyot and other FDP leaders such as Unita Blackwell, Fannie Lou Hamer, Victoria Gray, and Annie Devine. In addition, Holmes County was one of the strongest FDP counties in the state, with Hayes serving actively on the MFDP executive board. But MFDP positions weren't accepted automatically by the county.

No party line was handed down; the decision to run as Democrats or as Independents was ultimately up to the community and beat organizations. Everyone—the county FDP leaders, the candidates whether professional or not, the whole concerned black community—wanted to take what was the best path for victory. Everyone's goal was the same.

As chairman of the MFDP, Lawrence Guyot supported the Holmes movement and was in close contact with local leaders. He was an essential strategizer and political trainer.

Leaders and organizers presented arguments on both sides, and the meetings were many and long.

To run as a Democrat meant having the candidates' names on the ballot in the August 8 primary. If candidates won the primary, they would still have to be voted on again in November. Although the one-party history of Mississippi and the county showed that whoever won the Democratic primary won in November, because there was no opposition, history could not be depended upon in such changing times.

Running as Democrats meant turning out the black vote in both August and November. We knew it would be easier to turn out the black voters in August during the slack lay-by season than in November in the midst of cotton-picking and poorer weather. But to win a primary, one needed an absolute majority of the votes cast, over 50 percent. A plurality was not enough; it would require a run-off election within two weeks between the top two candidates. The experience in Alabama and other black-white primaries was that even blacks who won pluralities in the first primary vote got whipped overwhelmingly in run-off elections, because turning out the vote for a run-off is always more difficult than for the first election. Both whites and blacks have difficulty getting voters to return to the polls. To turn out inexperienced black voters twice in two weeks—for a reason many wouldn't understand—seemed an impossible feat.

Several other factors came into play. There was the off-chance that more than one white would run for an office against a black in November. If this occurred, only a plurality and not an absolute majority would be needed to win the general election, which would work in the blacks' favor. In addition, primary elections were handled through the white Democratic Party structure, and there was more opportunity for violating rules in August than in November. The official election commissioners administering the November general election were more subject to black pressure for black poll officials and federal pressure for fairness.

Finally, running in November would allow more time for registering voters. There were still several thousand unregistered blacks in Holmes County. The final deadline for registering to be eligible to vote in August was June 24 at the federal examiner in the post office, and the deadline for the November election was September 24. By waiting until November, the blacks would have more time to organize their voter registration. Gaining the entire summer to register black voters could yield perhaps as many as a thousand more voters for November.

To run as an Independent meant appearing only on the November ballot. Campaigning for one voting day would be less expensive than turning out the vote for two or three days. One of the main disadvantages was the effort needed to discourage black voters from participating in the primary. If blacks took part in the primary, they would have to vote for whites, which seemed detrimental to our goal. It took a great deal of time and effort to show people how to mark a ballot; once a voter marks an X for someone, for instance a white candidate in August, the voter is more likely to vote for the same candidate in November. Unlearning is a difficult thing.

Another consideration was that an all-white primary would probably produce the worst white from the frame of reference of the black community. The incumbents were known as cruel and unfair. It would be easier for a black candidate to win against a white with a known history of injustice.

Ultimately, not much seemed to be gained by running as Democrats. Yet, after four years of registration drives and stressing the importance of voting, it would be very difficult to justify urging nonparticipation in an election—especially an election like the August 1967 primary, the first time in history when black voters would be able to cast a vote for their own local officials. We considered organizing a voter education workshop on the same day as the primary, with everything from serious political education to picnics. We wanted an alternative place for the black voters to go and to build the strength and spirit of a black or Independent party. Finally all agreed—the executive committee, the major candidates, and the countywide meeting, that the black campaign for the 1967 elections would be run as Independents.

Their Stories: Robert G. Clark: The Day Is Coming

Robert Clark made these comments in a speech: "A friend of mine once introduced me to a crowd and told a story about traveling through Mississippi. This was back in the time around when the first freedom riders came in, as they call them. And that was a time. It was really dangerous times then. And he heard a noise. He drove along and he heard this noise, so finally he stopped his car and he got out of his car with his gun in his hand—he didn't know what to expect. Well, he walked back to his trunk and opened it to see what the noise was, and when he opened it he saw a great big rattlesnake back in the trunk. He was just about to take his gun and kill that rattlesnake when the rattlesnake looked up at him and said, 'Mister, please don't harm me. I'm just trying to get across the Mississippi line.'

"I'm quite aware that a saying of my grandfather's is coming true. It's almost at hand. I remember well the stories that my grandfather used to tell me when I was a boy. My grandfather, he was born during the time of slavery. He would tell how it was. How he never had a pair of shoes for his feet and how when he was sixteen all he wanted was an underdress. And he would tell how they come out and would feed them in a trough with milk and bread. And he would tell about how when the Yankees

Popular and very sharp, Robert G. Clark was the first black in the twentieth century to be elected as a state representative to the Mississippi House. He secured the highest office won by a black in all of Mississippi in 1967, the first year blacks voted. Clark served in the House until 2003.

came, how happy they all was to see the Yankees and how proud they was because they were free.

"There is one story that my grandfather talked about and he always talked about it late at night. I noticed that my grandfather was very careful how he picked the people that he would talk to about this story. From this I came to understand that this was something that my grandfather hated very much. It was a story about Reconstruction times here in Mississippi and how it was in that time. They had Negroes in lots of offices. Negroes had been elected to fill many posts in the government at that time. They had a Negro Sheriff in Hinds County and they had black men in many positions. My grandfather, he was the chairman of the Republican Party in Hinds County. They were having a raid on Clinton in Hinds County; they was killing Negroes. The black Sheriff of Hinds County and my grandfather were in Clinton that night and they had guns and they were shooting back, but they were overpowered. The black sheriff and the others got killed. My grandfather got evacuated at night and he ran away and he came to Holmes County. When he would tell it, you could see that he felt very bad about getting out that night and how he was sorry to have left his friends there killed.

"But my grandfather he loved Mississippi and he used to tell me then, he'd say 'Son, the old South and Mississippi is going to rise again and this will be a fine place to be. And the day will come when you and others who love Mississippi will stay and fight. You'll stay and fight to make it right. You will bring in the day when again Mississippi is great and strong and you can have a say in what affects your life and homes.' Well, that day is coming and it's coming soon because Mississippi is on the rise again."

14

Black and White Issues with SNCC Workers

Summer 1967

The spirited Edgar Love paid careful attention to the SNCC workers as early as 1964. In 1965 he helped out at the community center and talked about freedom to the plantation folks he lived with. He came from Refuge, a delta plantation where he lived with his parents in a house provided by "The Man." In those early years, hearing his steps was exciting to Henry and me because he was the first plantation person to join in the movement work. He came to learn more clearly about the movement, and he had the specific, passionate goal of organizing his people on dozens of plantations. He knew them better than any of the Holmes leaders and organizers.

In the dark of night he went onto the plantations and talked up the news of the movement, where it was going, how they might together change their condition. Then, by day, he returned to the center to report his progress and plans. It was risky and dangerous work; but his dream was to organize those poorest, most marginal people.

In 1966 Edgar's innate curiosity and desire to learn pushed him to pursue more movement action and leadership. He also started taking on work at the FDP office in Lexington with Henry. There he learned to handle such problems as registration attempts, harassment, and welfare and worked in the rest of the county communicating with and troubleshooting for movement leaders and people with problems. After the federal Voting Rights Act passed but before a federal registrar was assigned to the county, not much of a dent had been made in the thousands of

After being kicked off a white man's delta plantation for movement organizing and voter registration work, Edgar Love became a full-time movement staff worker. Here he speaks to a crowd, protesting the brutality of a black policeman we all called "Fats."

blacks still not registered. For the first time, the county FDP took on a bold advertising campaign.

I wrote a simple, pointed script aimed at those most fearful of attempting to register—the teachers, preachers, plantation workers, and town dwellers, and the FDP paid for a several-minute spot on WXTN, the Lexington radio station. One movement person in each of those categories read his or her lines over the radio announcing that he or she was a teacher, a preacher, or a plantation person or lived in a town and still was going to register to vote. Edgar was the first to read his script, "Hello, I'm Edgar Love. I live on a plantation and I'm going to register to vote. All plantation people have the right to register and no longer need to be afraid." When he returned home after the broadcast, he found out the white plantation owner had kicked him off the plantation, telling Edgar's dad that Edgar could no longer work or live there. In many ways he was relieved. Getting kicked off by "The Man" became freedom for Edgar.

That's when Edgar started as a full-time FDP organizer; he became an essential, all-around countywide local staff worker. He received subsistence movement pay of ten dollars a week from the FDP. Alone or with outside white volunteers, he took on the dangerous job of canvassing all the delta plantations, talking to people and showing them how to register. He drove them in the movement van to the courthouse and then, after the federal examiner came in, to the post office. During the latter part of 1966, he spent more time in the FDP office taking over for Henry and handling welfare and other problems of the people, getting out notices for meetings, and generally doing the day-to-day staff work. He became a replacement for Henry in the office; however, he was a worker much more than an organizer. Like Alec, he was constantly doing things rather than "getting things done" by building mechanisms, which was Henry's style of organizing.

Although Edgar was a staff person performing many of the tasks of campaign work, he was also a leader. He could legitimately function as a leader where Henry and other outsiders never should. By 1966 and 1967, when Black Power and bolder stances were being taken by blacks, Edgar was the first of the bold. He was of the right age and disposition to wear the new black pride.

The concept of keeping black organizers in black communities, and

whites in white communities was a major thrust of the Black Power statements beginning in 1966. Consequently, across the nation, whites had
gradually left the movement. In the Holmes movement, black and white
staff had sometimes had difficulty relating with each other. There was
tension in the 1964 Summer Project, when the first large wave of white
workers had been recruited.

In December 1966 SNCC expelled all of its white workers. Indeed,
the Black Power pronouncement of SNCC had been related in many
ways to the stifling effect of overbearing and overorganized white college
students on black workers and leaders in 1964.

In May 1966 H. Rap Brown became the leader of SNCC. He announced that the organization would continue its commitment to Black
Power, but he also openly advocated violence. He changed SNCC's
name, taking out the word *Nonviolent*. It became the Student National
Coordinating Committee. The Black Power message consequently lost
SNCC a large percentage of its financial support. Our support from the
outside for our work in Holmes County also suffered.

There were dangers in the Black Power message. "Once the black
power announcement was issued, everything was torn asunder in Mississippi," Guyot said. "Even though they caused a stir, black power zealots
had difficulty organizing around a slogan." It was especially difficult for
SNCC to organize new members.

SNCC supported great movement efforts in Mississippi, such as the
Freedom Elections of 1963, the Democratic Convention Challenge to
the segregated delegation in 1964, and the 1965 Congressional Challenge to the seating of the white congressional delegation, all of which
led to the passage of the 1965 Voting Rights Act. Despite these actions,
SNCC's strength had diminished quite significantly by 1966.

SNCC staff had almost completely pulled out of Mississippi in 1966
to work on local elections in Alabama and then to concentrate on black
college campuses and do some work in urban ghettoes. However, Holmes
County remained as one of SNCC's priority communities. For several
summers, specialized students in disciplines such as law and medicine
were recruited to come and work in the Mississippi movement. In 1967,
because Holmes had more black candidates than any other FDP county,
Ralthus Hayes, Walter Bruce, and other leaders argued that more than

one law student should be assigned to work there full time. They asked Henry to play his usual role of orienting and directing outside workers, but as with other movement work, Henry wanted to turn those functions over to key leaders.

In early June, two law students arrived—Tom, a young white man, and Pat, a young black woman. In accord with the FDP philosophy that whites should be as little visible in the campaign as possible, Tom was assigned to work on some of the nonpolitical problems related to Head Start, economic issues, and other projects Henry was developing.

Tom worked in the FDP office in Pecan Grove, a neighborhood where there were only four or five streets. The office was in a small shotgun shack with a front room and a back room. At one time a family's home, it was surrounded by overgrown trees and shrubs. The FDP office had a phone and freely gave black people access to it. Very, very few black people had phones in their homes. Two years earlier, the Council of Federated Organizations (COFO) workers had hand-painted for this office a wooden sign that proclaimed "Freedom Democratic Party—F.D.P." and nailed it up above the porch.

The FDP took a major step that year. At the beginning of the summer, we opened a new office in Lexington—a special campaign office for the coming elections, separate from the functions of the FDP office. It was a courageous step for us because the office was located in a public area of Lexington, on Beale Street, within a block of the courthouse square. It was in a commercial building in a white area. It had a couple of rooms with wooden flooring and mostly wood-sided interior walls. Over the wooden desk in the main room hung a photo collage of Martin Luther King Jr., John F. Kennedy, and Bobby Kennedy. The metal folding chairs were the main furniture, and a large black pay phone hung on the wall. Clark's campaign office was in a back room.

Pat was assigned to the campaign office to do full-time campaign work and handle any legal or other problems the candidates and leaders had. Generally she took over the communication functions that Henry had once fulfilled at the office; she effectively became the campaign secretary for the leaders during the summer. Tom also gave candidates help when Pat was overloaded.

Later in June, ten black workers arrived and stayed for varying lengths of time, most of them through August. Their numbers varied, as did their location in the county and their work. They were referred to as the "SNCC guys." They had been recruited from out of state by SNCC people in Jackson and therefore had a SNCC connection. None of them had the experience to be the kind of organizer Edgar Love had become. Most of the group were northern college students who, in terms of organizing experience or working with rural blacks, were not much different, except for their color, from the inexperienced, "green" summer volunteers who had come in previously. Only one of them, Shutes, had any experience in the southern movement, and that was in a nonrural part of Alabama.

White withdrawal and black organizing was an issue that was well understood by the white staff in Holmes. Henry's and my philosophy of transition represented a basic agreement with the SNCC philosophy. Yet, we were still in Mississippi. We knew that our presence may have been resented and looked upon suspiciously by some black workers around the state. The arrival of the black students in summer 1967 brought the issue into the open in Holmes, and the situation was strained, to say the least.

Henry had a great skill in knowing when to speak and when to be silent. Guyot said he admired Henry's way of handling the Black Power issue. "He just kept moving ahead. He didn't fight them; he didn't join them. He didn't train them, but he didn't interfere with their training either." Movement leaders seemed to take their cues from Henry. There was real fear that an internal conflict between blacks and whites would spoil the election, that Black Power would tear the movement apart, just when winning elections was within sight. It is possible that SNCC sent the ten workers to Holmes to shake up the agreeable relationships between local leaders and white organizers.

It was obvious to me that the SNCC group in Holmes thought Edgar was Henry's mouthpiece. They saw Edgar interact with Henry, meeting with Henry on strategy and getting advice on how to handle things. It was delicate. Edgar was the local organizer, and yet he wanted Henry's input. The SNCC students thought less of Edgar because of his high regard for Henry.

By that June, Henry and I had withdrawn almost completely from the election. Henry had started a new part-time coordinator position setting up the Holmes County Health Research Program for the University of Illinois. Demitri Shimkin, Alec's father, was key to the project. He developed the unique relationship between the university and Holmes County. Henry had the best of both worlds. He held an academic appointment, but he worked directly with the people in the county. The project hired Daisey Lewis, Bernice Montgomery, and Tom Griffin to work at the Milton Olive Program for Children. They studied health conditions and developed medical services.

Henry's new job meant that our financial situation was much improved and we were able to survive without donations from northern supporters. From the time we arrived in fall 1964, Henry and I had existed financially through the generosity of our supporters. Small groups and 132 individuals sent us money for those thirty-four months, totaling nearly seventy-nine hundred dollars. That made up our living and working expenses. Sometimes as many as twenty checks arrived in a single month. We received many in-kind contributions: medical and dental examinations and treatment, transportation, food, sometimes quite luxurious shelter during our much-needed vacation trips. There were thirteen people who gave us monthly donations during the entire time. Once a professor sent us $480. A Sunday school class in Duluth, Minnesota, sent us $19.25. Only about one-third of the supporters were people we knew before we came to Mississippi. All the rest were people we had never met. When Henry received the University of Illinois appointment, we sent all of our supporters a thank-you letter and a summary leaflet detailing their contributions.

Henry and I did not deal directly with the SNCC workers. Bruce and Hayes were their contacts and gave them direction. Henry and I didn't go out of our way to either relate with or confront the black students. Henry took the position that coordination of the students' efforts into the general overall campaign would have to be effected by the local leaders. When SNCC workers came to us at the direction of an FDP leader, Henry was quite willing to give them all the maps and background on the county that they wanted, but he didn't take responsibility for their orientation. He didn't push for black-white staff cooperation, for he understood the tensions and resentments that would be inherent in white guidance. He preferred to let the SNCC workers do their thing and let the leaders do the guiding and take the initiative. He withdrew from the political but did involve the local leadership in his economic, health, Head Start, and other work.

Shutes, the strongest of the black students, wore his thick, kinky hair in an Afro. He took the position that the presence of whites was not to be acknowledged. However, Henry was obviously respected by the local leaders, who didn't seem to agree with the "all whites are bad" viewpoint.

For staff like Edgar Love, the problem was identity. He very much identified with Shutes and the philosophy of blacks taking power. But he had lived and worked for over six months with Alec Shimkin, and the two had been through much together. Earlier, when Edgar had done movement education with plantation workers, he had related easily with white staff. And he still enjoyed learning from Henry. But Edgar's very manhood was being attacked, particularly when he was depicted as a flunky of Henry, who controlled all.

Overriding everything, however, was Edgar's intense involvement with working on the election of a black sheriff and the other black candidates. Edgar went along with the black pride and "talking black," but after several weeks of real problems, he concluded that Shutes and most of the others were more concerned with talk than action and not all that interested in working on the nitty-gritty of voter registration and directing block captains. Two other SNCC students took an interest in Edgar's campaign work, and they developed a working relationship.

Edgar returned to his full-time election work with Alec and using Henry as an adviser, and he helped the FDP organize a campaign caravan for July 4, 1967. Several cars and truckloads of leaders and candidates drove a campaign trail around the county, stopping in several communities for picnics and speeches. I went along to take photos and help out.

For Pat, the FDP-recruited black law student who had at first accepted guidance and direction from Henry, the effect of the black militants was even greater than for Edgar. She was a relatively middle-class northern black with no experience in the South, the movement, militant black philosophy, rural impoverishment, or the attacks on her bourgeois law school background. She had an inner conflict because she had friendly relationships with whites. For a while she seemed ready to leave altogether. Communication with Henry and me, and even with her fellow law student, broke down completely. When she finally decided to stay on, she never again related easily with the white workers. She spent time with Shutes and the others and took over the office coordinator role that Edgar had left when he took on more campaign activities.

The work the SNCC guys did do wasn't aligned with the elections or the campaign work. From the outside, their work looked unorganized. They tried to offer help to many communities, but lack of transportation and other factors made that difficult. They started work in Durant and later went to Lexington.

Their one positive project was running summer Liberation Schools for children from six to sixteen years old and older. The first school was set up in Bruce's hometown of Durant. SNCC's declining trust in white activists was matched by a declining interest in the study of American society in the classroom. Instead, the new schools placed an emphasis on African history and culture.

A controversy developed at the very beginning of the SNCC workers' efforts at the Durant Liberation School. Talk of a boycott had begun rather spontaneously. Shutes and the others, probably in the spirit of freedom and organizing, encouraged the kids to begin a boycott canvassing campaign. They didn't consult with Bruce, who was unquestionably the Durant movement leader. Holmes leaders had held a boycott of white stores in December 1965, and a successful boycott was held in Edwards, Mississippi, in August 1966. Bruce himself had pushed for a boycott earlier in the year. While under different circumstances Bruce might have welcomed the effort, he did not appreciate the SNCC students' total disregard of him. An additional problem arose when several of the strongest movement leaders refused to allow their children to attend the Liberation School classes because they believed a form of black racism and hatred for all whites was being taught. There was a fear that the controversial black-white issues the SNCC students brought up in the FDP office and the trouble in the Liberation Schools would negatively affect the election.

Holmes had a vested interest in getting out the vote, in entering the political system and making it work. The people risked everything they owned, and everything they would ever get in the future, on the 1967 election gamble, and they weren't about to lose it.

That June we heard the news that Thurgood Marshall had become the first black Supreme Court justice. Somehow, that made the stakes even higher. So much time and effort had been invested in voting rights and in the election campaign that the Holmes leaders knew they didn't want anything, including the SNCC students, to endanger the effort.

The generation gap between the students and the leadership was especially noticeable. In the black rural South, youth were expected to show great respect for the elders, and the SNCC guys weren't appropriately deferential. The predominantly middle-aged and older leaders of the Holmes movement must have looked pretty conservative to the young blacks, even though the young people were informed about the history of the area and the amount of movement work these middle-aged leaders had contributed.

Whites and blacks in Holmes County were aware of the unrest in the country. Earlier, the Watts riots of August 1965 had received much attention. In summer 1967, rioting again picked up and occurred across the United States. At the same time Holmes County was working with the SNCC students, rioting was on the television news practically every night. During these months, which came to be called "the Long, Hot Summer," the nation saw more than forty urban racial uprisings—including actions in Newark; Detroit; New York; Washington, D.C.; Baltimore; Chicago; Atlanta; and Buffalo, N.Y.

The national unrest affected Holmes. There was controversy surrounding the SNCC students on many levels. Yet the black students were able to bring up issues that white workers couldn't, such as black unity and how whites can't fully relate to the black experience. Although these issues were not necessarily directly related to the elections, they were questions the Holmes black community, like all black communities in the late 1960s, had started discussing. On the summer campaign issues, particularly those related to participating in or staying out of the primary, the black students voiced their opinions.

The movement was able to deal with the SNCC students that summer without having a major white-black confrontation that would have spoiled the elections. "The students were creatively contained," Guyot said. "That shows leadership. Thank God they didn't cause any more trouble than they caused."

The best effect was that the black students, in a different and often stronger way than Henry or I could do, had pushed local movement leaders to take more control of the election campaign.

With Lexington leaders Lucille Davis and Lela Mae Walden, Edgar Love and others marched around the courthouse to Lexington City Hall. Outside worker Alec Shimkin also marched. The marchers were attempting to remove a brutal black policeman from the Lexington force.

In fall 1967, after the black SNCC students returned to college, Edgar spearheaded a boycott of Lexington businesses. A group called the Negro Consumers of Lexington printed an open letter to white businessmen and leaders in the *Lexington Advertiser.* It called for the formation of a biracial committee to discuss ending police brutality by the black policeman "Fats." The letter told the white merchants (and community) to put their white children back into the public school and to welcome black patrons to the community's cafés, offices, waiting rooms, and washrooms by removing the discriminatory Jim Crow signs. It also called for better jobs, better roads, more money for schools, the end of harassment, the end of Ku Klux Klan scare tactics, and respectful treatment of blacks. One of the statements read, "We are not satisfied with having officers like Willie 'Fats' Jordan, the first black, white-lackey police officer, and Mr. 'Meter Man Mack' bully over us. We do not approve of lawlessness."

A list of businesses that respected blacks was circulated, and the boy-cott continued for a year or more. The boycott took much of Edgar's time, and he was in and out of jail several times. "Policeman Fats" was particularly cruel. Edgar gathered people together to protest the brutality and attempt to remove Fats from the Lexington force. Edgar led a march that included local Lexington leaders Lucille Davis and Lela Mae Walden and out-in-the-county folks such as Eugene Montgomery, teenagers, and Alec Shimkin. Marching to and around the courthouse, they ended at City Hall, where they confronted Sheriff Andrew P. Smith, Deputy Billie Joe Gilmore, and another white policeman.

By October, Edgar was back in the field, traveling the county, con-tacting precinct leaders, talking with block captains, attending meetings and rallies, and assisting with the campaign. Edgar and others planned a campaign caravan for October 28 to cover one hundred miles.

On his own, Edgar led desegregation drives of local cafés and public places and refused to back down or cringe in the face of the white threats. He was quite the hero to the teenage set. Even when older folks com-plained of his boldness and called it "craziness," an undercurrent of pride and respect for his courage could be felt. Their label of "crazy" often was more an expression of fear for his safety than a judgment of him or denial of the rightness of his actions.

His work, flare, and style increasingly made him the target of white wrath. He truly was in danger. He was constantly being followed and harassed and often jailed. However, he gave the police many openings by committing minor infractions. It was common knowledge that various local black people had been offered money to pull a trigger on Edgar.

With his streak of crazy wildness, Edgar was bullheaded and strong and had a vision of what was right, just, and fair. He often took the heat, becoming the lightning rod that attracted the fiery hatred of the whites. By doing so, he became a target as well as a shield and was a role model for young and old.

Their Stories: Edgar Love and the Tchula Shootout

Edgar recounted the Tchula shootout for me the day after it happened:

"I was at the door of the van, getting in, standing there, and this guy comes up. Fact is I didn't see him coming. I just sort of felt him behind me. He comes up close and says, 'You is that nigger that's in all that civil rights working, aren't you?'

"And I said, 'That's right. That's me.'

"And he says, close up, 'Okay, nigger, you've had it. We're gonna get you.'

"And he just keeps talking and says, 'Look up, there at that window, nigger. You see them two men there? They gonna shoot you.'

"I didn't look over there. I didn't know that maybe he wasn't just trying to make me look over so he could get up closer to me or something. But then I saw these two guys getting out of their truck. One of them had an automatic shotgun. I don't know what the other had. They was parked right up side the van. I don't know how that happened. I just didn't know they were there. I must be slipping. My mind's not right, not watching for these things any more, or something. Anyway, the two guys are coming out of the truck and around, one around one side, and the one with the automatic, he's coming around the back and standing there. When I saw him, I reached into my jacket and felt for my pistol. And then, when I saw the guy coming round, I pushed my pistol out.

"And the one that was up close, talking—the Lacy Chapman guy [Lacy Chapman was a local white]. He looks down and says, 'Why, look at that nigger. What you got there? What you gonna do with that thing, nigger?'

"I said, 'That's my pistol. I'm gonna shoot you. That's what I'm gonna do, man.'

"And he yells over to them, 'Watch it, fellahs. This nigger here's got a pistol.' And the one starts backing away behind the truck again, the one with the shotgun, backing away so he could raise up his shotgun and fire—shoot, but out too far from me where I could get him with my pistol.

"Then I saw these others—one coming up from one street and another coming in from along another street, and they was all over, closing in. I started thinking then, you know, these motherfuckers was going to kill me. I didn't have nothing but five shots in my pistol. I had a whole box of shells, but they was up in the van. I thought to myself, I gotta figure out a way to get outta here 'cause them motherfuckers can shoot me, blast me with what they had and kill me dead. So I started running down the street.

"I was way the hell up by the goddamn Chinaman's. I ran down the street, peeped into Knott's [a black café], but didn't see nobody there. I mean there was one fellah in there, but he wasn't nobody that would stand up or do anything—just one cat who didn't have no gun, nothing. But I saw Dorsey." Dorsey was the black sort-of-assistant to the Tchula police officer, Bob Gillespie.

"I ran up there to Dorsey, and I say, 'You got your gun, Dorsey? Get your gun. Where's your gun?'

"Dorsey said, 'Yeh, I got my gun. What's the matter, Edgar?' So I ran on down and Dorsey followed and I got to Mansoor's. That's the man that saved me. I mean I owe my life to that white man. He stood up." Tony Mansoor was a longtime Tchula shopkeeper, a Middle Eastern man, thus not quite white in the 1960s southern social structure, but not quite colored either.

"We went on into Mansoor's store and I told him, 'They out there and they gonna kill me.' Mansoor's wife is pregnant and all, and she was there shaking, oh and ah. They went by, and she saw them through the window and said, 'Yes, they is out there.'

"Mansoor, he comes up from the back, and he got his pistol. I went over behind the belts. Dorsey, he said, 'I'll cover the door.' I stayed down low behind the counter. They hadn't seen me duck into Mansoor's. They looked all over Tchula for me. Then they come back to Mansoor's. Some one had told them I was in Mansoor's and they came back looking for me.

"Chapman came in and said, 'Come on, where's that nigger? We're going to kill that nigger, and you better give him to us, Tony, or we'll get you too.' I was crouched down low, way down behind the counter. Mansoor, he was talking to him, telling him he should go on home.

"But Chapman kept saying that he was gonna kill that nigger, so then I just stood right up. I got up from behind the counter and I said, 'Here I am. You're not gonna get me.'

"I had my pistol on him. I was up behind where he was. He raised his hands out some, turned around to look at me, and said, 'Come on out there, nigger. We gonna get you out there.'

"And I said, 'Hell, no, I ain't gonna let you kill me.' I said, 'Stay where you are, man, or I'm gonna shoot you.' He stayed where he was, didn't come any closer. I mean I had him scared. I was gonna shoot that bastard, you know what I mean. I mean I wanted to shoot that motherfucker right there. But, I thought if I shoot him, they're really gonna get me. The whole town of Tchula was gonna come down on me if I shoot him. So I was bluffing him. You know, some of these cats I tell this to, they say, 'Hell, if it had been me, I woulda shot that motherfucker dead right there.' They say they wouldn'ta stood like that. But they would've shot that bastard right then. Hell . . . I don't know. All I know is that they had the whole town out there, and I woulda been dead. But I jes' kept bluffing him. I had him in front of me, and he didn't come no closer. He thought I would shoot him. He said, 'Come on, nigger. Come outside. We gonna fix you.'

"There was lots of people there. In and out of the store. Nobody was doing nothing. Marshall Moore was there. But what can a guy do when he's scared. He couldn't do nothing. They would have killed him too. Hell, Mansoor, he called Sheriff Smith, told him to come on down, there was going to be a shoot-out in Tchula. And you know what that bastard said? He said he wasn't coming over to Tchula. They could get me and kill me for all he cared.

"And you know what Chapman's wife did? She came in, talking, trying to tell me to go on out and let her husband kill me. She said, 'You go on out there and give yourself up.'

"I said, 'Man, you better get her outta here. That bitch is crazy. Just get her on outta here, 'cause I ain't gonna let nobody kill me. So just get that motherfucking bitch outta here. She must be crazy telling me that. I ain't going out nowhere where no goddamn motherfuckers can shoot me.'

"What finally happened was Bob Gillespie [a Tchula police officer] came. He came in and handed me the piece of paper. Showed me the warrant and said he was going to take me. I read it. It just said that I, Edgar Love, was pointing and aiming at Lacy Chapman. I said, 'Naw. I ain't going nowhere. You're not gonna take me out into that street where them motherfuckers is gonna kill me.' Gillespie, he whispered up close that he was going to protect me. He was doing it to protect me, take me out of town.

"I said, 'Naw, I ain't gonna give my gun up. You're not gonna do nothing but take me out in that street, and then say you couldn't do nothing about it when all them motherfuckers started shooting to kill me.'

"But then I looked up and saw [Howard] Bailey. He was there in the store too. He had come in. He wasn't there at the beginning. But I guess he had come into Tchula and then heard what was going on, and he had come in to Mansoor's. Bailey, he gave me the sign, so I gave my gun to him and went on out with Gillespie. They carried me over to Lexington and put me in jail."

Their Stories: Alec Shimkin's Reflection

Alexander Shimkin, a white outside volunteer, wrote this note and left it in a voter data file. These are some of his comments:

"As the heat of the Mississippi summer grows upon us, we find ourselves—or at least I find myself—coming to the very end of an era. Since I was barely twenty, I've devoted almost every moment of my life to the movement; what passed before those days hardly matters—for it was school and athletics and preparation for the life of an Army officer. But my own longing for something else—human companionship, perhaps—led me to the brink of despair, and the rejection of what I had done as being essentially worthless. In the very flood tide of the movement, I joined at Selma when the whole nation apparently stood behind the freedom movement. Now the waters have flowed back to the sea.

"In that time was a very great suffering, and some very great joy. The joy came in the bitterest moments; for under the hand of death the barriers that keep people silent, alone, afraid of one another, are broken down, if only for a while. At times—as when through my error a man died—there was grief too great to be borne. But in time one becomes hard, and emotion is dulled. At last you begin to feel that you no longer feel, that you no longer think, that you no longer perceive the light of the sun or the stars or the wood, but only work. The forces of evil do not seem to grow less; yet because I was born white, because I cannot alter that fact, I feel at times that even our victories—the movement's victories—are in a sense the sign that my own life, as I have known it for

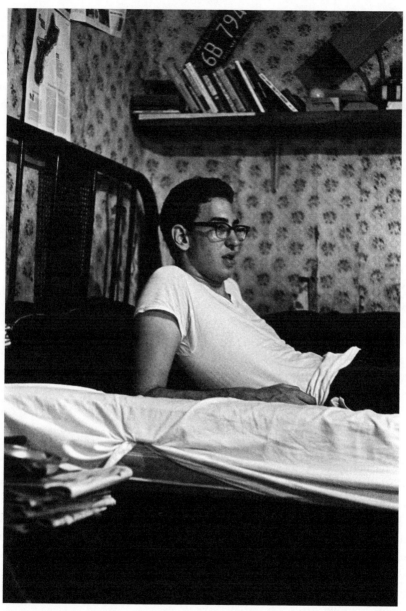

Alec Shimkin, a northern college student and outside worker, takes a break at the Lorenzis' Balance Due shack. Shimkin focused on 1967 elections work with Edgar Love.

the past two and a half years, is passing. Intellectually I agree, of course, with the philosophy that SNCC has laid out. But emotionally, to tear oneself from the midst of people one has struggled with is a terrible process. I have a detached enough view to see that, historically, my personal feelings are quite irrelevant. I also concede that in a sense, the flow of events, the flow of hatreds, can no more be controlled by me than the rising of the sun; for the seeds were laid before I was born, before my grandfathers were born.

"Perhaps the barrenness of my life outside the movement leads me to this state of mind—the fact that I do not feel myself to be particularly useful outside the narrow sphere; that I have too stark and grim a vision of America to believe that such instruments of power as the poverty program or the Peace Corps actually help people. I do accept the idea that white America is racist, that it needs to be educated, that whites need to work to civilize their own people. I cannot however—and this has been a long struggle in my mind—accept the idea that all personal relationships between persons of different races must be ended in the interest of revolutionary struggle. At times I am haunted by the idea that evil may take the place of (admittedly greater) evil; what is certain is that many things I have prized, are coming to an end. I sometimes think of those who died in the high years of the movement, and feel that they are fortunate to lie in the bitter earth.

"There are some things which are so deep within me that I cannot speak them. Yet I've been fortunate; I've done the things of which I've dreamed. I've made some friends—all but a very few have been in the movement. Those from days before are now scattered beyond recall. Indeed, I have no regrets. But I sense that our days of being useful ARE drawing to an end. This country is so deeply racist that it is almost impossible to ever truly break away from the prison of flesh into which one was born. We feel a sense of detachment from the world now. The world in which we once lived, the conventional world, is not attractive for we have seen IT as the enemy. In the world of the movement, our time is swiftly drawing to a close. All we have is to live our lives in relationship to the people we love.

"Once having lived in the movement at its height, the conventional rewards of success seem of little moment. As the year draws to a close it will mean the death of what we've been, we the few whites still working in the movement.

"We came because—among other reasons—these cries for help that we heard were addressed to the whole world. But at this time and at this place, we are the whole world. Now these days are ending. In passing from the strange dark earth of Mississippi, only love remains as a value to endure."

15

The Success of the 1967 Holmes County Elections

September–November 1967

Excitement was building. We had stuck to the decision to run as Independents in November, and the black slate numbered twelve. The candidates included Robert G. Clark for state representative, Robert R. "Bob" Smith for sheriff, Mary Lee Hightower for circuit clerk, T. C. Johnson for Beat 1 supervisor, Tom Griffin for Beat 1 justice of the peace, Ed McGaw for Beat 1 constable, Ward Montgomery for Beat 2 supervisor, John Henry Malone for Beat 3 supervisor, Willie James Burns for Beat 4 supervisor, John Daniel Wesley for Beat 4 justice of the peace, Griffin McLaurin Jr. for Beat 4 constable, and Ralthus Hayes for Beat 5 supervisor.

The education campaign to encourage people not to vote in the primary had been progressing smoothly until it was sideswiped by Hazel Brannon Smith. She announced she was running for the state senate in the Democratic primary on August 8. Smith, the editor of the *Lexington Advertiser,* was respected by many movement leaders for her editorials supporting civil rights. Those same leaders were now angry because she didn't honor the strategy to skip the primary to vote for black Independent candidates in November. She confused the issue, making people argue about whether to vote in the primary for her.

In order to keep the newly registered black voters away from the polls on primary day, the Holmes County Independent Campaign office sponsored an Independent Voters Workshop. Here's how the flyer read: "On August 8 come to your independent voters workshop. Practice marking ballots for our candidates for November. The names of our candidates

Old Pilgrims Rest leader Howard Taft Bailey (*left*) brought word of the move-ment to his hill community. Later, during the 1967 elections, he made sure can-didate petitions, such as this one from supervisor candidate T. C. Johnson (in hat), were signed properly before they were turned in.

will not be on the August 8 primary ballot. There is no reason for us to go to the polls. Some people are saying that if you don't vote in August then you can't vote in November. But that is a lie. You do not have to vote in the August 8 primary in order to vote in November. Charles Evers of NAACP and Lawrence Guyot of the FDP both say none of the candidates for governor and lieutenant governor are worth voting for. Black people don't need to vote on August 8. Our candidates are independents. Let's save our votes for November 7." Note the reference to the NAACP and the FDP. Those factions had come together for this important election season in order to maximize the black vote.

Most blacks stayed away from the primary. Hazel Brannon Smith didn't succeed. She finished second in the race for nomination in the state Senate, but two weeks later she lost the run-off election to incumbent state senator Ollie Mohamed.

Henry was busy with his new job, and I stayed behind the scenes, documenting significant events. The candidates campaigned at cafés, grocery stores, and community meetings and often by speaking in a public place from the back of a flatbed truck.

The movement leadership had paid for advertising in the past and it was successful. I helped write a radio script for all twelve Independent candidates. They were each encouraged to make a ninety-second tape at the radio station they chose for advertising. The stations suggested were WXTN in Lexington, WOKJ in Jackson, and WDIA in Memphis. The TV stations suggested were WLBT in Jackson, WABC in Greenwood, and WJTV in Jackson. The newspapers were the *Jackson Daily News*, the *Jackson-Clarion Ledger*, and the *Memphis Commercial Appeal*.

Robert G. Clark's message went like this:

Attention: Holmes County voters. This is Robert G. Clark, your independent candidate for state representative, post one. I'm a candidate for your state representative because I want to bring opportunities to the people of Holmes County. Over three quarters of us live in the rural Holmes County where the income is lower than the income of any other rural people in any other county in the state. But we are poor only because we have been deprived of opportunities. I want the opportunity as your state representative to open up better opportunities for all. We need larger checks for dependent children so they can have the opportunity to be fed and clothed and schooled. We need training programs for adults so they can have the opportunity to get good jobs. We need more and better jobs so that all can have the opportunity to provide decently for their families. On Tuesday, November 7, over six thousand new voters have their first opportunity to vote for opportunity. Don't miss it. Join them in voting for Robert T. Clark for state representative, post one. On Tuesday, November 7, make your mark for Robert Clark. Thank you very much.

All the work of campaigning would be lost if blacks were cheated at the polls. The Independent campaign office was so concerned about the inclusion of black poll watchers that they sent letters to the federal

Reverend Willie B. Davis waits across from the 1967 Holmes Freedom Democratic Party Campaign Office on Beale Street.

government and to the state of Mississippi and the Holmes County election committee. A press release openly called for fairness at the polls and showed Holmes citizens that the 1967 election would be under scrutiny. The press release said letters were "signed and sent by the twelve Negro candidates who are running as independents in the November 7 elections. The twelve seek offices ranging from the beat positions of constable, justice of the peace and supervisor, and the countywide positions of sheriff and circuit clerk, to the district position of 19th District state representative, post one."

The letter urged the election commission, Mr. J. W. Moses, chairman, to appoint fairly and proportionally Negro officials, clerks, and managers for each polling place in Holmes County in the November 7 elections. It continued, "Unfair representation of Negroes at the polling tables in November would throw the whole election into question and legal action would be taken. We await written reply from the election commissioners who will be meeting within the next few weeks."

Television and newspaper reports that fall were disheartening. Not only did the men who murdered Schwerner, Chaney, and Goodman get light sentences, between three and ten years, but the lawyers for white candidates were winning in court. Legal maneuvers throughout Mississippi wiped out gains by black candidates. Election officials played all kinds of games, keeping candidates' names off the ballot because they had voted in the primary and denying nominating petitions for trumped-up reasons. The legislature kept changing the rules, and as a result, seventeen Mississippi candidates were disqualified, including Mrs. Fannie Lou Hamer, who was running for a seat in the Mississippi Senate.

One month before the election, in October 1967, Hayes expressed his belief that if Henry had worked on the elections, they would be doing better. Even if blacks were successful in electing six or seven or eight or nine of their candidates, Hayes said he would always believe they would have done better—would have elected ten or eleven or all twelve candidates—had Henry worked on the elections. Despite his understanding of all the Lorenzi justifications for not participating as workers or even organizers, Hayes still thought Henry should have done more.

On Election Day in November, Henry worked in the central movement office while I drove in a tour with several of the candidates, mak-

Etha Ree Rule, a woman with an infectious smile, volunteered daily in the Lexington campaign office.

ing the rounds of the county's fourteen polling places. When the major work was over, Henry and I did join in the overall excitement and final effort. The day would be a victory, even if no black candidates won, because more than one hundred black candidates contested offices across the state and nearly two hundred thousand blacks were registered to vote in Mississippi.

That night in Mississippi, twenty or so black winners were announced, along with eighty white winners. The Holmes movement had two huge victories: Griffin McLaurin Jr. won the seat of Beat 4 constable and Robert G. Clark became the state representative of the two-county district in the Mississippi state legislature.

Henry and I opened the sealed envelopes we had each prepared. They included our predictions of the election outcome. Both of us thought four candidates would win, and while we both had predicted wrong, we were pleased that two had succeeded.

The Jackson newspaper gave a minuscule amount of space to the black victory, emphasizing the election of John Bell Williams for governor. By contrast, the headline "Negro Elected to All-White Mississippi Legislature" appeared in the Thursday, November 9, edition of the *New York Times* above an article stating:

> The triumph of Robert G. Clark, a thirty-seven-year-old Negro educator with a Masters degree in sociology from Michigan State University, who was elected to the state House of Representatives, was a dramatic breakthrough for the state's slowly emerging Negro political forces. No Negroes have sat in the domed, marble walled chamber of the house since the state's white Redeemers disenfranchised the former slaves and stamped out the last remnants of Reconstruction around the turn of the century. Mr. Clark won his seat by defeating James P. Love, a sixty-five-year-old Holmes County planter and cattleman, who had held it for more than ten years and who had served as chairman of the educational committee. The representative elect, who is a part-time instructor at Holmes County Junior College and a former executive director of a local anti-poverty program, was backed by the militant Freedom Democratic Party, a predominantly Negro

group. In addition to his masters degree, Mr. Clark finished most of his work on a Ph.D. at the University of Michigan before returning to Holmes County, a part of the state's delta region.

Henry and I were happy to have stayed to see Clark elected. We stayed long after most white, outside workers had left Holmes, primarily because we had been accepted by movement members and we knew our place as outsiders and whites. From the beginning, we had been conscious of our role as organizers of mechanisms and structures that could carry on without dependence on outside workers.

The 1967 elections were the strongest kind of success. Those two strong black victories were the culmination of the Holmes County movement. From the beginning the Holmes County movement had been dynamic. Led by landowning black farmers, its members welcomed SNCC workers and white volunteers, like Henry and me, and organized an effective political force. Holmes County was a showcase of black organization and dedication, and the 1967 election was its high point.

Not only did we elect two candidates to office, but we also won on other critical fronts. We won because the middle class and the landless poor worked together. We won because the factions—the FDP-led coalition and the NAACP—recognized that white supremacy was the real enemy and set aside their political and personal differences to support the common goal. The black leaders won by taking their fate in their own hands. They won by running their own campaign. Freedom's thunder cracked through the ugliness of Mississippi racism and its blatant cruelty.

Representative Clark was the first black since the 1800s to sit in the Mississippi State House. His was the highest office won by a black in all of Mississippi in 1967, the first year African Americans voted. The eleven other local people who ran were victorious just by running for office, by doing what no one else had done in any of their lifetimes, by being a critical element in bringing change.

Their Stories: Mary Lee Hightower

Mary Lee Hightower was talking to me after Robert Clark's inauguration: "When Robert Clark was inaugurated into the Mississippi House of

Representatives, Mr. Clark's aunts and uncles were there, along with his nephew Richard and a cousin. They weren't going to let but six in, but we all had tickets and there were seven or eight of us. Mr. Bailey and I went in. But Mr. Anthony, Mr. Bruce, and Mr. Patterson didn't get in. They stayed out in the lobby or sat in their cars and waited around. Mr. Bruce didn't want Mr. Clark to have to go back to the hotel alone.

"It started around noontime, and we didn't get through 'til around three o'clock. We were all up in the balcony. We couldn't get a seat. Every time we tried to sit down, some of them white people would tell us them seats was reserved. We finally fixed them and just went down by the railing and stood along it and the ones behind couldn't see. After we did that, one of the white men gave me his seat. He said, "Say lady, would you like to sit here? Here, take my seat." So then I sat down and all the whites got up and left from that whole section. So we all sat down."

Their Stories: Robert G. Clark, at a Farmers Co-op Meeting

Inside the community center, Howard Taft Bailey's farmers co-op meeting had already started in the main room. Three long rows of folding chairs extended from one side wall to the other, with no center aisle. The thirty or so local farmers, mainly men, sat facing forward, with their backs to me as I entered. Mrs. Epps and Alice and one or two other women were the only ladies present. We had come to hear Robert Clark, the newly inaugurated state representative. The listeners were all quiet and bundled up with their coats left on, because the heater was not throwing enough heat to take the chill off. Clark had been speaking for a while in his loud, almost shouting-sounding voice, carefully and with unique near-mispronunciation throughout his words ringing, almost grating.

Noise of laughter and loud talking from the library filtered in. Finally round Dave Howard, the Mileston farmer on whose land the community center was built, lifted up his arms slightly, one finger extending just over his head, and raised himself slowly with concentrated care. With a sticky-sweet smile plastered on his face, he walked backwards, tiptoeing, and finally with grim determination, twisted around, holding his breath, and turned to leave the room. After a few moments the noise from the library stopped, and Howard returned, carefully tiptoed in, and sat down in his seat.

Robert G. Clark was the first to fully use the new campaign office. Besides this desk in the meeting room, Clark had his own desk in a smaller, back-room office.

Clark spoke mainly about the need for getting together with co-ops, diversifying from cotton crops, going into cucumbers for pickles. "The whites up in those offices will tell you that you can't make any money on cucumbers. They point to some white man, Liberto, and say he lost five thousand dollars on his cucumber crop one year and they don't say it actually, but what they're really saying is, that if Liberto can't make it, then no Negro better try, because the Negro certainly couldn't make money on such a hard crop. But what they don't tell you is Liberto didn't have a proper workforce, he didn't have people that will go out and pick those pickles at the right time. You need to watch pickles, pick them when they're right, watch them every day and get them just when they're ripe for picking. You could make a lot of money on that kind of crop. There is okra and sweet potatoes, too. I want to tell you that the sweet potato is the best crop there is. You could make more money per acre on sweet potatoes than you can on any other crop."

He talked more about co-ops and the need for farmers to get together and start making new crops and learning about them and getting away from cotton. When he finished, he sat down to a good amount of applause.

In the library, the cause of all the previous noise was just four people playing whist at the desk: Nutchie and Jim, Dorothy Vinko, and Pump Rucker. They were laughing and having a good time, and the transistor radio on the window sill was still blaring tinnily with soul-WLAC-Nashville, Tennessee, music.

Their Stories: A Late-Night Meeting with Robert G. Clark

Clark and I sat in his car and talked. The light from the radio, loudly narrating the events of a pro basketball team, was the only light in the black leather interior of the car. The bucket seats and the rich carpet, all bright black and gleaming new, were part of the lemon-yellow new car, borrowed by Clark from somebody in Jackson. Clark's eyes and teeth and bright white shirt were really all that could be distinguished inside the car. He was excited, exuberant, and filled with boyish delight. His words spilled out on their own and in response to my many interrupting questions.

I hadn't seen him since the morning after the election. We had talked long-distance right before New Year's on the night he heard that Love had dropped the challenge against his being seated.

We talked of his seating, his daily routine, his plans, vacation, and the pup he had given me a few months earlier, after Puppydog was killed. He mentioned the departure of Alec, who had left Mississippi after the elections. He said he had left my "Some People" story in Jackson, implying that it was too valuable to leave in irresponsible hands.

Clark is smooth and has a warm way of making the person he is talking to think that he thinks that person is very important to him. He also has a way of seeming very cool but so disorganized and busy, busy, that you must be taking up his time, his valuable important time, speaking of trivia with him. It's almost as though he has read a lot of books and knows all the proper rules, like involving a lot of people, playing up to local leaders, patronizing local machines, and so forth. He spouts the rules to local leaders. This is either a sign of his nonsophistication or the reverse, letting people feel "in," to see a part of him and know his techniques.

He was his normal energetic, ecstatic, flurried self. "Yes, yes, they dropped the challenge against me, and gave me no trouble at all. Old Love wanted to take it on, but I heard John Bell called it off. They just recognized how bad it would look. Our lawyers were really running him. My seat is right up there in the very front row—there's an empty seat next to me, that's right, that's where the speaker of the house sits. Of course, he's always up in front.

"I've been getting lots of mail, that's right, lots of mail. No, not only from people in the county. It's from all over the country, people send me congratulations and good wishes. Also I've had three I believe, of the other kind. You know, 'dear nigger, why don't you, dirty so-and-so black' they carry on just like that, saying what they're going to do to me, calling names and such as that.

"This pistol, well you know why I carry it. I don't think anything big is going to come up, but there always is some danger from some nut or someone. I rode through that parade in a Cadillac. I didn't get to go to the inaugural ball. That was by invitation only and naturally I didn't get invited to that. And then for the inauguration speeches, the announcement they sent around, said it started at noon. I got there at 11:30 and it was already going on. You see how it is. They just try any way they can. You got to keep calling and asking and pushing.

"Well for the parade, they said it was a certain time, and Alan and I got there three hours ahead of time. We were the first car there. The colored policeman came up to tell us to move, you know, they were getting ready to start and then he said, 'Oh I'm sorry, you are Representative Clark. I didn't realize this was you. You're in the parade.'

"This is the first year that they had it that the state didn't provide cars for the parade. This year the legislators had to use their own cars. Well, I didn't want them to have any excuse whatsoever. So I called up Al and I told them to find me a good, sharp Cadillac and he did. You should've seen that. We just rode in that car. Of course, we weren't the first car in there once they got lined up. But the people were really something, these white fellows, some of them riding standing up, you know, waving out one side and the other.

"I was just sitting there, driving, you know, and when our car would pass, all those people just cheered and shouted. Yes, yes, it was good."

16

Changed Lives

Celebrating the Movement and Its People

We rarely celebrated. We just kept on working. The files Henry and I so carefully packed were full of the struggle, the lawsuits, the posters, the data, the agendas, and the strategy. It is rare to find information on the final project outcomes of any of the initiatives.

Although they deserved it, I don't remember any event to honor the First Fourteen and others who tried to register in those earliest days: Alma Mitchell Carnegie, Sam Redmond, John Daniel Wesley, Reverend Jesse James Russell, Rosebud Clark, and Hartman Turnbow, Annie Bell Mitchell, Charlie Carnegie, Norman Clark, Chester Hayes, Ralthus Hayes, Jack Louie, Ozell Mitchell, Joe T. Mitchell, Reverend Nelson Trent, and the others. They were respected and their stories were told in meetings, at kitchen tables, and on front porches, but there was too much to do to stop and celebrate.

In the early days, the Holmes County Community Center at Mileston embodied the movement work, and hope, and excitement. Standing there, just off the highway and the train tracks, visible to all who passed by, the HCCC shouted to the world that there were people taking charge of their lives. It was a symbol of democracy and self-government, of education and health care. It was a symbol of defiance to the system.

The FDP, too, picked up and carried on that enthusiasm and energy as leaders built the movement throughout the county.

When Ralthus Hayes and Henry asked me to read my "The Some People" story at a 1967 election kick-off meeting, it was for a purpose. We wanted to unite the grassroots leaders and the professionals in an election effort. I read, and those in that crowded meeting room heard my tribute to their actions. And finally, we celebrated.

Robert Cooper Howard (*left*) and Burrell Tate (*next to Howard*) lighten a Countywide Meeting with their laughter.

We celebrated the civil rights leaders of Holmes County who did something more than just live as their mothers and fathers had before them. They changed their lives—and not just each individual, not just their families, not just Holmes County—they worked to change the lives of all people.

It was an honor and an education to work alongside them.

Afterword

Henry and I spent nearly two additional years in the county after the elections, but we stayed out of the political realm as much as possible. Henry was engaged in his economic and health research programs. He and Demitri Shimkin led an innovative and extensive study of Holmes County, making it perhaps the most thoroughly researched county in the state. Some of their work was funded by the Department of Health, Education, and Welfare. I spent much of that time photographing, recording, and interviewing local people and writing descriptions of them and their activities.

The Head Start program in Mileston, one of the very first in the United States, expanded and prospered and is still strong.

The health clinic, started by Josephine Disparti in the kitchen of the Holmes County Community Center, became a model for comprehensive community health centers, which serve more than 30 million Americans today.

Robert Clark served for thirty-six years in the Mississippi state legislature, running the House Education Committee. In the final ten years of his tenure, he served as Speaker Pro Tempore. His son, Wandrick Bryant Clark, won his seat in 2003. Since the 1967 elections, hundreds of Holmes black men and women have been elected as school board members, mayors, sheriffs, and other public officials.

Three years after we left the county in 1969, Henry and I returned to show off our one-month-old son Aaron to the local people. Then I did not return until months after Henry's death in 1982, when I went back to Holmes to share in mourning for Henry with Holmes leaders. I also helped on Robert Clark's campaign for the U.S. Congress, which turned out to be unsuccessful.

Over the years I visited often, spending time with local friends such as Rosie Head Howze, Walter Bruce, Robert Clark, Hartman Turnbow, the Montgomery family, and Norman Clark. I celebrated at two family "Appreciations"—one for Howard Taft Bailey and the other for Bernice Patton Montgomery.

Several times in the 1980s and 1990s, long-distance-truck-driving Edgar Love stopped in D.C. to visit me and Aaron. Then in 1999, three years after I moved to Duluth, Minnesota, Edgar Love, Walter Bruce, and Zelma Williams Croom came to Duluth. They spoke at the premiere of my Holmes County photography exhibit "The Some People of That Place" at the Tweed Museum of Art on the University of Minnesota Duluth (UMD) campus.

In 2001 I brought to Holmes for the very first time that same photographic story of their movement, in an expanded touring form. The FDP displayed the one-hundred-piece exhibit for nine months. The black school superintendent provided buses for every school child through all twelve grades to come to Lexington to see it.

Zelma came back in 2004 to speak at the University of Wisconsin–Superior's Multicultural Center opening of the "The Some People" touring exhibit. She returned in 2008 to speak about the Mileston Head Start to UMD students in early childhood education.

Acknowledgments

After Henry and I left Mississippi, many people assisted as I worked to get the Holmes County story into a publishable form. During the final five years, I worked closely with Cheryl Reitan, a cofacilitator of my writing group. Cheryl, a gifted editor, writer, and arranger, became as passionate as I am in believing in the vital importance of the work in Holmes County to the civil rights movement. Supremely energetic and persistent, she possessed a keen desire to make the book accessible. I'm very fortunate to have found Cheryl when I needed her. We worked with the hundreds of pages I had already written and the hundreds of documents I had saved to use in a final manuscript. Her interest, generosity, discipline, and pushiness allowed me to see how I could use my on-the-spot 1960s records of the voices and lives of local people to tell their story.

I'd like to mention three inspirational resources that sustained me through the decades as I wrote this book: *Sing for Freedom: The Story of the Civil Rights Movement through Its Songs*, edited and compiled by Guy and Candie Carawan (Bethlehem, PA: Sing Out, 1990); *Local People: The Struggle for Civil Rights in Mississippi*, by John Dittmer (Urbana: University of Illinois Press, 1994); and *Memories of the Southern Civil Rights Movement*, photography and words by Danny Lyon (Chapel Hill: University of North Carolina Press, 1992).

I have dedicated this entire work to the Holmes County community and its leaders. I'll never forget the special qualities of several of the First Fourteen: the spirited being of Alma Mitchell Carnegie; the sweetness and strength of her brother Ozell Mitchell; the power and heart of Hartman Turnbow; the solid, rational constancy of Ralthus Hayes; and the gentle, pure goodness of Norman Clark. The strength and courage of others also deeply inspired me—Charlie Carnegie, Rosebud Clark, Chester Hayes, Jack Louie, Annie Bell Mitchell, Sam Redmond, Reverend

Jesse James Russell, Joe T. Mitchell, John Daniel Wesley, and Reverend Nelson Trent.

I must name some of the other Holmes leaders with whom I worked closely and who taught me much: Eugene Montgomery, Bernice Patton Montgomery, T. C. "Top Cat" Johnson, Edgar Love, Howard Taft Bailey, Walter Bruce, Rosie Head, Tony (Anthony Leonard) Jones, Alice Mae Epps, Elease Gallion, Thelma "Nutchie" Head, Zelma Williams, Nancy Epps, Daisey Montgomery Lewis, Mississippi State Representative Robert G. Clark, Edith Quinn, Mary Lee Hightower, Emmitt "Bay" Rule, John Malone, Ed McGaw Jr., Willie James Burns, Robert R. "Bob" Smith, Vernon Tom Griffin, Griffin McLaurin Jr., Lucille Davis, Burrell Tate, Vanderbilt and Cora Roby, Lela Mae Walden, Matilda Burns, and Robert Cooper Howard. And Otha Lee Wright, Dino West, and Chrissie Epps are but a few of the children who marked my heart. Sam Epps and Dimp Walden are two of the older boys who shared their wisdom with me.

Lawrence Guyot is the organizer and leader who was most helpful to Henry and me during the sixties. We stayed in touch over the years, and he focused his special support and encouragement on me and my writing. Constance Curry, John Dittmer, and Ben Bagdikian have in varying ways been my mentors, advisers, and editors. Other outside volunteers, workers, and organizers who were most helpful to us in our earliest years were Mary Brumder, Abe Osheroff, Jim Boebel, Don Hamer, Larry Stevens, John Allen, Josephine Disparti, Harriet Tanzman, Jan Hillegas, Alec Shimkin, Lisa Marshall, Ed Brown, Sam Howze, Joe Lewis Harris, Hollis Watkins, and Ed King. Attorneys Al Bronstein, Mel Leventhal, Marian Wright (Edelman), Henry Aronson, and Armand Derfner are only a few of those so-essential-to-survival 1960s civil rights lawyers.

From the 1970s through the mid-1990s I lived in Washington, D.C., and a variety of friends gave particularly supportive, spiritual strengths: Loret "Lolly Lune" Ulmschneider, Alda Curtis, Judith Treesberg, Sue Silber, Deb George, Deb Friedman, Jane Mara, Kate McEvoy, Lorraine Sorrel, Ellen Isaly, and the special friends of the New Family commune and the First Things First Books for Women collective. Colleagues at my editing position at the Center for Strategic and International Studies lent me their kind support for my own manuscript: M. Jon Vondracek, Nancy Eddy, Jean Newsom, and Mihn LeMau.

Duluth's restorative outdoor beauty has been a blessing. I am also grateful for the Duluth arts community, especially for my live-work studio and community at the Washington Studios Artist's Cooperative, the Norcroft Women's Writing Retreat, the Blacklock Nature Sanctuary, the Arrowhead Regional Arts Council, Lake Superior Writers, Poetry Harbor, and my writing group.

Individuals who sustained me emotionally and sometimes financially include Judy Sausen, Lyn Clark Pegg, Carla Blumberg, Barb Neubert, Jill Hinners, Mary Brumder, Ellen Pence, Amanda McCormick, Graham Barnes, Tony Ferguson, Linda Glaser, Liz Minette, Jean Sramek, and Ann Klefstad. Special friends who actually assisted me in producing the book include Becky Norlien, Mali Lorenz, Erin Cartwright, and Amy Wilcox from Loaves and Fishes, who sent me an intern.

In the end, and from beginning to end, I must thank my families: my Sadoff, Harris, Sheffer, and Abram families and Henry's Lorenzi, Shaffer, and Malacarne families. Our son Aaron has been ever present and ready to share his personal and academic truths. Most essential of all is Henry John (Lorenzi) Sojourner. I am thankful for his being and having been and for the memory of him, which has been with me always.

Chronology of Movement Events in Holmes County and the United States

Cheryl Reitan and Kimberly Stella

May 7, 1955: NAACP leader Reverend George Wesley Lee is assassinated in Belzoni, Mississippi (Humphreys County), after registering to vote and encouraging others to register. "41 Lives for Freedom," *The Civil Rights Memorial,* Southern Poverty Law Center, 2005, www.crmvet.org/mem/41lives.htm, accessed April 2, 2010.

1961: Freedom Riders come through Jackson, Mississippi. All are jailed in Jackson and then sent to the Parchman Prison Farm. "Freedom Ride 1961," in *The Student Voice 1960–1965: Periodical of the Student Nonviolent Coordination Committee,* ed. Clayborne Carson (Westport, CT: Meckler, 1990), 45 (April and May 1961).

October 1, 1962: Campus riots break out in protest of James Meredith's enrollment in the University of Mississippi–Oxford. Meredith is the first black person to study at the University of Mississippi. The riots cause two deaths and seventy-five injuries and necessitate protection from federal troops until Meredith graduates in 1963. Claude Sitton, "Negro at Mississippi U. as Barnet Yields; 3 Dead in Campus Riot; 6 Marshalls," *New York Times,* October 1, 1962, 1.

1962–1963: Holmes County black farmers go to Greenwood in adjoining Leflore County to attend SNCC-organized Freedom Meetings. Wesley C. Hogan, *Many Minds, One Heart: SNCC's Dream for a New America* (Chapel Hill: Univ. of North Carolina Press, 2007), 86–87.

March 1963: Bob Moses and another SNCC worker meet with Mileston citizens to talk about voter registration and going to the courthouse to try to register. Letter by Howard Taft Bailey to the Board of Trustees, Holmes County Community Center, Mileston, January 7, 1965.

April 1963: The First Fourteen attempt to register at the courthouse in Lexington. Soon afterward, Hartman Turnbow's home is firebombed. He is arrested for arson. "5 Negroes in Vote Drive Charged with Arson in Mississippi Blasts," *New York Times,* May 10, 1963, 14.

May 3–5, 1963: Martin Luther King Jr. is arrested in Birmingham. "Racial Strife," *New York Times,* May 5, 1963, 191.

June 11, 1963: Medgar Evers is assassinated in Jackson. Myrlie Evers, "He Said He Wouldn't Mind Dying—If . . .," in *The Autobiography of Medgar Evers,* ed. Myrlie Evers-Williams and Manning Marable (New York: Basic Civitas Books, 2005), 304–8.

August 28, 1963: The March on Washington for Jobs and Freedom draws 250,000 to D.C. "Program of Rights March," *New York Times,* August 28, 1963, 21.

September 15, 1963: Four young girls are killed in a Birmingham church bombing. Claude Sitton, "Birmingham Bomb Kills 4 Negro Girls in Church; Riots Flare; 2 Boys Slain," *New York Times,* September 16, 1963, 1.

November 1963: Black residents of Holmes County join with other black Mississippians to cast ballots in the mock Freedom Vote. "The Student Voice, November 11, 1963: Over 70,000 Cast Freedom Ballots," in Carson, *The Student Voice,* 77.

November 22, 1963: President John F. Kennedy is assassinated. "Ambush Building Chosen with Care," *New York Times,* November 23, 1963, 8.

May 1964: White newspaper publisher Hazel Brannon Smith condemns violence against civil rights activists and blacks in the *Lexington Advertiser,* her Holmes County weekly. She is awarded a Pulitzer Prize for courageous journalism. "Pulitzer Prizes," *New York Times,* May 5, 1964, 42.

Summer 1964: The Council of Federated Organizations (COFO) Freedom Summer begins. The project attracts nearly one thousand outside volunteers. Most are white college students, among them law students, but also included are lawyers, clergy, and doctors. They come to Mississippi to work in the movement, in most cases for the summer. Joe Street, "Reconstructing Education from the Bottom Up: SNCC's 1964 Mississippi Summer Project and African American Culture," *Journal of American Studies* 38, no. 2 (August 2004): 273–96.

June 1964: The Holmes County movement welcomes more than thirty outside volunteers as part of Freedom Summer. They teach literacy, political organizing, and voter education in Freedom Schools, churches, and makeshift community centers in Mileston, Tchula, Old Pilgrims Rest, and Sunnymount–Poplar Springs. California carpenters Abe Osheroff and Jim Boebel begin work on a community center at Mileston, built with twenty thousand dollars that Abe raised. Daniel Perlstein, "Teaching Freedom: SNCC and the Creation of the Mississippi Freedom Schools," *History of Education Quarterly* 30, no. 3 (Autumn 1990): 297–324.

Holmes County blacks are turned away when they try to attend a Democratic Party precinct meeting. They elect themselves delegates to the state convention of their own Mississippi Freedom Democratic Party (MFDP). Claude Sitton, "Mississippi Freedom Party Bids for Democratic Convention Role," *New York Times,* July 21, 1964, 19.

June 21, 1964: James Chaney, Andrew Goodman, and Michael Schwerner are murdered in Neshoba County. Philip Benjamin, "Families of Rights Workers Voice Grief and Hope," *New York Times,* August 6, 1964, 16.

July 2, 1964: President Lyndon B. Johnson signs the Civil Rights Act into law. E. W. Kenworthy, "President Signs Civil Rights Bill; Bids All Back It," *New York Times,* July 3, 1964, 1.

August 1964: Holmes County residents attend the state MFDP convention. Hartman Turnbow is elected as one of the delegates to the Democratic National Convention. "Over 800 Meet at MFDP Convention," in Carson, *The Student Voice,* 45 (August 12, 1964).

August 9, 1964: Armed guards are posted at movement homes and churches after an attempt was made to blow up the construction site of the Mileston Community Center. Civil Rights in Mississippi Digital Archive: Freedom Summer Incident Summary by City or County, http://digilib.usm.edu/crmda_incident2.php, accessed November 23, 2011.

August 25, 1964: The Democratic Party holds its national convention in Atlantic City, New Jersey. E. W. Kenworthy, "Alabamians Push into Convention," *New York Times,* August 25, 1964, 1.

August 29, 1964: Johnson signs into law the Economic Opportunity Act of 1964. The act creates the Office of Economic Opportunity on August 30, 1964. Todd Steven Burroughs, "The Administration of Lyndon B. Johnson," in *Encyclopedia of African American History, 1896–Present,* ed. Paul Finkelman and Cary D. Wintz (New York: Oxford Univ. Press, 2009).

October 18, 1964: The Holmes County Community Center at Mileston opens. "Mileston Opens Community Center," in Carson, *The Student Voice,* 197 (October 18, 1964).

October 30–November 2, 1964: The MFDP holds a statewide Freedom Vote with 80,000 voting throughout the state and 2,500 in Holmes County. Victoria Gray, Fannie Lou Hamer, and Annie Devine are on the ballot and get elected to the U.S. House of Representatives in the Freedom Vote. Black Holmes citizens vote. Freedom vote tallies, COFO press release, November 4, 1964, Historical Manuscripts and Photographs, Univ. of Southern Mississippi Digital Collections, http://digilib.usm.edu/u?/manu,124, accessed March 11, 2010.

November–December 1964: The federal agency dealing with the farmers' cotton allotments, the Agricultural Stabilization and Conservation Service (ASCS), holds county-level elections for the cotton allotment board. For the first time, black farmers learn from COFO workers that blacks can vote in the ASCS elections. They run candidates. One wins and is later harassed. *News-Sheet on the Lorenzis,* Holmes County, MS, September 27, 1966, 3.

December 7, 1964: The Holmes County Community Center opens a kindergarten. The local movement gives out ten tons of clothing donated by the National Council of Churches. *Holmes County Community Center at Mileston Newsletter,* January 14, 1965.

January 1965: More than forty Holmes movement leaders travel to D.C. to support the Congressional Challenge; they get firsthand national political experience. More than six hundred MFDP supporters hold a silent march in front of the House of Representatives. Mike Thelwell, *The Student Voice,* July 1965: "MFDP–Congressional Challenge," in Carson, *The Student Voice,* 225.

January 28, 1965: Josephine Disparti, a northern nurse assigned to Mileston by the Medical Committee for Human Rights, sets up a clinic in the community center. *Holmes County Community Center at Mileston Newsletter,* May 10, 1965.

January–February 1965: Lawyers from around the country come to Holmes County to help the MFDP present depositions in the Congressional Challenge. In Greenwood, Mississippi, more than six hundred Holmes movement members present evidence to the House Committee on Election Procedures about being prohibited from voting. Chana Kai Lee, *For Freedom's Sake: The Life of Fannie Lou Hamer* (Urbana: Univ. of Illinois Press, 1999), 110–13.

February 21, 1965: Malcolm X is assassinated. Paul L. Montgomery, "Harlem Is Quiet as News Spreads," *New York Times,* February 22, 1965, 11.

Spring 1965: The Holmes County FDP opens an office in Lexington. *News-Sheet on the Lorenzis,* September 27, 1966.

March 7, 1965: Protesters are beaten and fifty are hospitalized in Selma, Alabama, at the Bloody Sunday March. Roy Reed, "Alabama Police Use Gas and Clubs to Rout Negroes," *New York Times,* March 8, 1965, 1.

March 29, 1965: Henry and Sue Lorenzi, Hartman Turnbow, Mrs. Epps, and Mrs. Sanders return from a speaking engagement in Iowa. While fixing a flat tire, they are threatened with rifles by a crowd of whites. The three black movement leaders flee into the woods. *Newsletter from Sue and Henry Lorenzi to Donors and Friends,* Lexington, MS, April 1, 1965.

Spring–Summer 1965: Talks begin at the community center about starting cooperative businesses. A small group of people start a leather workshop. *Holmes County Community Center at Mileston Newsletter,* November 11, 1965.

Hundreds more blacks continue to try to register. The twenty-one-question registration form is changed to six questions, and more begin to "pass the test." By summer's end nearly six hundred are registered. Barbara Brandt, "The Voting Bill—How Does It Work," in Carson, *The Student Voice,* 228 (August 30, 1965).

April 2, 1965: Duluth, Minnesota, citizens send a truckload of goods to Holmes County, Mississippi, including canned goods, a new set of encyclopedias, and money. The shipment follows their late-1964 truckload of clothing for families in need. "Duluth to Send Goods to Negroes," *Duluth New Tribune,* April 2, 1965.

May 1965: The Holmes County school board receives two petitions calling for school integration—one from 467 black parents, the other from 445 black students. Black plantation workers sign petitions asking for schooling for their children. Many are forced off the plantations, becoming homeless and jobless. Petition to Board of Education of Holmes County, Superintendent of Education for Holmes County, May 3, 1965;

and Petition to the School Board for the Holmes County Public Schools, April 1965.

Summer 1965: Federal District Judge Harold Cox orders Holmes County to desegregate its schools, four grades per year, starting with the earliest grades. Gene Roberts, "Mass Integration Is Quiet in South," *New York Times*, August 31, 1965, 1.

June 1965: Head Start opens in Holmes County Community Center at Mileston, then in Tchula, Sunnymount–Poplar Springs, Old Pilgrims Rest, and Second Pilgrims Rest. All five movement communities are assisted and become part of CDGM. Findlay, "The Mainline Church and Head Start in Mississippi," 238.

Child Development Group of Mississippi (CDGM) Head Start schools run out of funds only a few months after starting in summer 1965. Some local communities open their centers on a volunteer basis; they and some new communities begin working to get re-funding from the government. James F. Findlay, "The Mainline Church and Head Start in Mississippi: Religious Activism in the Sixties," *Church History* 64, no. 2 (June 1995), 243.

June 8, 1965: More than five hundred people march in Lexington in support of the MFDP and black voting rights in Holmes County, and more than six hundred black citizens of Holmes County, most of them recently registered, are not allowed to vote at their precincts in a special statewide election. Paul L. Montgomery, "472 Are Arrested in Jackson March; 5 Charge Beating," *New York Times*, June 15, 1965, 1.

July 1965: Holmes County citizens join the MFDP Freedom March in Jackson. More than one hundred are arrested and jailed at the state fairgrounds. Some are badly beaten and, on national television, charge the police with brutality. "200 from Holmes County Join in Freedom March in Jackson Mississippi," *Lexington Advertiser*, June 24, 1965.

August 4, 1965: Congress passes a national voting rights bill that the president, two days later, signs into law. On the day of the law's passage, movement people send scores of sworn statements, affidavits, and testimony about the unfair registration process and ask for a federal registrar. E. W. Kenworthy, "Johnson Signs Voting Rights Bill; Orders Immediate Enforcement; 4 Suits Will Challenge Poll Tax," *New York Times,* August 7, 1965, 1.

August 11, 1965: The Watts riots break out in Los Angeles. Peter Bart, "New Negro Riots Erupt on Coast; 3 Reported Shot," *New York Times,* August 13, 1965, 1.

September 1965: Nearly 190 Holmes County black children, the highest number in the state, enroll in grades one to four in the county's public, formerly all-white schools. Many white children withdraw from the Lexington and Tchula desegregated schools. Whites set up private academies for white students. Eventually, the NAACP files a lawsuit against the school board for using state funds for private academies. Black children remain in the desegregated schools in spite of harassment. John Herber, "School Integration Pace May Triple," *New York Times,* September 5, 1965, 34.

Crosses are burned at homes and businesses in the county. White men wearing capes like those of Ku Klux Klansmen ride in a parade at night with lights on inside their cars and trucks to frighten blacks and sympathetic whites. *Holmes County Community Center at Mileston Newsletter,* November 11, 1965.

Mississippi passes a new law that keeps more than five hundred black children out of Holmes County schools and thousands out all over the state. Parents and children protest in Washington. A lawsuit is filed that Mississippi quickly loses, and all the children are allowed back into school. Gene Roberts, "Mississippi Law Bars Hundreds from Schools," *New York Times,* September 11, 1965, 11.

Henry M. Aronson, Marian E. Wright, and other attorneys file a motion in the U.S. District Court in Jackson, Mississippi, for a temporary restraining order and preliminary and permanent injunctions for denying plaintiffs admission to public schools. *Willie Earl Carthan, et al. v. Mississippi State Board of Education, et al.,* U.S. District Court, Southern District of Mississippi, Jackson Division, September 1965.

September 17, 1965: Holmes County residents raise more than fifteen hundred dollars to send sixty Holmes FDP members to Washington to support the MFDP Congressional Challenge. They talk, march, lobby, and mix with representatives from all over the nation. Sitting in spectators' seats in the House of Representatives, they watch the final vote on their Challenge, which does not pass. After a year and a half of work, the Challenge is over. Lee, *For Freedom's Sake*, 110–13.

Fall 1965: Work on the annual farmers' ASCS elections yields big victories—six black farmer candidates win places on the committee and four become alternates. Also, a month-long official investigation is made of the county ASCS election officials and their office. *News-Sheet on the Lorenzis*, September 27, 1966, 6.

The house of Aaron Malone, whose children have enrolled in the formerly all-white school, is attacked. His wife is shot as she stands inside holding a baby in her arms and comforting the rest of the children around her. A bullet to her knee cripples her. *Holmes County Community Center at Mileston Newsletter*, November 11, 1965.

Some young people in Lexington start a boycott of stores. "An Open Letter to the White Business Men and Leaders of Lexington," *Lexington Advertiser*, December 16, 1965.

November 8, 1965: The U.S. attorney general sends a federal registrar to Lexington in response to the affidavits filed over a four-month period charging continued discrimination by the circuit clerk. More than two thousand people get registered to vote in just two months. "Federal Examiner Comes to Holmes County," *Lexington Advertiser*, November 25, 1965.

February 1966: Nearly one thousand movement people come together in a Poor Peoples Conference to discuss housing, land, jobs, and food. Protest arises because Mississippi refuses to give out the $20 million worth of food for the needy from the federal government. Fifty men, women, and children from the meeting, including Mrs. Alma Mitchell Carnegie from Holmes, march and demonstrate at the Greenville Air Base. "Mississippi Air Base Occupied by Negroes in Search of Jobs," *New York Times*, February 1, 1966, 23.

Head Start school funding starts up again as the program receives new financing for six months. Between September 1965 and February 1966, the schools operated on a volunteer basis. A total of nine centers are funded: Mileston, Tchula, Sunnymount–Poplar Springs, Old Pilgrims Rest, Second Pilgrims Rest, Mount Olive, Long Branch, Pickens, and Goodman. The new centers fix up buildings, recruit children, and hire staff. Findlay, "The Mainline Church and Head Start in Mississippi," 243.

March 7, 1966: Approximately five hundred blacks and thirty whites meet. The Community Action Program (CAP) poverty programs are restructured to allow significant community input. "Holmes CAP Advisory Group," *Lexington Advertiser,* March 10, 1966, 1.

March 25, 1966: The U.S. Supreme Court outlaws the poll tax. "Court's Final Word on Poll Taxes: 'No,'" *New York Times,* March 27, 1966.

Spring 1966: Busloads of people from Holmes County and other Mississippi movement communities go to the U.S. Capitol to demand a hearing regarding Head Start funding. Funding Bill HR 15111 passes on September 29, 1966. Maris A. Vinovskis, *The Birth of Head Start* (Chicago: Univ. of Chicago Press, 2005), 123.

The Holmes movement watchdogs antipoverty funds. More than five hundred people crowd into the courtroom of the Holmes County Courthouse for an Office of Economic Opportunity (OEO) CAP meeting. Blacks are elected to committees, and more communities invite FDP and Head Start workers to help with OEO programs. "Anti-Poverty Program Meeting Overflows Court House Here: Program to Continue," *Holmes County Herald,* March 10, 1966, 1.

April 4, 1966: Six candidates file to run in the state Democratic Party primary. The MFDP candidates include Reverend Clifton R. Whitley, who is running for a seat in the U.S. Senate. The other candidates run for the U.S. House of Representatives: First Congressional District, Dock Drummond; Second Congressional District, Ralthus Hayes; Third Congressional District, Reverend Edwin King; Fourth Congressional District, Clint Collier; and Fifth Congressional District, Lawrence Guyot. Mississippi Freedom Democratic Party press release: Six Candidates File to Run in the State Democratic Party Primary, April 4, 1966, and Emergency Bulletin: Primary Elections.

June 4, 1966: Right before Election Day, a recently activated Holmes Ku Klux Klan tries to scare blacks away from voting. They hold a night-time rally—complete with a twenty-five-foot flaming cross and a speech by the Grand Dragon of the State of Mississippi. "Dear Faithful Few," *Holmes County Community Center at Mileston Newsletter,* June 18, 1966.

June 6, 1966: James H. Meredith is shot by a sniper after beginning a lone civil rights march, known as the March against Fear. Meredith began walking from Memphis, Tennessee, to Jackson, Mississippi, on June 5. The Meredith March continued from northern Mississippi, where Meredith was shot, to Jackson. Jonathan Randal, "Onward They March and It's No Fun," *New York Times,* June 18, 1966, 20.

Many from Holmes join the March against Fear. SNCC worker Willie Ricks gives a speech on black power at the courthouse rally in Lexington. Drew Hanson, *Dream: Martin Luther King, Jr., and the Speech That Inspired a Nation* (New York: HarperCollins, 2005), 187.

June 7, 1966: On Election Day for the 1966 primary elections, 2,500 black voters turn out in a steady stream to vote at Holmes County's polling places. Black voter registration in Holmes County tops 4,500. Reverend Clinton Whitley, running for the U.S. Senate, won majorities in two predominately black river counties, Claiborne and Jefferson. "Dear Faithful Few," June 18, 1966.

Summer 1966: The FDP organizes block captains and precinct leaders in every beat. "Dear Faithful Few," June 18, 1966.

August 31, 1966: Several stores in Edwards, Mississippi, are threatened with closure because of a boycott. Groups throughout Mississippi demand that every public place be open to blacks as well as whites. "Edwards, Miss., Stores Hurt: Negro Girl Leading Successful Boycott," *Providence (MS) Journal,* August 31, 1966, 6.

Fall 1966: Holmes public schools become more integrated. The school board and white citizens are prohibited from using government funds for private schools. "Schools Open in Holmes County," *Holmes County Herald*, September 15, 1966, 1.

Blacks serve on juries and learn more of the legal system. "Circuit Court to Begin Here Monday," *Holmes County Herald*, September 29, 1966, 1.

October 15, 1966: The Black Panther Party for Self-Defense is founded by Huey Newton and Bobby Seale in Oakland, California. Huey P. Newton, *Revolutionary Suicide* (New York: Harcourt Brace Jovanovich, 1973).

November 8, 1966: General elections are held for U.S. senators and representatives. Three blacks run for office, including Clifton Whitley, running for the U.S. Senate. None win. "Eastland, Montgomery Win, Whites Win Local Positions," *Holmes County Herald*, November 10, 1966, 1.

November 14, 1966: The FDP works again on the ASCS election and tests the new block captain organization. "Community Committeemen named in ASC Election," *Holmes County Herald*, November 24, 1966, 1.

December 1966: SNCC votes on a narrow margin to expel all whites from the organization. John Dittmer, *Local People: The Struggle for Civil Rights in Mississippi* (Urbana: Univ. of Illinois Press, 1994), 408.

March 1967: H. Rap Brown is elected as chairman of SNCC. The organization removes the word *Nonviolent* in its name and changes the name to the Student National Coordinating Committee. Walter C. Rucker and James N. Upton, *Encyclopedia of American Race Riots* (Westport, CT: Greenwood Press, 2006), 625.

June 1967: The FDP focuses seriously on gearing up and strengthening the organization for the coming 1967 elections. *Mississippi Freedom Democratic Party Newsletter*, no. 1, October 1, 1967.

June 17, 1967: Thurgood Marshall becomes the first black Supreme Court justice. Roy Reed, "Marshall Named for High Court, Its First Negro," *New York Times,* June 14, 1967, 1.

July 1967: The Long Hot Summer includes riots in Detroit and other cities. Irwin Isenberg, *The City in Crisis* (New York: H. W. Wilson, 1968), 7.

October 20, 1967: Seven Ku Klux Klansmen, including Imperial Wizard Sam Bowers of Laurel and Neshoba County Deputy Cecil Price, are convicted of federal civil rights violations in the deaths of James Chaney, Andrew Goodman, and Michael Schwerner. They receive prison terms of from three to ten years. "Verdict Pleases a Victim's Family; Parents of Goodman Rejoice at 'Landmark Decision,'" *New York Times,* October 21, 1967, 18.

October 28, 1967: The twelve Independent black candidates launch a campaign caravan to cover one hundred miles in Holmes County. Holmes County Independent Campaign Office, press release, October 25, 1967.

November 7, 1967: Robert Clark is the first black to be elected to the Mississippi State House of Representatives since Reconstruction. Griffin McLaurin Jr. wins a constable position in Beat 4. Walter Rugaber, "Negro Elected to All-White Mississippi Legislature," *New York Times,* November 9, 1967, 33.

April 4, 1968: Dr. Martin Luther King Jr. is assassinated in Memphis. Earl Caldwell, "Guard Called Out," *New York Times,* April 5, 1968, 1.

Index

Page numbers in italics refer to photographs. All locations are in Mississippi unless otherwise indicated.

Abernethy, Tom, 159
African Americans. *See* blacks
ACLU. *See* American Civil Liberties Union (ACLU)
AFSC. *See* American Friends Service Committee (AFSC)
Agricultural Stabilization and Conservation Service (ASC) (ASCS), 184; annual elections, 74–75, 133, 193, 200
Alabama, 12–13; Birmingham church bombing in 1963, 4, 10; civil rights movement in, 180, 195, 244; 1966 elections in, 174, 195, 230, 232, 233, 242; Selma Bloody Sunday in 1965, 128. *See also* Lowndes County (AL)
Alexander, Angie, 20
Alexander, Doris, 20
Alexander, Florence, 20
Alexander, Jereldine, 20
Allen, John, 45, 58
American Civil Liberties Union (ACLU): Lawyers' Constitutional Defense Committee (LCDC), 96
American Friends Service Committee (AFSC): loan program, 149–50
antipoverty programs, 117–18, 144, 147–49, 150, 162
Aronson, Henry, 96, 103, 115

ASC. *See* Agricultural Stabilization and Conservation Service (ASC) (ASCS)
ASCS. *See* Agricultural Stabilization and Conservation Service (ASC) (ASCS)

Bailey, Elner, 179
Bailey, Howard Taft, *57,* 104, 129, 147, 149–50, 254, 267, 276; and 1967 Holmes County local elections, 195, 202–5, 225, *260*
Balance Due, Lorenzi home in, *7,* 134–35, 182, *206, 255;* visitors to, 217–21
Ball, John: at First Fourteen registration attempt, 29, 31, 33, 38; and voter education meetings, 24, 28, 40
Barrett, Pat, 61, 62, 229
Beddingfield, (Mrs.), 15, 74, 101–2
Beddingfield, Nathaniel, *15*
Birmingham, AL: church bombing in 1963, 4, 10
Blackmon, Florence, *68*
Black Panther Party, 180, 195, 232
Black Power movement, 177, 179–81, 241–42, 244, 248. *See also* Student National Coordinating Committee (SNCC); Student Nonviolent Coordinating Committee (SNCC)
blacks: electing to local offices, 158, 196, 198–99, 203–5, 225–35, 246, 259, 263, 265, 275; use

blacks: electing to local offices *(cont.)* of term, 14–15; voting rights of, 128–31, 133, 148, 163, 166, 239, 242. *See also* children, black; churches, black; farmers, black; civil rights movement; civil rights movement, Holmes County; civil rights workers; preachers, black; professionals, black; schoolteachers, black; voter registration; whites: violence against blacks
Blackwell, Unita, 232
Blanton, C. H., Jr., 115
Block, Sam, 38, 42; and Amzie Moore, 28; at First Fourteen registration attempt, 39
Bloody Sunday (Selma, AL, 1965), 128
Board of Education of Topeka, Brown v., 105
Boebel, Jim, 18; and community center construction, 16, 48, 49
Bond, Julian, 164
Booker, Fannie, 218
Booker, Warren, 226
boycotts, 114, 133, 193, 247, 249–50, *249*
Boyd, Napoleon, 130
Brown, Charlie, 130
Brown, Ed, 52, 53, 60, 157
Brown, H. Rap, 242
Brown, R. Jess, 96
Brown v. Board of Education of Topeka, 105
Bruce, Walter, *49, 197,* 267, 275, 276; as FDP leader, 147, 245, 247; and 1967 Holmes County local elections, 195, 196, 198, 199–200, 242, 267
Brumder, Mary, 9, 11, 56, 72; civil rights work, 12, 15, 16, 18, 19,

45, 86, 184; and Henry Lorenzi's arrest, 52, 53
Burns, Willie James, 67, 105; and 1967 Holmes County election, 204, 229, 259
businessmen, black: movement involvement, 199, 200

Caldonia, (Mrs.), 59–60
Canton, March against Fear incident in, 178–79
CAPs. *See* Community Action Programs (CAPs)
Carmichael, Stokely, 58, 164; and Black Power movement, 177, 179–80; and March against Fear, 174, 178
Carnegie, Alma Mitchell, 20, 38, *68, 69,* 95, 98–102, *99,* 105, 202, 219; at Greenville air base occupation, 143–44, 145; at Greenwood meetings, 24, 98; and March against Fear, 175, 178–79; one of First Fourteen, 29, 36, 42, 273, 277; at Poor Peoples Conference, 141, *142,* 143–44
Carnegie, Charlie, 95, 99–100; one of First Fourteen, 31, 273, 277
Carter, Jessie Lee: school desegregation experiences, 113
Carter, Pearlie C.: school desegregation experiences, 113
CDGM. *See* Child Development Group of Mississippi (CDGM)
Celebrezze, Anthony, 82
Central Mississippi Incorporated (CMI), 148, 149, 154
Chaney, James: murder of, 4, 46, 94, 263
Child Development Group of Mississippi (CDGM), 117, 118, 120, 145, 148, 162, 164

children, black: in Pecan Grove, *89,*
90, 121–24, 122, 123, 125, 161;
from plantations, 117, 118; and
school desegregation, 103–15;
violence against, 4, 10. *See also*
Head Start program, HCCC;
kindergarten, HCCC
churches, black: movement activities,
91, 93, 95; violence against, 46,
114; voter registration meetings
in, 147–48, 160, 164, 165, 166,
190. *See also* preachers, black;
National Council of Churches
Delta Ministry; Sanctified Church
(Mileston); Second Pilgrims
Rest Church; St. John's Church
(Lexington)
Civil Rights Act of 1964, 103
civil rights movement, 9, 180; issues
between blacks and whites in, 239,
241–48; Lorenzis' commitment
to, 4–5, 10–11. *See also* voter
registration
civil rights movement, Holmes
County, 23–36, 45, 81, 145, 149,
248; blacks' involvement in, 78,
88, 199–200, 202–3, 226–28,
241, 273; communication
methods, 45–46; expansion of,
60, 109; farmers' involvement in,
23–24, 88; leaders in, 273–74;
local control of, 61, 98, 181; and
March against Fear, 175, 177–79;
and 1967 local elections, 265,
266; school desegregation work,
103–5. *See also* First Fourteen;
Third Sunday Countywide
Meetings; voter registration
civil rights workers, 46, 120, 195;
Black Power movement's approach
to, 241–42; harassment of, 52–54,
60, 81, 86–87; Neshoba County

killings, 4, 46, 94, 184; violence
toward, 51–52, 75–77, 78, 215–
16; white, 23, 32, 45, 55, 181,
266. *See also* Freedom Democratic
Party (FDP), Holmes County;
Student National Coordinating
Committee (SNCC); Student
Nonviolent Coordinating
Committee (SNCC)
Clark, C. L., 226
Clark, Inez, 65, 66
Clark, Kayrecia, 65, 178–79
Clark, Lewis, 65
Clark, Marvis, 65
Clark, Norman, 58, 63–66, *64, 72,*
130, *227,* 276; and 1967 Holmes
County local elections, 204, 229,
243; one of First Fourteen, 31, 63,
273, 277; school desegregation
work, 104, 105
Clark, Richard, 65
Clark, Robert G., 235–37, *236,*
267–71, *268;* and farmers' co-op
meeting, 267, 269; inauguration
of, 266–67, 269–71; and 1967
Holmes County local elections,
230–31, 259, 261, 265–66; as
state legislator, 275; Sue Lorenzi's
meeting with, 269–71
Clark, Rosebud, 63–66, *64,* 118; one
of First Fourteen, 29, 273, 277
Clark, Wandrick Bryant (son of
Robert G.), 275
CMI. *See* Central Mississippi
Incorporated (CMI)
coalition building, 200, 202–3,
211, 214, 225–26, 228, 231,
266. *See also* elections, 1967
Holmes County local; grassroots
organizing
Coffey, Mildred: school desegregation
experiences, 113

COFO. *See* Council of Federated Organizations (COFO)

Collier, Clinton: and 1966 Mississippi primary, 160, 162–63, 165

Colman, Bob: and 1967 Holmes County local elections, 195, 196

Colmer, William, 160

colored, use of term, 15. *See also* blacks

Community Action Programs (CAPs), 143, 148, 149, 150, 153–54, 169, 231

Congressional Challenge (MFDP): in 1964, 49–51, 74; in 1965, 59, 81–98, 242

Congress of Racial Equality (CORE), 5, 60, 145, 174; Lorenzis' relationship with, 61

Cooke, Robert, 117

CORE. *See* Congress of Racial Equality (CORE)

Cotton, Dorothy: and SCLC citizenship schools, 67

Council of Federated Organizations (COFO), 11, 12, 16, 28, 174; Freedom Ballot/Freedom Vote in 1963, 50, 55; Freedom Summer Project in 1964, 23, 45, 49, 69, 75, 81; Lorenzis' relationship with, 5, 16, 48, 52, 54, 60–61, 134; orientation meeting, 49, 54–56, 159; violence against workers, 51; work with Holmes County FDP, 55, 88, 135, 243

Cox, Harold: school desegregation rulings, 62, 105, 115

Croom, Zelma Williams, 276. *See also* Williams, Zelma

Cunningham, Phyllis, 75

Curry, Constance, 149–50

Dahl, Kathy, 75

Davis, Caldonia, 61, *68*

Davis, Lucille, *249*, 250

Davis, Sarah, 61

Davis, Shadrach "Crook," 61–63; and 1967 Holmes County local elections, 204, 229

Davis, Shadrach, Sr., 61

Davis, Willie B., *189*, *262*

Delta Ministry. *See* National Council of Churches Delta Ministry

Democratic Party, 202; and 1964 National Convention, 50–51, 59, 70, 215–16; unresponsive to blacks, 85, 166, 180. *See also* Congressional Challenge (MFDP); Mississippi Freedom Democratic Party (MFDP)

Democrats, blacks running as, 232, 233, 235. *See also* blacks: electing to local offices

desegregation, 180, 250; school, 103–15

Devine, Annie, 164, 232; and March against Fear, 174, 178; as MFDP convention delegate, 82–83; and 1964 Freedom Election, 59, 70

Devine, George: and Mississippi state election in 1966, 164

discrimination, 50, 112–13, 143, 145, 164, 289. *See also* racism; segregation

Disparti, Josephine, 75–76, 93, 120–21, 275

Doar, John, 32

Drummond, Dock, 159, 198

Dulaney, Mister: and 1967 Holmes County local elections, 230

Dulaney, P. K., 24

Duluth (MN): donation to HCCC, 74; Sue Lorenzi's residence in, 276

Durant, school desegregation in, 108, 112–13, 114, 115, 117; voter

education meetings in, 196, 198, 247
Durant Liberation School, 247

Eastland, James O., 50, 159
Eaton, Eleanor, 150
elections: Alabama state (1966), 174, 195, 230, 232, 233, 242; ASCS annual, 74–75, 133, 193, 200; Freedom Ballot/Freedom Vote, 50, 55, 56, 59, 70, 81, 82–83; Mississippi state (1966), 159–60, 162–66, 173, 195–205
elections, 1967 Holmes County local: block captain–precinct leader system, 166, 195, 196, 198, 199; education for, 149, 159, 231–32; electing black officials, 148, 158; FDP involvement, 265–66; fund-raising for, 165, 198, 214; organizing for, 157–66, 173, 195, 196, 198, 205, 234, 250; platforms, 160, 162; poll watchers, 165, 166, 198, 199, 261, 263; running black candidates, 158, 196, 198–99, 203–5, 225–35, 246, 259, 265; run-off votes, 233–34; staying out of primaries, 233–34, 248, 259–60; success of, 259–66
Ellis, Irene, 130
Ellis, Steve, 122, *125*
Epps, Alice Mae, 118, 165, 219–20, 267
Epps, Nancy (Mrs.), 86–87, 267
Epps, Sam: on Henry Lorenzi, 208–9
Erwin, Lula Turner, *151*
Evers, Charles, 202, 232, 260
Evers, Medgar, 202; assassination of, 54

farmers, black: acreage allotments for, 75, 133; landowning, 27, 46, 88,

229, 266; plantation workers, 24, 50, 61, 141, 229, 246; project, 67, 74, 230. *See also* Agricultural Stabilization and Conservation Service (ASC) (ASCS); plantations; sharecroppers
Farmers Home Administration (FHA), 27, 164, 169
FDP. *See* Freedom Democratic Party (FDP), Holmes County
Federal Compliance Oath (school desegregation), 104
FHA. *See* Farmers Home Administration (FHA)
First Fourteen, 18, 26–36, 92, 109, 129, 177, 273, 277. *See also individual members*
Fisher, Marie, 130–31
Forte, Irma, 111
Forte, Lila, 76
Freedom Ballot/Freedom Vote: in 1963, 50, 55, 56, 70, 81; in 1964, 50, 56, 59, 70, 82–83
Freedom City/Strike City. *See* Greenville: Poor Peoples Conference in
Freedom Democratic Party (FDP), Holmes County: COFO's work with, 55, 88, 135, 243; Freedom Day, 88–89, 91–93, 97; growth of, 85–86, 147, 273; local leadership, 199–200, 225, 241; Lorenzis' work with, 135, 205, 214, 225, 244–45, 260–61; and March against Fear, 165, 173, 175, 177; and 1967 local elections, 173, 196, 202–5, 227, 243, 246, 260, 265–66; organization of, 147–48, 150, 157, 165; Pecan Grove office, 88, 107, 135, *158,* 231, 243; and school desegregation, 107–8, 110; voter registration

Freedom Democratic Party *(cont.)*
    efforts, 130, 131, 241. *See also*
    Mississippi Freedom Democratic
    Party (MFDP); Third Sunday
    Countywide Meetings
Freedom Meetings. *See* Greenwood:
    voter education meetings in
Freedom Riders/Rides, 9, 23, 34,
    235
Freedom Schools, 55–56, 247
Freedom Summer of 1964, 48–
    49, 55, 88, 96, 242; COFO
    involvement in, 23, 45, 49, 69,
    75, 81
Freeman, Orville, 82
Free Southern Theatre, 71
Friends of the Children of Mississippi,
    198
fund-raising: Black Power movement's
    effects on, 180–81, 242; for 1967
    Holmes County local elections,
    165, 198, 214. *See also* North
    (U.S.): donations from
Fusco, Liz, 55–56

Gallion, Elease, *151;* as HCCC young
    adult worker, 69, 70; as Head
    Start teacher, 117, 118; and
    March against Fear, 175, 179
Garner, (Dr.), 220
Gibson, Earvin, 104, 105
Gilmore, Billie Joe, 250
Goodman (town): school
    desegregation in, 110, 112; voter
    education classes in, 87
Goodman, Andrew: murder of, 4, 46,
    94, 263
grassroots organizing, 69–70, 88,
    120, 134, 144–45, 147, 174,
    273. *See also* coalition building;
    elections, 1967 Holmes County
    local; Freedom Democratic Party

(FDP), Holmes County; voter
    registration
Gray, Victoria, 59, 70, 82–83, 164, 232
Great Society. *See* War on Poverty
Greenberg, Polly, 118
Greensboro (NC), Woolworth's lunch
    counter sit-ins in 1960, 23
Greenville, 75; Poor Peoples
    Conference in, 141, 143–44
Greenville Air Base, occupation of,
    143–45
Greenwood, 28, 53, 74, 84–85, 160,
    261; doctors in, 19, 220; voter
    education meetings in, 24, 36,
    38–39, 69, 98, 129, 160
Griffin, Vernon Tom, 191, 245;
    and 1967 Holmes County local
    elections, 226–27, 229, 230, 259
Groves, E. G.: and 1967 Holmes
    County election, 198
Guyot, Lawrence, 50, 147, 160,
    174, 232, *233;* on Black Power
    movement, 242, 244; and
    Congressional Challenge of 1965,
    81, 93; at Hartman Turnbow
    arrest, 32, 62; on Henry Lorenzi,
    205, 207; and 1967 Holmes
    County election, 260; as SNCC
    worker, 28, 159, 248

Hall, Carsie, 96
Hamer, Don, 3, 45
Hamer, Fannie Lou, *82, 83,* 232;
    beatings suffered by, 215–16; as
    Freedom Vote candidate, 59, 70;
    and March against Fear, 174, 179;
    as MFDP convention delegate,
    82–83; 1964 Democratic National
    Convention speech, 50; and 1967
    Holmes County local elections, 263
Hayes, Chester: one of First Fourteen,
    31, 273, 277

Hayes, Ralthus, 36–40, *37,* 61, 67, 91, 147, 205, 245; arrest of, 93–96, 97; coalition building by, 200, 202–3; and March against Fear, 174, 175; and 1966 Mississippi state primary, 159, 160, 162, 163–64, 165, 166; and 1967 Holmes County local elections, 195, 196, 204–5, 225, 228, 231, 242, 259, 263; one of First Fourteen, 31, 35, 91, 273, 277; school desegregation work, 104, 105; voter registration work, 24, 67, 131

Hayes, Sandra Faith, 94

Head, Calvin "Butchie," *73*

Head, Dorothy Jean, 110–11

Head, Micheal, *15*

Head, Patricia, *47*

Head, Pecolia, *47,* 69

Head, Robert, *47,* 105; and community center construction, 16, 48, 51

Head, Rosie, *151,* 165; birthday party for, 150–52; as HCCC young adult worker, 65, 69, 70; as Head Start teacher, 117, 118; on Henry Lorenzi, 207. *See also* Howze, Rosie Head

Head, Thelma "Nutchie," *71,* 118

Head Start program, HCCC, 115, 117–20, 144–45, 243, 275, 278; CAP involvement in, 149, 150, 169; local leadership of, 149, 162, 164, 229, 246; Milton Olive, 204; teachers of, 103, 106, 107–8, 110, 111, 117–18, 162; whites' attempts to take over, 148–49

Henderson, West, Sr., 105–6

Henry, Aaron, 55, 70, 159–60

Herron, Matt, 58

HEW. *See* U.S. Department of Health Education and Welfare (HEW)

Highlander Folk School (SC), 67

Hightower, Mary Lee, 266–67; and 1967 Holmes County local elections, 230, 259

Hightower, Sammie Lee: school desegregation experiences, 114

Hill, Mary Alice: school desegregation experiences, 113

Hill, Sarah Ruth, 112–13

Holmes County: children in, 121–24; Countywide Meetings in, 188, 190–93; FDP in, 93, 147–48, 150; Freedom Schools in, 56; Freedom Summer of 1964, 48–49; Freedom Ballot/Freedom Vote in 1963, 50, 55; health research project in, 244–45, 260, 273, 275; Lorenzis' move to, 12, 14–19, 45, 51; NAACP in, 202; school desegregation in, 103–15; SNCC efforts in, 242–43, 266; voter registration in, 23–43, 56, 77, 86, 87, 127–35, 133. *See also* civil rights movement: Holmes County; elections, Holmes County local in 1967; Lexington; Mileston

Holmes County Community Center (HCCC, Mileston), 67–77, *68, 119,* 134, 205, *212,* 273; construction of, 16, 45, 48–49, 51; fund-raising activities, 70–71, 72, 74; grand opening, 56–59; guarding, 77, 115, 153; health clinic, 75, 76, 87, 120–21, 275; kindergarten, 69–70, 115, *116,* 117–20; library, *71, 73;* local control of, 61, 135; Lorenzis as managers of, 59, 70–71, 77; voter education meetings, 67–69, 70. *See also* Head Start program, HCCC

Holmes County Courthouse
(Lexington), 28, *83,* 91–93, *176,*
177
Holmes County Health Improvement
Association, 76, 77
Holmes County Health Research
Program (University of Illinois),
244–45, 260, 273, 275
Holmes County Herald (newspaper),
35, 92–93, 106; coverage of First
Fourteen, 29, *30,* 31, 34
Holmes County Service Fund (AFSC
loan program), 149–50
Hooker, Ed Wilburn, 20
Hoover, Curtis "Ollie," *146*
Howard, Dave, 16, 48, 267
Howard, Flora, 16, 18, 111
Howard, Robert Cooper, 105, *227,*
274
Howmiller, Elaine, 86
Howze, Rosie Head, 275. *See also*
Head, Rosie
Howze, Sam, 133
Humphrey, Hubert, 70

ICC. *See* U.S. Interstate Commerce
Commission (ICC)
Inc. Fund. *See* Legal Defense and
Education Fund Inc. (Inc. Fund,
NAACP)
Independent candidates, blacks
running as, 198–99, 232–35, 263.
See also blacks: electing to local
offices
Independent Voters Workshop
(Holmes County), 259–60

Jackson, (Dr.), 220
Jackson: CDGM base in, 118;
COFO office in, 48, 51, 61;
Congressional Challenge march
in, 93–98; MCHR in, 75; media

in, 261, 265; MFDP office in,
162, 165, 232; voter education
meetings in, 98
Johnson, June, 50
Johnson, Lyndon B., 50, 70, 117,
128, 143
Johnson, Thomas C. (T. C.), *260;*
and 1967 Holmes County local
elections, 204, 226–27, 228, 230,
259
Jones, Anthony "Tony" Leonard, 134
Jordan, Willie "Fats," 249, 250

Kenney, Mike, 45
Keppel, Francis, 105
kindergarten, HCCC, 69–70, 115,
116, 117–20
King, Edwin "Ed," 54–55; and 1966
Mississippi state primary, 159–60
King, Martin Luther, Jr.: and March
against Fear, 174, 178
Kohn, Mary Helen, 117, 118
Ku Klux Klan, 115, 160, 166

landowners, black. *See* farmers, black:
landowning
law enforcement, harassment by,
52–54, 60, 81, 85, 86–87, 93,
249–50
lawyers: black, 96, 229; civil rights,
61, 96–97, 103, 104–5, 107, 110,
115
Lawyers' Committee for Civil Rights
under Law, 96–97
Lawyers' Constitutional Defense
Committee (LCDC, ACLU), 96
Lee, George Wesley (Rev.): killing of,
78
Legal Defense and Education Fund
Inc. (Inc. Fund, NAACP), 96,
105, 115
Levin, Tom, 118, 120

Lewis, Daisey Montgomery, 105, 148, 193; and coalition building, 200; as HCCC director, 57, 59, 60, 205; and loan programs, 149–50; and Milton Olive Program for Children, 245

Lewis, Lee Henry, 105

Lexington: business boycott in, 249–50, 249; civil rights movement in, 91, 247; Countywide Meetings in, 188, 190–93; doctor in, 220; media in, 241, 261; school desegregation in, 108, 110, 114. *See also* Balance Due, Lorenzi home in; Holmes County Courthouse (Lexington); Pecan Grove

Lexington Advertiser (newspaper), 35

Liberation Schools, 247. *See also* Freedom Schools

Lorenzi, Henry John, 96, 150, 158, 206, 275; arrest of, 52–54, 55; biographical information, 5–6; and COFO orientation, 49, 54–56, 159; and community center construction, 16, 45, 48–49, 51, 70; FDP work, 135, 205, 214, 244–45, 260–61; as HCCC manager, 56, 59, 70–71, 72, 77, 134–35; in Linn County, Iowa, 86–87; and March against Fear, 174, 175; marriage to Sue, 9–12; move to Mississippi, 3–5, 12–19; and 1967 Holmes County local elections, 165–66, 195, 196, 198, 200, 204; organizing work, 145, 147, 241, 243, 244, 266; relationship with COFO, 5, 16, 48, 52, 54, 60–61, 134; remembrances of, 205, 207–9; work on Holmes County Health Research Program, 244–45, 260,

273. *See also* Balance Due, Lorenzi home in

Lorenzi, Silvio, 74

Lorenzi, Susan (Sue) Harris Sadoff, 7, 86, 149, 150; arrest of, 93–96, 97; biographical information, 5–12; and COFO orientation, 49, 54–56, 159; dangers faced by, 51–52; in Duluth, MN, 276; FDP work, 135, 205, 214, 225, 244–45, 260–61; fund-raising activities, 70–71, 72, 74, 97; as HCCC manager, 59, 70–71, 72, 77; in Linn County, Iowa, 86–87; and March against Fear, 174, 175, 177, 178–79; marriage to Henry, 9–12; move to Mississippi, 3–5, 12–19; and 1967 Holmes County local elections, 165–66, 196; organizing work, 145, 147, 266; relationship with COFO, 5, 16, 48, 52, 54, 60–61, 134; school desegregation work, 107–8, 110; "The Some People of That Place," 211–14, 273, 275, 276; trip north, 214–15; work in Mileston, 55, 56. *See also* Balance Due, Lorenzi home in

Louie, Gloria Jean: on Henry Lorenzi, 208

Louie, Jack, 24, 129; one of First Fourteen, 31, 273, 277

Louie, Mattie, 24, 129

Love, Edgar, 249, 276; boycott of Lexington businesses, 249–50; and 1967 Holmes County election, 246, 247, 250; organizing work of, 134, 239, 240, 241, 244; and Tchula shootout, 250–54

Love, James P., 265

Lowenstein, Al (Allard), 48; *The Brutal Mandate,* 9

Lowndes County (AL): 1966 state election in, 174, 232; voter registration in, 179, 180, 195

Malcolm X, assassination of, 86
Malone, Aaron: school desegregation experiences, 103–4, 114
Malone, Dan, 130
Malone, James, 130
Malone, John Henry: and 1967 Holmes County local elections, 204–5, 228–29, 259; school desegregation work, 105
Malone, Linda: school desegregation experiences, 103
Malone, Marie: school desegregation experiences, 103–4
Malone, William: school desegregation experiences, 103–4
March against Fear (Meredith March), 166, 173–79, 180, 195
Maroney, (Mrs.), 220–21
Marshall, Ruthie B., 112
Marshall, Thurgood, 38, 202, 247
Matthews, Lucinda, 105, 111
MCHR. See Medical Committee for Human Rights (MCHR)
McChriston, Joseph, 152–54, 153
McClellan, Henry B.: and 1967 Holmes County election, 230; obstruction of black voter registrants, 27, 40, 61, 62, 127, 129, 130–31, 157
McGaw, Ed: and 1967 Holmes County election, 230, 259
McGee, Nanny, 137
McGee, Penny, 137, 138
McGee's Café, 122, 135–39, 136, 138
McIntyre, Leola, 20
McIntyre, Northalee, 24
McKissick, Floyd: and March against Fear, 174

McLaurin, Catherine, 118, 151
McLaurin, Griffin, Jr.: and 1967 Holmes County local elections, 230, 259, 265
Medical Committee for Human Rights (MCHR), 75, 118, 120–21
Meredith, James: integration of University of Mississippi, 23, 34, 173; and March against Fear, 166, 173–74, 179; shooting of, 166, 174, 178
MFDP. See Mississippi Freedom Democratic Party (MFDP)
Mileston, 14, 16, 20, 28, 45–61, 72; Beddingfield's store, 15, 74; civil rights movement in, 23, 46, 59–60, 78, 229; FHA project in, 169; Lorenzis' work in, 49, 54–55, 56, 134–35; medical clinic in, 120–21; voter education meetings in, 24, 27, 38, 40, 48, 52, 58, 67–69, 77–78, 88, 129, 228; Wong's store, 74. See also First Fourteen; Holmes County Community Center (HCCC, Mileston)
Milton Olive Program for Children, 204, 205, 245
Mississippi: civil rights movement, 23, 32; Constitutional Convention of 1890, 148; Lorenzis' move to, 12–19; NAACP work in, 200, 202; and 1966 state elections, 159–60, 162–66, 173, 195–205; redistricting in 1965, 163, 165; school system, 84–85, 103–15; SNCC efforts in, 51, 242; voter registration, 83–84, 85. See also Holmes County; and individual towns
Mississippi, U.S. v., 84–85
Mississippi Freedom Democratic Party (MFDP), 144, 174, 232; Congressional Challenges, 49–51,

74, 81–98; Freedom Ballot/
Freedom Vote, 50, 55, 56, 59, 70,
81, 82–83; and 1964 Democratic
National Convention challenge,
50–51, 59, 70, 81, 82–83, 89; and
1966 Mississippi state elections,
159–60, 162–66, 198–99. *See also*
Freedom Democratic Party (FDP),
Holmes County
Mitchell, Annie Bell, 20, *26, 68;* one
of First Fourteen, 26, 31, 273,
277
Mitchell, Joe T.: one of First
Fourteen, 31, 273, 277
Mitchell, Ozell, *25;* NAACP
membership, 202; one of First
Fourteen, 26, 31, 40, 273, 277;
school desegregation work, 104,
105; at voter education meetings,
24, 38
Montgomery, Bernice Patton,
34, *128,* 187, 188, 245, 276;
movement involvement, 88, 129,
199, 231; and 1966 Mississippi
state election in, 164, 165; voter
registration story, 127–28
Montgomery, Eugene, 34–35,
182–88, *183,* 250, 276; movement
involvement of, 88, 129; and
1966 Mississippi state election,
165; and 1967 Holmes County
local elections, 226, 227; visiting
the Lorenzis, 217–18; voter
registration story, 127
Montgomery, I. H., 226
Montgomery, Ward: and 1967
Holmes County local elections,
226, 228, 259
Montgomery-Whatley, Zelpha, 127–28
Moody, "Mister" (state patrol officer),
53, 58
Moore, Amzie, 40; and Sam Block, 28

Moore, James, *49*
Moore, Marshall, 253
Morey, Hunter: and 1966 Mississippi
state election, 164
Moses, Bob, 28, 32, 40; and
Congressional Challenge of 1965,
81, 83; trial of, 62–63
Moses, J. W., 263
Mount Olive, voter education
meetings in, 45, 61, 147
movement, the. *See* civil rights
movement; civil rights movement,
Holmes County

National Association for the
Advancement of Colored People
(NAACP), 5, 38, 46, 174;
Duluth, Minnesota, chapter, 74;
in Mississippi, 159, 200, 202, 203;
and 1967 Holmes County local
elections, 228, 232, 260, 266. *See
also* Legal Defense and Education
Fund Inc. (Inc. Fund, NAACP)
National Council of Churches Delta
Ministry, 75, 144–45, 198
Negro, use of term, 15. *See also*
blacks
Negro Consumers of Lexington, 249
Neshoba County, 101; FDP in, 165;
killings of civil rights workers in
1964, 4, 46, 94, 184
night riders, 75, 115; voter
registration retaliation, 18, 31–33,
35, 36. *See also* violence
North (U.S.), 83, 134; donations
from, 70–71, 74, 81, 85, 86, 97,
214, 245
Norvell, Aubrey James: shooting of
James Meredith by, 178

Old Pilgrims Rest, voter education
meetings in, 61

Osheroff, Abe, 18, 19, 53, 54, 68, 71, 74, 77; and community center construction, 16, 45, 48, 49, 51; at HCCC grand opening, 56, 59

pastors, black. *See* preachers, black
Pecan Grove: children in, *89,* 121–24, *122, 123, 125,* 137, *161;* FDP office in, 88, 107, 135, *158,* 231, 243; McGee's Café in, 122, 135–39, *136, 138;* residents of, *161.* *See also* Balance Due, Lorenzi home in
Pittman, (Rev.), 192
plantations, 14; children from, 117, 118; evictions from, 134, 141, 241; owners' control over black workers, 70, 118; Roosevelt administration break up of, 27–28, 46; voter registration work on, 160, 239, 241; workers on, 24, 50, 61, 141, 229, 246
police. *See* law enforcement, harassment by
Polk, LePlause, 226
poll taxes, 75, 85, 127, 128, 129
poll watchers, 165, 166, 198, 199, 261, 263
Ponder, Annelle, 50
Poor Peoples Conference (Greenville), 141, 143–45
Poor Peoples Corporation, 134
Poussaint, Alvin, 121
preachers, black: movement involvement, 78, 88, 199, 200, *201,* 203, 226, 241. *See also* churches, black; Trent, Nelson: one of First Fourteen
President's Committee. *See* Lawyers' Committee for Civil Rights under Law
professionals, black: movement

involvement, 88, 199–204, *201,* 225–26, 273

Quinn, Edith, 129, *132*

racism, 4, 51, 148, 181, 247, 256, 266. *See also* discrimination; segregation
reciprocity bonds, 32
Reconstruction, 237, 265
Reconstruction Act of 1867, 148
Redmond, Laura, 19–20
Redmond, Lonnie, 21
Redmond, Sam, 19–22, 24; one of First Fourteen, 29, 42, 273, 278
Reiss, Mike: on Henry Lorenzi, 209
Richardson, Helene, 121
Ricks, Willie, 177
Robinson, L. E., 200, *201*
Roby, Vanderbilt and Cora, 45, 129, 147
Rule, Etha Ree, *264*
Russell, Jesse James, 67, 69; at HCCC grand opening, 56, 59; one of First Fourteen, 29, 77–78, 273, 278

Sadoff, Susan Harris. *See* Lorenzi, Susan (Sue) Harris Sadoff
Saffold, Jodie, 226
Sanctified Church (Mileston): voter education meetings at, 24, 48, 58, 67
Sanders, Emma: in Linn County, Iowa, 86–87; and 1966 Mississippi state elections, 198
schools: desegregation of, 103–15; in Mississippi, 84–85
schoolteachers, black, 59, 61; Head Start, 103, 106, 107–8, 110, 117–18, 162; movement involvement, 84, 88, 199–200, 202, 227–28,

241; and 1967 Holmes County local elections, 226, 227, 230, 231
schoolteachers, white: reactions to desegregation, 111, 113, 115
Schwerner, Michael "Mickey": murder of, 4, 46, 94, 263
SCLC. *See* Southern Christian Leadership Conference (SCLC)
Second Pilgrims Rest Church: arson fire, 114; voter registration meetings in, 198, 199, 226
segregation, 23, 33, 84–85, 105, 121. *See also* discrimination; racism
Sellers, Cleve: and March against Fear, 174
Selma (AL), Bloody Sunday, 128
Seymour, (Rev.), *158*
sharecroppers, 27, 74, 141, 144. *See also* farmers, black; plantations
sheriffs, black candidates for, 158, 196, 204–5, 226–29, 230, 246, 275. *See* law enforcement, harassment by; Smith, Andrew P. (sheriff)
Shimkin, Alexander "Alec," 200, 217, 218, 231–32, 246, *249*, 250, 254–57, *255*
Shimkin, Demitri, 200, 245, 275
Shriver, Sargent, 117
Silver, Andy, 12
Simpson, Euvester, 50
Sims, William, 104
Smith, Andrew P. (sheriff), 53, 58, 61, 77, 177, 250; and First Fourteen voter registration event, 29, 32, 38–39, 40, 42–43
Smith, Hazel Brannon, 35; and 1967 Holmes County election, 259, 260
Smith, Joe (Lexington), 226
Smith, Joe (Tchula), 46, 200, 202, 228
Smith, Robert R. "Bob": and 1967 Holmes County election, 226–27, 228, 259

SNCC. *See* Student National Coordinating Committee (SNCC); Student Nonviolent Coordinating Committee (SNCC)
Sojourner, Henry. *See* Lorenzi, Henry John
Sojourner, Sue. *See* Lorenzi, Susan (Sue) Harris Sadoff
Southern Christian Leadership Conference (SCLC), 5, 67, 174
Square, Ben, 24
Stein, Joe, 218
Stevens, Larry, 45, 157; and Henry Lorenzi's arrest, 52, 53
St. John's Church (Lexington), 191–93
Strike City. *See* Freedom City/Strike City
Student National Coordinating Committee (SNCC), 242
Student Nonviolent Coordinating Committee (SNCC), 5, 23, 51, 180, 195, 256; black-white issues in, 239, 241–48; and Congressional Challenge, 85; Freedom Ballot/Freedom Vote, 50, 55, 56, 59, 70, 81, 82–83; in Holmes County, 24, 28–29, 31, 33, 54, 242–43, 266; Lorenzis' relationship with, 52, 61, 134; organizers for, 60, 69, 81, 98, 133, 157, 159, 174, 177. *See also* Black Power movement; Carmichael, Stokely
Sunnymount, voter education meetings in, 61, 88, 147
Sutton, J. T., 111–12, 129
Sutton, Rosie Bell, 112, 129

Tardy, Paul, 92
Tate, Burrell, 167–72, *168*, 192, *274;* and 1967 Holmes County local elections, 227, 231

Tate, Mrs. Burrell, 167–72
Tchula, 14, 46, 74, 228, 250–54;
    NAACP chapter in, 202; school
    desegregation in, 108, 110–12,
    113, 114
teachers. *See* schoolteachers, black;
    schoolteachers, white
Third Sunday Countywide Meetings,
    33, *49,* 188, 190–93, 203, *212,*
    228, 229, *274*
Tougaloo College, 28, 54, 77, 159, 179
Trent, Nelson: one of First Fourteen,
    29, 31, 34, 273, 278
Turnbow, C. Bell, 18–19, 75, *119*
Turnbow, Hartman, 1, 69, 213, 275;
    at HCCC grand opening, 56, 59;
    in Linn County, Iowa, 86–87; and
    1967 Holmes County election,
    200, 205, 225; MFDP delegate,
    50; one of First Fourteen, 29,
    34, 39, 42, 273, 277; oratorical
    abilities, *17,* 18, 33, *49,* 61, 71,
    129; organizing by, 24, 188;
    reprisals for voter registration
    attempts, 19, 31–34, 35, 36, 60,
    75, 77, 84; trial of, 62–63

Udall, Stewart, 82
U.S. Department of Health Education
    and Welfare (HEW), 160, 162,
    275
U.S. House Committee on Election
    Procedures, 83–84. *See also* voter
    registration: federal examiners
    overseeing
U.S. Interstate Commerce
    Commission (ICC), 23
U.S. Justice Department, 29, 32,
    39–40, 40–41, 43
U.S. Office of Economic Opportunity
    (OEO), 117, 118, 141, 143–44,
    148. *See also* antipoverty programs

U.S. v. Mississippi, 84–85
University of Mississippi, James
    Meredith's integration of, 23, 34,
    173

Vaiden, harassment of civil rights
    workers in, 87, 216
Vance, Maude C., *68*
violence: toward blacks, 4, 10, 21,
    86, 87, 93, 160; toward civil
    rights workers, 4, 51–52, 75–77,
    78; school desegregation–related,
    103–4, 108, 112–13, 114–15;
    voter registration retaliations,
    27, 60, 85, 129, 166, 175, 178,
    215–16. *See also* law enforcement,
    harassment by; night riders
voter registration, 55, 84; early
    attempts, 18, 23–43, 157;
    education meetings for, 27, 56,
    67–70, 77, 86–87, 149, 165–66;
    expansion of, 98, 107, 127–35,
    157–58, 173, 234, 241, 265;
    federal examiners overseeing,
    84, 128–29, 130–31, 133, 157,
    166; literacy tests, 67, 75, 89,
    128, 131, 204; marching for,
    174, 175, 179; poll taxes tied
    to, 75, 85, 127, 128, 129; Third
    Sunday Countywide Meetings,
    33, *49,* 188, 190–93, 203, *212,*
    228, 229, *274. See also* elections,
    1967 Holmes County local; First
    Fourteen; Freedom Summer
    of 1964; Greenwood: voter
    education meetings in; Holmes
    County: voter registration
    in; Mileston: voter education
    meetings in; violence: voter
    registration retaliations
Voting Rights Act of 1965, 128–31,
    133, 163, 166, 239, 242

Wade, Mary T., 113
Walden, Lela Mae, 165, 219–20, *249,*
250
Walker, Prentiss, 160
Walls, Kelly, 226
War on Poverty, 117, 143
Watkins, Hollis, 28, 40, 159
Wax, Mel, 86
Weatherly, Patricia, 121
Weathersby, Chick, 39, 185
Wesley, John Daniel, *41,* 219; and
1967 Holmes County election,
229, 259; one of First Fourteen,
29, 39, 40–43, 273, 278
West, Dino, 121, 123–24, *125,* 137
White Citizens Council, 35, 92
whites, 166, 263; attempts to take
over Head Start programs, 148–
49; as civil rights workers, 23, 32,
45, 55, 181, 266; responses to
school desegregation, 103–15;
violence against blacks, 21, 86–87,
103–6, 108, 129, 160, 175, 215–
16; ways of dealing with, 14, 217.
See also night riders
Whitley, Clifton R.: and 1966
Mississippi elections, 159, 165,
166, 198, 199
Whitten, Jamie, 159
Wiley, Austin, 45, 129, 147, 226
Wilkins, Roy: and March against Fear,
174
Williams, Annie, 112
Williams, Clemma, 70, 115
Williams, Dearies, 104
Williams, Elsie, 112
Williams, Jesse, 114, 226
Williams, John Bell, 159, 265
Williams, Johnny B., 130
Williams, Link, 129
Williams, Minnie, 105
Williams, Zelma, 70, 103; as Head

Start teacher, 115, 117, 118, 120;
and March against Fear, 175, 179.
See also Croom, Zelma Williams
Winona, violence against civil rights
workers in, 215–16
Wise, Stanley, 174
Wright, George and Willie Mae, 45,
88, 129, 147
Wright, Marian, 96, 103, 115
Wright, Otha Lee, 122, *123,* 123

Young, Andrew, 67, 179
Young, Jack, 96
Ydyke, Elmira P., 111

Zinn, Howard, 85

Civil Rights and the Struggle for Black Equality
in the Twentieth Century

Series Editors
Steven F. Lawson, Rutgers University
Cynthia Griggs Fleming, University of Tennessee

Freedom's Main Line: The Journey of Reconciliation and the Freedom Rides
Derek Charles Catsam

Subversive Southerner: Anne Braden and the Struggle for Racial Justice in the Cold War South
Catherine Fosl

Constructing Affirmative Action: The Struggle for Equal Employment Opportunity
David Hamilton Golland

Becoming King: Martin Luther King Jr. and the Making of a National Leader
Troy Jackson

Civil Rights in the Gateway to the South: Louisville, Kentucky, 1945–1980
Tracy E. K'Meyer

Democracy Rising: South Carolina and the Fight for Black Equality since 1865
Peter F. Lau

Civil Rights Crossroads: Nation, Community, and the Black Freedom Struggle
Steven F. Lawson

Freedom Rights: New Perspectives on the Civil Rights Movement
edited by Danielle L. McGuire and John Dittmer

This Little Light of Mine: The Life of Fannie Lou Hamer
Kay Mills

After the Dream: Black and White Southerners since 1965
Timothy J. Minchin and John A. Salmond

Thunder of Freedom: Black Leadership and the Transformation of 1960s Mississippi
Sue [Lorenzi] Sojourner with Cheryl Reitan

For Jobs and Freedom: Race and Labor in America since 1865
Robert H. Zieger